The culture of violence

Note to the reader from the UNU

The UN University launched in 1990 a programme of research and training on Governance and Conflict Resolution with a view to producing a coherent framework and building knowledge and competence for resolving internal conflicts caused by ethnic, cultural, and linguistic differences. The programme has examined the underlying conditions for internal conflicts, particularly where this is manifested through direct violence. It has also focused on the conceptual and theoretical problems related to such conflicts, early warning of potential conflicts, and conflict transformation.

The present volume addresses the question of culture that legitimizes violence and the impact of routinized violence upon culture, through theoretical reflections and empirical case-studies. This volume should contribute to better understanding of the culture–violence interface, which has remained a much-neglected area of study. The papers included here are the revised versions of papers presented at a UNU symposium on the subject in Lima, Peru, in October 1991.

The culture of violence

Edited by Kumar Rupesinghe and
Marcial Rubio C.

**United Nations
University Press**

TOKYO • NEW YORK • PARIS

The views expressed in this publication are those of the authors and do not necessarily reflect the views of the United Nations University.

United Nations University Press
The United Nations University, 53–70, Jingumae 5-chome, Shibuya-ku, Tokyo 150, Japan
Tel: (03) 3499-2811   Fax: (03) 3406-7345
Telex: J25442   Cable: UNATUNIV TOKYO

Typeset by Asco Trade Typesetting Limited, Hong Kong
Printed by Permanent Typesetting and Printing Co., Ltd., Hong Kong
Cover design by David King and Judy Groves

UNUP-866
ISBN 92-808-0866-4
04850 P

Contents

Contents

Introduction

Kumar Rupesinghe

The works in this volume, the fruit of a conference sponsored by the United Nations University on **The Culture of Violence**, held in Lima, Peru, in October 1991, provide a multifaceted approach to the interface between cultures and violent phenomena, an examination of theories of violence, and selected case studies related to ethnic and human rights, drugs, and urban crime. The emphasis of the collection is on the situation in South America but is not strictly limited to that region either in content or scope. In fact, the Latin American experience of violence and the transformation of violence contains parallels with experiences in many other areas of the globe and lessons for all.

The concepts of violence and culture and the interrelationships between them do not allow neat definition. Hence, the reader will find a variety of approaches and emphases, including a nuanced exploration by Felipe MacGregor and Marcial Rubio C. of the Galtungian triangular relationship between structural, cultural, and direct violence; Bruce Kapferer's exploration of the influence of Buddhism as a cultural system on legitimizing violence in Sri Lanka; Francisco de Roux's argument that a culture of violence is a contradiction in terms because "violence acts against culture." As I point out in my chapter, there are a multitude of definitions of culture. These range from "learned behaviour" to "ideas in the mind," "a logical con-

1

struct," "a statistical fiction," "a psychic defence mechanism," and so on. As with culture, there are major difficulties in arriving at definitions of violence. While many definitions have been given to inter-state war, violence and internal wars within the state are in an early stage of conceptualization. This being the case, it is not surprising that there is no consensus when it comes to framing discussions of "cultures of violence."

Although the authors in this work bring to their contributions different approaches, common threads in the tapestry of the relationship between culture and violence, both explicit and implicit, are discernible. Whether we are describing the roots of violence in Uganda, the content of mobilizing myths in Sri Lanka, the clash of cultures between indigenous people and those of European ancestry in the South American case studies, the uses of state terrorism in the New World Order, or violence in the culture of the United States, we are constantly confronted with the importance of the interplay of the modern on traditional social, political, and economic organization.

Another major historical development running through these works is the loss of the monopoly of violence by the state, whether in Colombia, Uganda, or Sri Lanka. Several of the authors also delve into what to many is one of the most difficult phenomena to grasp and work with when looking at ways to mitigate or resolve violent conflict – the absence of a discourse of rationality in many violent situations.

While the studies demonstrate the historical and geographical particularities of the cases under discussion, they also indicate that modernization and the global information revolution, while vastly increasing the potential for human understanding and cooperation, have also accelerated the disintegration of traditional cultures, widened the actual and perceived chasms between advanced technological societies and those struggling to provide the basic necessities of life, and, for millions around the globe, raised expectations which will be unattainable for generations to come, if ever.

In my paper, I have tried to outline what I believe is one of the fundamental points of departure for increasing our understanding of present-day violence – coming to grips with the dynamics of this global clash between traditional cultures and the "celebration of the modern."

Historically, economic, political, and social modernization processes have often met with fierce resistance around the world. The more pervasive and rapid onslaught of modernization and Westernization which has been generated by the global communications revolution has obviously accentuated actual and potential conflicts between "Westernized" élites, those aspiring to gain the material benefits of a modem lifestyle, and those seeking to preserve and even extend traditional values and systems.

Although Colombian, American, Ugandan, or Sri Lankan society may be seen as extremely violent in comparison with other societies in the world, it should be borne in mind that even the most seemingly intractable violent societal conflicts, like political conflicts between states and within states, are not static processes, but are moving through stages from conflict formation to the transformation to peace. Chile is one example, in the South American context, where a once-terrorized society has embarked on a healing process that holds the promise that the traumas of violent social and political conflict can be successfully treated when injustices are acknowledged, processes are put in place to prevent them recurring, and a culture of reconciliation and peace is actively promoted.

A recurring theme in this work is the need to deepen our understanding of the nature of violence within individual cultures and societies and increase our ability to share the new-found knowledge on how to mitigate or resolve violent conflicts. Felipe E. MacGregor, S.J., and Marcial Rubio C. help expand the debate on the theoretical framework for any discussion of violence in their "Rejoinder to the Theory of Structural Violence," which examines Johan Galtung's seminal thinking on the subject. While accepting many of the aspects of Galtung's general definition of violence as being present "when human beings are influenced so that their actual somatic and mental realizations are below their potential realizations," the authors suggest that the definition is too broad, since other elements of reality, such as natural disasters, unpredictable events, and accidents, can also reduce a person's effectiveness. They also contend that the quantity and quality of violence is important to any definition, for instance the difference between straightforward physical aggression and torture. The co-authors set forth their own general definition of violence as "a physical, biological or spiritual pressure, directly or indirectly exercised by a person on someone else, which, when exceeding a certain threshold, reduces or annuls that person's potential for performance, both at an individual and group level, in the society in which this takes place."

On structural, institutional, and direct violence, MacGregor and Rubio once again seek to expand on Galtung's constructs by defin-

3

ing personal or direct violence as that "in which the aggressor can or may be identified," while structural violence "happens to a person from and within a society's structures which are shaped, maintained, and eventually transformed with margins of plasticity by the human beings, and in many cases this also includes the victims, all of whom are shaped by the same structures." Institutional violence, a "sub-species" of structural violence, "is that type of structural violence which is found formally or truly embedded in the institutions and is accepted, or at least tolerated, with the complicity of the people." On the relationship between culture and violence, MacGregor and Rubio assert that "structural violence is made up of social rules of the game which have an economic, social, political, cultural, or ideological content, according to the case, and which are generally accepted by both the beneficiaries and victims. In other words, it is convenient and correct to distinguish between structural and cultural violence, but we do not consider that this involves phenomena of an excluding taxonomy, because many of the rules of structural violence actually belong to the realm of culture and ideology."

In their summary of general conclusions, the co-authors note that the concept of pacifying societies by eliminating structural violence presupposes a transformation of structures. However, they stress that it is necessary "to discern with some care those aspects of structure that most generate violence, as well as the efficient consequences of annulling or changing them." They also underline that structural violence is not limited to poverty and injustice, but also "a whole set of institutions and social rules." Finally, they make a strong case for the need for interdisciplinary studies of structural violence to broaden our understanding of it, with the aim of bringing peace and improvement to human society.

Bruce Kapferer situates his contribution, "Remythologizations of Power and Identity: Nationalism and Violence in Sri Lanka," in the context of the 1988 and 1989 violence involved in the Marxist Janatha Vimukthi Peramuna's insurrection against the national government, which had already been fighting a Tamil guerrilla movement in the north and east of the country since 1983. The author explores "the content and pattern of the violence as this is ... organized in relation to ideological conceptions of identity." Kapferer is also interested in the way "violence (here, specifically physical destruction) as an instrument of power and oriented through ideology can become a totalizing force."

Kapferer examines the reconstruction and distortion of ancient Buddhist myths through a prism of modernization and rationality acquired during the colonial and post-colonial periods and describes how the cosmic kingship myths were given a meaning unrooted in empirical evidence. They remained, nonetheless, potent as generators and sustainers of violence. While pointing out the perversity of the use of the kingship myths as a mobilizing agent for violence in a Buddhist society in which non-violence is a primary value, the author notes that the rationalizing processes of the modern world have imbued Buddhist nationalism with the "overarching importance of 'power'." In the struggle between the state and the Sinhalese JVP, exercise of that power meant enforcing submission to a Sinhalese-dominated hierarchy of power, as well as the demonization of enemies and the use of annihilation – an intertwining of pseudo-historical cultural constructs and a desire to preserve, through the use of violence, the dominance of the power of the modern state. In August 1989, the author notes, placards were placed throughout Colombo and the provinces in which JVP figures were depicted as demons surrounded by the dead. The population was exhorted not just to kill JVP members, but to use the punishment of the ancient kings, impaling with a stake through the anus. Another form of annihilation has been the burning of bodies in petrol-soaked tyres. As for the JVP, it resorted to appeals to "traditional" village values and staged executions of government supporters, as well those it considered to have breached local morality or customs. What is revealed in this discussion of events in Sri Lanka is not a culture of violence, but the reinterpretation of mythological aspects of the culture to meet political ends, in this instance the violent suppression of violent opponents of the state and resistance to that suppression.

Francisco J. de Roux, S.J., looks at the impact of drug trafficking on Colombian culture and concludes that the Colombian drug trade has not created a culture of violence but rather has flourished in an institutional and cultural vacuum with social, economic, and ethical aspects. De Roux hypothesizes that during the past four decades Colombia's institutions were misaligned with the expectations and needs of Colombians. Moreover, Colombians had to adapt to living in a society in which they lacked political and economic influence and which provided them with little protection from the guerrillas, drug traffickers, and paramilitary forces that took root in this environment.

De Roux provides a number of insights in relation to the institutional, social, and economic vacuums he describes. In the first instance, the historical lack of credible state institutions in vast rural areas of the country spread during the 1970s to urban centres, where populations had increased dramatically, while economic opportunities declined sharply. Rural guerrilla movements sought to fill the institutional vacuum by providing social services and security, but when the financial toll on *campesinos* rose too high, peasants and local landowners formed their own private armies to defend their lives and property. Eventually, drug traffickers, local armies, and the military joined forces to fight the guerrillas and in 1988 mercenaries were brought in by drug traffickers to train local paramilitaries. Meanwhile, in urban centres, the cocaine cartels had enlisted gangs of youths eager to attain economic mobility, a sense of belonging, a means of escape, or power and security. In the latter case, drug trafficking profits bought sophisticated weapons, adding to the level of violence.

As for the moral vacuum, de Roux suggests that while the country was and remains nominally Catholic, beginning in the early 1960s it underwent a rapid process of secularization which removed a source of guidance from Colombian society as a whole and which was not accompanied by a growth in civil ethics that would have been able to guarantee the development of a pluralistic society capable of protecting the rights of its members. The brutality and scope of the drug-related violence, including assassinations of judges, journalists, and politicians, "effectively silenced the moral conscience of Colombian society."

However, it was the growth in power of the extralegal groups and the astronomical death toll for a country "at peace" – 24,000 dead as of 1991 – which turned public sentiment around and prompted political action against the drug trade, in spite of the recognition that it had contributed enormously to Colombia's economy – an estimated US$1–4 billion annually, according to de Roux. A government clampdown on drug traffickers, negotiations with guerrilla groups and paramilitaries, the signing of a new constitution, and the growth of grassroots social movements opposed to the violence had begun to show promise of a more peaceful society in late 1991. Ominously for other fragile states in the region, however, the drug producers had begun to move their operations to other countries.

In "Ethnic Violence: The Case of Bolivia," Xavier Albó provides a detailed description of the various strata of Bolivian society and argues that ethnic relations inherited from the colonial structure continue to be a source of structural violence. At the heart of the problem, asserts Albó, is the unequal status of the various ethnic groups and the "subjective prejudices attached to this stratification." For the author, ethnic violence in Bolivia "is not of the apartheid type, but acts in a less formal and sometimes paternalistic way, permeating most situations and domains of society." Because of its insidiousness, ethnic prejudice makes rational settlement of social and economic differences more difficult.

Albó describes ethnicity as referring to two factors – race and culture; and culture as referring to "behaviour – such as language or religion – that is transmitted to the members of a given social group through the process of socialization or enculturation." If the focus is put on race, then the problem becomes one of racism, whereas if the focus is on ethnicity, the problem is one of ethnocentrism. However, the author notes, ethnic violence can stem from either one and "it is quite common that cultural differences are reinterpreted as racial."

In Bolivia, indigenous groups made up at least 68 per cent of the total population of 7 million in 1976, when the last national census was taken. Albó provides a listing of the categories Bolivians use to describe their own and other groups within society – *gente decente* or "decent people," used by whites of themselves; *mestizos* and *cholos*, the first implying persons of mixed blood who have accepted the white lifestyle and the second, more derogatory, term for those indigenous people who have abandoned some, but not all, of their traditional way of life; *indios* or *campesinos*, who have been regarded as Indians since the birth of the colony but have been renamed "peasants"; and *collas* and *cambas* – Andean highlanders and lowlanders, respectively. Another "ethnically loaded" word is the Andean peoples' pejorative descriptor for whites as *q'ara*, or "people without blood in their faces."

In effect, the stratification evident in how Bolivians describe each other can be seen as a symptom of social and economic stratification in which the lower ranks of society are at best neglected and at worst repressed. Although Albó notes that ethnicity has become a banner for grass-roots political mobilization, the intertwining of negative ethnicity, class, and gender perceptions presents formidable obstacles to social change.

Edward Khiddu-Makubuya examines the violence and conflict in Uganda from a historical perspective, and then delves into responses and possible approaches to "creative management of these trends." His article analyses the initiatives of the National Resistance Movement since it took power in January 1986 and began waging what Khiddu-Makubuya terms an "active armed-cum-political struggle in an essentially rural setting among peasants." This effort has been backed and buttressed by political "conscientization and enlightenment" with the stated aims of instutionalizing democracy, security, the consolidation of national unity and the elimination of all forms of sectarianism, the building of an independent, integrated, and self-sustaining economy, the elimination of corruption, the restoration of social services and the rehabilitation of war-ravaged areas of the country, redressing the dislocation of segments of the population, and so forth. The author also reviews the emergence of new institutions, including a code of conduct for the army, the establishment of grass-roots Resistance Councils and Committees, a Human Rights Commission, an Inspector General of Government, control of the intelligence community, the establishment of a Ministry of Constitutional Affairs and the Uganda Constitutional Commission, pressing forward with policies to bring development to Karamoja in the north-east of the country, removing the barriers to Ugandan women's participation in public life, and aiding Asians expelled by Idi Amin to return.

In spite of these positive developments, he notes that conflict and violence have persisted, particularly in the north of the country; freedom of the press, while affirmed by the government, has not been absolute; education has been put on the back burner under the International Monetary Fund's structural adjustment programme; Uganda's Muslim community has been riven by doctrinal and leadership disputes; and "the outstanding example of silent violence, which has currently reached epidemic proportions" in Uganda, is AIDS, with an estimated 1.5 million victims out of a total population of 16.6 million. "The deterioration in health services and other infrastructure over the years and the moral collapse which has occurred as a consequence of violent conflict have almost certainly aggravated the spread and incidence of AIDS in Uganda."

Referring to the pervasiveness of violence in Ugandan society, the author notes that "conflicts have been accompanied by practically all forms of violence – regime, anti-systemic, tribal, political, economic, religious, and others. Nearly every class of Ugandan society has been touched by this process, and there is hardly a single part of the country which has not reverberated with some form of conflict or violence." Khiddu-Makubuya sees a need for further research on the causes of violence within Uganda, in particular on Ugandan society and cultures; élites; the government; the causes and processes of violence; gender issues in violence; and the design of a working peace system. Perhaps more importantly, he sets out a number of ideas for "management of the process of power on the basis of nationalism and democracy," with the primary goal of the development of an orderly process of governmental succession which eliminates "conquest as a mode of accession to power." Strengthening the constitution as a tool for the mediation of conflict is crucial for a long-term political settlement, he argues. "A democratic, nationalist, and development-oriented constitution must be put in place, with an emphasis on realistic separation of executive, judicial, and legislative powers; on popular participation at all levels; and on general application of the principles of justice to all major political issues." The constitution should incorporate a comprehensive Bill of Rights guaranteeing human rights, but should also enshrine economic, social, and cultural rights, including regional economic equalization, minority rights, and women's rights. Other issues which need to be addressed are how to safeguard the constitution against *coup d'état*, the size and function of the military and police, the encouragement of cultural tolerance and pluralism, the restructuring of education, the development of a coherent national language policy based on a spirit of cultural pluralism, and increased accessibility of the courts. Ultimately, what needs to be generated and nurtured is a national ethos of dialogue, compromise, and tolerance. "Despite the ready availability of arms in Uganda, all politically relevant strata of society must begin to learn to talk before shooting."

Luis Pedro España N. describes a nation which has slipped from relative prosperity and social and political stability to one riven by crisis, in "Violence and the Welfare State: The Case of Venezuela as an Oil Country." The main focus of his examination is the decline of the Venezuelan economy, marked by the refusal of the international banking community to provide any more credit in 1983, followed by the rapid decline in oil prices, the mainstay of the Venezuelan economy and social welfare system.

While at the time of writing political violence had not reappeared with the "relative change from bonanza to depression," social violence had done so, in the form of what España terms "indirect" or "implicit" violence, as well as "direct social violence," which has

9

taken the form of "delinquency, self-defence, taking advantage of the defenceless, the invasion of others' property and rights, a system of complicity, lack of justice, and generalized fear." He notes that the lack of credible political alternatives should sustain the current political system, while individual economic actors are likely to maximize their efforts to innovate "on the margins of formal legality," thus increasing social violence.

The ongoing crisis, España asserts, assumes increased poverty, decay of institutions of government, and a loss of credibility in the system's methods of resolving conflicts and disputes. Among the alternatives for eradicating violence, the author suggests, are a restructuring of society aimed at eradicating poverty, or else police repression. The latter would imply a militarization of society and an increase in the violence while not addressing the underlying problems. The new *pacificación* or peace-building process in Venezuela should, at the micro level, involve the state's guaranteeing public security and exercising its legitimate control of violence. But it should act at the same time on reforms at the macro level. "The state should convert itself into an instrument of compulsion that does not go beyond the principle of the democratic state."

Miles D. Wolpin, in his article "State Terrorism and Death Squads in the New World Order," stresses that the dominance of the United States in the wake of the collapse of the Soviet Union should not be confused with the "success" of the capitalist system in providing basic needs or equitable development in the third world. Growing public-sector austerity, increases in unemployment, declines in real wages, excessive indebtedness, and a global decline of economic pluralism, Wolpin suggests, will increase structural violence.

Thus the present era is characterized by demoralization of egalitarian alternative development movements, national self-determination aspirations, and an intensification of mass relative deprivation. This is exacerbated by growing economic insecurity contrasted with the opulent lifestyles that are conveyed by ... (the) media ... and exposure to comprador elements within their own societies. As relative deprivation escalates, we may expect a rise in ethnic and other ascriptive conflicts.

Wolpin notes, however, that as long as such conflicts pose no threat to a given state stratified system, the forces capable of being used in direct institutional violence – regime terrorism and death squads – should remain latent. Where state terrorism and death squads are most likely to emerge, according to the author, are within the new democracies of Eastern Europe, where minorities will react to the suppression of equal rights and former state terrorist personnel have not been incapacitated. Globally, economic stagnation will heighten the chances of repression of old and new popular movements, but the likely reaction is not to be through regime terrorism, because of global human rights norms, but rather through covert forms such as death squads. Pessimistically, Wolpin predicts that for decades to come human rights norms will have little effect on these covert activities.

For the purposes of his discussion of violence and culture in the United States, Robert Brent Toplin divides violence into four categories: collective and political violence; criminal violence; psychopathic violence (in which he groups assassination, mass gratuitous violence, and serial killings); and violence in foreign policy. Toplin states that the concern with the connection between culture and violence in American society stems from the 1960s, when, after a quarter-century of relative domestic tranquillity, the United States found itself plunged into consensus-shattering upheaval caused by escalating involvement in the Viet Nam war and demands by blacks for racial equality. Through the latter half of the 1960s, limited incidents of bombings and violent black and student protests received wide media and public attention, but after four students were killed in a fusillade from National Guardsmen on the campus of Kent State University, commitments to wind down the war in Viet Nam defused the confrontational atmosphere and protests declined dramatically in the early 1970s.

Toplin argues that the civil rights movement "could not achieve all its goals, but it did bring many of the most glaring racial abuses to an end." By the 1990s, Toplin asserts, the United States had taken measures to remove a great deal of the racial tension between whites and blacks in the country by ensuring "equality under the law and seeking ways to integrate its major minority population into the mainstream of economic, political, and social activities." The author notes that at the beginning of the 1990s, black mayors were in office in most of the major US cities. In sum, Toplin sees the political and collective disturbances in the United States in this century as episodic rather than epidemic, largely because American society has lacked long-term religious, ethnic, and linguistic divisions.

In contrast to incidents of collective or political violence in the United States, criminal violence has surged since the 1960s. Here Toplin touches on a number of speculative hypotheses for the increase, including poverty, drug dependence, the rise in single-parent families, the argument that the media, in particular Hollywood films, have influenced the criminally violent and led them to participate in "copycat" crime, and the status consciousness of poor young males seeking upward mobility. He also discusses the increase in ownership of firearms in the United States and the rising firearm homicide rates. By 1980, half the households in the country reported owning at least one gun. In 1988, the United States recorded 8,915 gun murders, compared with seven in Great Britain, 13 in Australia, and eight in Canada. As for the legacy of the Wild West, Toplin contends that the real levels of violence on the frontier were less than those in present-day East Los Angeles or central Detroit, suggesting that there is no continuous violent tradition spanning the nineteenth and twentieth centuries.

In the area of foreign policy, the author traces American involvement in wars through three centuries, but finds no common thread until after the Second World War, when the United States emerged as the dominant military power in the world, a role that was to be sustained and justified by its ideological opposition to communism. In both the prevalence of criminal violence in American society and in its aggressive foreign policy, Toplin concludes, can be seen reflections of a culture of violence.

Irene Rizzini, in her contribution, "Children in the City of Violence: The Case of Brazil," observes that "a deep vein of violence is entangled in the history of our continent and resides in our collective unconscious." This vein of violence includes the decimation of indigenous peoples, the importation of African slaves and their resistance, violence in rulers' strategies for conquest and domination, the violence of economic backwardness, and the "enormously unequal distribution of income in Latin America and, in particular, Brazil."

In Brazil, social and economic impoverishment in recent decades have created new multitudes of marginalized people, especially in the big cities. The 1980s are now regarded as a lost decade, in which social inequality intensified. Violence is increasingly present in the lives of Brazilian citizens, with muggings, attacks, kidnappings, torture, drug trafficking vying with attempts to legalize the death penalty.

In this general climate of violence, "extermination," particularly of children "in the name of defending society," has become the most serious problem. It is estimated that about half of Brazil's 60 million children and adolescents live in domestic situations of relative or absolute poverty, in which monthly family incomes range from one-half to one-quarter of the minimum salary of US $80. Rizzini notes that most of the "street kids" work as roaming vendors to supplement family incomes; others steal, beg, traffic in drugs, or prostitute themselves. It is estimated that thousands of these children have been killed at the hands of professional killers, "frequently connected with police contracted to eliminate these children." The "extermination groups" or "death squads," which often practise extreme brutality – torture and dismemberment – are motivated by the need to keep Brazilian cities "safe," the author notes.

While domestic and international outrage at the killings has fostered positive changes in legislation and social services, Rizzini contends that the judicial system has not responded vigorously enough either in investigating cases, punishing perpetrators, or protecting potential victims. She argues that what is needed is structural modification of the living conditions of the continually impoverished.

Tony Mifsud, S.J., in "Human Rights and Dictatorship: The Case of Chile," describes the central role of the Roman Catholic Church in combating human rights abuses and protecting the victims of the Pinochet regime. Helping the persecuted and restoring "peace based on justice became leitmotifs of the Church's preaching, teaching, and practice." These activities were later taken up also by other groups opposed to the military regime, in a pluralistic movement which used the concept of solidarity to combat the individualism brought on by insecurity in a climate of fear, civic impotence, and the "indignation of a sorrow that cannot be made public."

While the "social truth" of the Pinochet years of repression and gross abuses of human rights has become accepted, Mifsud states that "the question of penal justice is still unresolved." He suggests that the perpetrators of human rights violations must face legal prosecution if the process of reconciliation is to be completed. However, he acknowledges that "power," "force," and "legitimacy" are still not fully invested in a single political agent or institution and that the Chilean armed forces remain capable of intervening. Strict justice cannot bring back to life the dead and the missing or repair the physical and psychological damage suffered by the tortured, Mifsud suggests. But at the same time, impunity for abuses of human rights must not be consecrated. Ultimately, ensuring that "never again" will ideology and force be used in Chile to justify human rights abuses will mean creating "a culture of respect for human rights" through education, conviction, and commitment.

1

Forms of violence and its transformation

Kumar Rupesinghe

Introduction

My paper intends to discuss the interplay between modernization and violence and will pay some attention to identity conflicts as a crucial arena for violence and war. It will argue that the globalization of culture will reinvigorate the search for identity and this may often take violent forms. The end of the Cold War may mean the elimination of some forms of potential violence, such as nuclear war between the superpowers, but "internal conflicts" within defined state boundaries may increase in salience and intensity. The challenge facing the global community, therefore, is to address forms of violence which are used as a means of resolving conflicts.

1 The celebration of modernity

An interesting feature of global thinking has been the celebration of modernity. Modernity may best be defined as a metaphor which encompasses a vision of rationality and culture which is not bounded and which is transnational. The triumph of modernity has been a constant theme since the day Christopher Columbus "discovered" the Americas. From the time of the Spanish Conquest, the dominant discourse has been the attempt to incorporate traditional cultures and their peoples into the modern project. Throughout the centuries, the modernization project has had many convolutions. These have been the subject matter of sociology and the evolution of this particular science is rooted in explaining the transition to modernity. Whether it was Comte, Saint-Simon, Durkheim, Weber, Karl Marx, or Adam Smith, the project which they described and analysed was the consequence of modernity. They all had a notion of momentous revolutionary change for the future, whether this discourse was articulated in terms of tradition and modernity or in terms of the evolution of capitalism. What did not assume a central notion in their writing was the evolution of modernity with violence.

Resistance to the modernization project, with its many-sided manifestations, has seen the birth of new and complex social movements. The thrust of early protests against industrialization, anti-colonial movements, working-class movements, or the modern religious and fundamentalist movements has been to resist and transform the modernization project. It is the interaction between the forces of modernity and the tension inherent in their articulation which is significant and interesting.

During the post-war period a range of scholars has celebrated modernity. Two who immediately come to mind are Walt Rostow and Talcott Parsons. Scholars of modernity cannot be characterized as left or right on the political spectrum. In the 1960s there were serious and celebrated interventions on the issue, particularly by Herbert Marcuse and Marshall McLuhan. The most interesting formulations were advanced by Bill Warren in *Imperialism: The Pioneer of Capitalism* (London: Verso, 1981), in particular his suggestion that imperialism, as the highest stage of capitalism, had spread capitalism to all corners of the globe and become a truly globalizing and civilizing project.

A simultaneous theoretical discussion took place among futurists such as Toffler (writing on the global village) and a variety of scholars who advanced theses equating global culture with a hegemonic cultural order. Here, global culture was seen as the rapid spread of consumerism and the communications revolution. An interesting contribution in this area came from Giddens, who refers to modernity as the type "of social life or organisation which emerged in Europe from about the seventeenth century onwards and which subsequently became more or less worldwide in their influence."[1] The theoretical schools associated with global culture represent another variant of this thinking.[2]

The end of the Cold War inspired new interventions such as those of Francis Fukuyama (the end of history), Moeller (the end of war), and others, who linked modernity with what they perceived as a triumph of democracy, neoliberalism, and even the end of war. It is worth noting that Moeller emphasizes the role of culture as a factor in people's rejection of war in the democracies. The Hegelian notion of dialectics as a movement of history and progress would stop with the demise and downfall of the communist alternative. What is to be noted in the discourse on modernity is that none of the classical thinkers or the current ones has paid much attention to the role of violence in the modernization project. Each one refers to violence as perhaps a necessary evil, but very few have attempted to focus on the centrality of violence and its possible autonomy. The signal honour for this notion may be attributed to Machiavelli and to the school of Machiavellians in historiography, who accorded centrality to the notion of violence.

Peace research, it seems, has been formed through a dialectical process. One impetus has been the intellectual challenge posed by Machiavelli and his legacy – a perspective that includes the utility of violence against humans. Another factor has been the moral challenge posed by the history of the twentieth century: the two world wars, the rise of nuclear weapons, the danger of conventional military conflicts, and the inability to resolve conflicts. Together, these problems have formed a set of traumas for humankind and for peace research.

In Wallensteen's view, Machiavelli is a relevant starting point for an analysis of the roots of peace research. In the Machiavellian world, six principles appear to be fundamental; violence is omnipresent and inevitable; violence is instrumental; in politics, violence is the ultimate source of power; conflicts are resolved through power and violence; the state and the government are the primary actors of importance; the state is independent *vis-à-vis* other states. For peace research, these principles lead to six crucial areas of contention with Machiavelli and his legacy.[3]

The core terms of peace research are conflict, violence, and peace. But conflict is too wide a field. Peace research differs from the strategic, historical, or sociological understanding of conflict in its focus on violence. Violence plays the same organizing role in peace research as poverty in political economy or illness in public health. Our primary concern is violence. Wars represent the most visible form of violence. But most violence occurs in less public arenas. A staggering amount of physical and mental mistreatment takes place within ordinary families and in daily life. The physically stronger force their will on the physically weaker. Children are battered, wives beaten, and women raped. Only recently, and only in the most developed societies, has this hidden violence been studied and revealed to the public.

If we accept that the discourse of rationality is associated with modernity, then certainly modernity is in crisis. The most explicit manifestations of this crisis are in the extraordinary degradation of the environment, in the violence perpetrated on living organisms, and in the consequences of human action on the very survival of the species. This crisis is also explicit in the weapons and ideologies of violence which have made the twentieth century the bloodiest in history. It is not only the head counts of the casualties of inter-state wars, but the genocides, ethnocides, and democides of internal wars where governments have killed their own people, which are of great importance. Acts of ethnocide have also meant the elimination of many cultures, linguistic forms, and customs which have been the common wealth of the world.

It is this crisis of modernity and its relationship to violence which is the subject of my reflections. The question may be posed in the following manner. Are there limits to the discourse of rationality? Or will rationality eventually turn or be turned against itself and destroy itself? Or can and will the logic of rationality give way to other modes of thinking from other cultures and traditions which can transform object–subject, superego and other Cartesian categories into a processual understanding of an organic culture and civilization of non-violence in the widest possible sense? Surely developments since the end of the Cold War directly pose the question of whether we need a new or regenerated utopian project which can ultimately transform the violence of this century into greater peace and harmony in the next. At the very least, the elimination of violence and a world of civic order based on respect for human rights should be central to the agenda for the twenty-first century.

There is no doubt that the globalization process characterized by economic, environmental, and political processes is having an impact on many societies. Powerful tendencies are at work exacerbating conflicts. The widespread diffusion of consumerism has accentuated cultural homogenization and modernization, creating a rise in expectations. On the other hand, the process of homogenization is strongly resisted by some cultures and peoples, leading to a localization and internalization of conflicts.

The great conflicts of the twentieth century are too well known to us to require elaborate repetition. However, what is significant in such projects is their universal character. These ideological movements do not address themselves to a particular ethnic group or nation but to human beings, *per se*. What is distinctive about these visions – whether they are projects involving self-determination, capitalism, or democracy – is their common acceptance of modernization in the context of nation-building, socialism, or capitalism. They all subscribe to the building of a future. Notions of ethnicity or some forms of fundamentalism may refer to a primordial past or a restoration of a past glory.

2 The experience of violence

It is a fact that more people have died through violence and war when no official war has been declared than in situations of declared belligerence, and there is a great likelihood that such forms of violence will increase in the future. It is important not to confuse appearance with reality. Internal wars have led to massive civilian casualties, destabilized societies, and created millions of displaced persons and refugees. Melko, for example, notes that while there have been only two major conflicts in the developed world since 1945 (the Greek Civil War and the Hungarian Revolution), more than 14 million people have been killed in the third world, compared to fewer than 100,000 in the developed world.[4]

According to Rummel, absolutist governments have killed more of their own people – as well as other people – than have been killed in all civil and international wars put together. The seven most lethal democides of this century alone total, in Rummel's words, "... 143,166,000 men, women, and children shot, beaten, tortured, knifed, burned, starved, frozen, crushed, or worked to death; or buried alive, drowned, hung, bombed, or any other of the myriad ways these governments have inflicted death on helpless citizens or foreigners."[5] What Rummel is focusing on are not acts of war but war crimes and peacetime crimes perpetrated by states. Unarmed, non-resisting civilians are arbitrarily put to death by those who wield centralized, unchecked, and undisciplined power to gain a variety of ends, ranging from ethnic or racial purity to national unity and rapid development, or to Utopia itself.

Furthermore, the United Nations High Commissioner for Refugees (UNHCR) estimated in 1989 that there were in the world over 17 million refugees, largely victims of internal armed conflicts, and another 20 million internally displaced persons. There are those who suggest that this total may double by the end of the twentieth century.[6] Refugees are but one indicator of the extent of direct violence. The figures for other victims of violence, such as children, are truly staggering.

There is no evidence that internal wars are on the decrease. All the evidence points to an increase in the scale, intensity, and frequency of such violent conflicts. Moreover, studies have not emphasized enough the increase in violence and criminality in many societies. Violence has become endemic, along with militarization.

Types of internal conflict

We need to distinguish between the various types of internal conflict which generally result in serious or violent hostilities. From the data available on conflicts we may make the following classification with regard to internal conflicts:

1. **Ideological conflicts** between the state and insurgent movements, where the social inequality between classes is dominant;
2. **Governance and authority conflicts** concerning the distribution of power and authority in society. Demands from the opposition are for regime changes and popular participation;
3. **Racial conflicts**, evident in South Africa, the USA, Western Europe, and elsewhere;
4. **Identity conflicts**, where the dominant aspect is ethnic, religious, tribal, or linguistic differences. Often these conflicts involve a mixture of identity and the search for security. In the latter case, the main contention often concerns the devolution of power and such conflicts are likely to increase. Identity conflicts can be subdivided into territorial conflicts, ethnic and minority conflicts, religious assertions, and struggles for self-determination;
5. **Inter-state conflicts**, which are typically cases of traditional inter-state wars.

Various linkages may exist between the conflicts so defined, or we may find a mixture of several. The above classification is, however, static. What is required is to conceptualize the various interrelations between them. A typology is a way of grouping instances of conflict so that common characteristics and systematic differences are revealed. But this is only a statement of purpose. Similarity and difference are cultural constructs. Typologies derive from theories. They are tools rather than verities. To choose a conflict typology is to choose a way of looking at the world of conflict. It does not exclude other ways. It may well be that there are several types of conflict which are waged simultaneously; or that a country faces two or more types of conflict – for example, identity conflicts based on the demand for autonomy, and governance and authority conflicts. In 1989 in Sri Lanka five armed conflicts were being waged simultaneously. In Colombia and Lebanon, also, several armed conflicts were being waged. Given the analytical problems in defining the specificity of these conflicts, some scholars term them protracted social conflicts or intractable conflicts.[7] What is distinctive about this typology is that conflicts may be multiple in character. While a typology enables us to delineate each specific type analytically, in the real world there is a dynamic interaction between the various categories which enables us to call these conflicts protracted social conflicts. Others would prefer to use the term "intractable conflicts." It is the sources of intractability which need to be identified.

I will not discuss here all the types of conflicts mentioned above, but will concentrate on identity conflicts, which are of special relevance to this discussion.[8]

Identity conflicts

Identity conflicts are the most pervasive and the most violent of conflicts. Identity has been defined as an abiding sense of selfhood, the core of which makes life predictable to an individual. To have no ability to anticipate events is essentially to experience terror. Identity is conceived of as more than a psychological sense of self; it encompasses a sense that one is safe in the world physically, psychologically, socially, even spiritually. Events which threaten to invalidate the core sense of identity elicit defensive responses aimed at avoiding psychic and/or physical annihilation. Identity is postulated to operate in this way not only in relation to interpersonal conflict, but also in conflict between groups.[9]

Ethnicity is a variant of identity. Ethnicity is not a static concept but a dynamic one, in that ethnicity and ethnic boundaries can be continuously redefined, given certain factors. Perry Anderson suggests that ethnicity is largely imagined but is a myth of powerful significance. The politicization of ethnicity is a long historical process, in which a crucial factor is the interaction between centre and periphery. Polarization does not seem to take place until a certain point has been passed: before this point, there will normally be instances where conflict resolution could be achieved through compromise and accommodation.

Ethnicity itself can be enhanced and reformulated under conditions of modernization. Myths of origin, enemy images, demonizing the other, are old and traditional myths of long historical duration. Most ethnic groups do have a myth of origin, a history of the group, chosen enemies, and stories of traumas. But what is it that gives these symbolic elements meaning and, in certain contexts, a possibility of actualization? When do self-fulfilling prophecies become actualized? Here, the intersection between modernity and the revival of myth and ritual is of considerable interest.

Religious fundamentalism

Religion in all its manifestations continues to be a source of identity and meaning in a turbulent and modernizing world. In today's world, religion is deeply involved with internal conflicts. In spite of predictions that religion would disappear with continuing modernization, it continues to provide a primary source of meaning and identity to many people, whether Christians, Muslims, Jews, Buddhists, Hindus, or others. This religious revival is of significance, and many have applied the loose concept "religious fundamentalism" to it. Some scholars have labelled other religious expressions as fundamentalist – often meaning something unlikeminded, something dark and malevolent, or not sharing one's concept of rationality. Judaism, Christianity, Islam, and Buddhism have strong ontological components of exclusion and have indeed been strong forces of mobilization. The Christian and Islamic projects are in conflict because their goals are so similar. Spreading the Gospel to the heathen and gathering the unbelievers to the One True Faith are understood as commands from on high. Judaism also has a claim for exclusivity in its concept of the "chosen people." The faithful constitute distinct, exclusive communities that confront each other as competitors for the soul of humanity. It is this exclusiveness and the claims inherent in such concepts of exclusion that are potentially conflictual. Among the most interesting sociological explanations advanced for the rise of Islamic fundamentalism or puritanism is Ernest Gellner's view of Islamic fundamentalism as the transformation of the central "great tradition" of Islam into the majoritarian folk tradition: "It allows it to assume a triple role in affirming a continuous old identity, in reduplicating a humiliating past and poverty, and in rejecting the foreigner. And yet it also provides a charter for purification and self-discipline."[10]

Another approach is provided by the authors of a major comparative study of ten fundamentalist movements, who understand fundamentalism as involving "a view of the universe and a discourse about the nature of truth that encompasses and transcends the religious domain. For that reason, every movement or cause is potentially fundamentalist."[11]

An important sociological clue to the revitalization of identity and its salience is the concept of relative deprivation. Ted Robert Gurr suggests that the necessary precondition for violent civil conflict is relative deprivation, defined as

actors' perception of discrepancy between their value expectations and their environment's apparent value capabilities. Value expectations are the goods and conditions of life to which people believe they are justifiably entitled. The referents of value capabilities are to be found largely in the social and physical environment: they are the conditions that determine people's perceived chances of getting or keeping the values they legitimately expect to attain. I assume that perceived discrepancies between expectations and capabilities with respect to any collectively sought value – economic, psychosocial, political – constitute relative deprivation.[12]

Another of Gurr's propositions is equally of value when looking at the revitalization of identity. The occurrence of civil violence presupposes the likelihood of relative deprivation among substantial numbers of individuals in a society. Concomitantly, the more severe relative deprivation, the greater the likelihood and intensity of civil disobedience.[13]

What is significant about these theses is that modernization enhances and increases the sense of relative deprivation. What is particular about modernization is the entire drive towards modernity. This can take many forms. Consumerism, for example, projects a fantasy world which can never be achieved. It is at this point of interaction that the psychological need for identity becomes strongest, because the chimeric goal cannot be achieved and one's own language and/or culture are in the process of being reduced in status. We need only to look at demographic forecasts to glimpse the potential magnitude of the problem, seeing that young people, in particular, caught in these clashes of cultures, are so ready and willing to join the ranks of so-called fundamentalist movements.

Another aspect which is worth investigating is the role of the mass media in the recreation and the actualization of these mythologies. In most societies, the mass media play a decisive role in mobilizing myths and demonic images of the other. Normally, demonization is not carried out through the secular press, but by other means. In some cases, national television and radio are mobilized to re-create and excite myths or stories of past traumas, whether imagined or real.

3 The role of culture

Culture has many definitions. It may be defined as behaviour peculiar to *Homo sapiens* together with the material objects used as an integral part of this behaviour. Specifically, culture consists of language, ideas, beliefs, customs, codes, institutions, tools, techniques, works of art, rituals, ceremonies, and so on. Given the evolution of the concept, there is no agreement on its definition. Kroeber and Kluckhohn cite 164 definitions of culture, ranging from "learned behavior" to "ideas in the mind," "a logical construct," "a statistical fiction," "a psychic defense mechanism," and so on. For the purpose of this note, we use "culture" as an abstraction which provides symbolic meaning. In this sense, culture has different specificities and can be different in different historical societies. *Homo sapiens*, unlike other animals, is influenced by culture. Culture provides meaning for our existence and influences our action. It is only *Homo sapiens* who incorporates this unique influence.

The word "violence" is related etymologically to the word "violation." Great difficulties are encountered in searching for definitions of violence. War has been the subject of many definitions and many studies, but violence and internal wars within the nation state are still in an early stage of conceptualization. In *Violence and Its Causes* (Paris: UNESCO, 1981) Galtung complained how little scientific work has been done on the subject, given the significance of violence.

Galtung defines the idea of violence as "anything avoidable that impedes human self-realization." Human self-realization, in turn, is defined as satisfaction of human needs. Galtung has made a distinction between direct and structural violence. Direct violence is the use of physical force to affect, or in response to, the actions of other human beings. Structural violence, on the other hand, is the result of social structures which affect people indirectly. In the literature, less significance has been given to cultural violence. Cultural violence can be defined as the denial of identity, security, and symbolic meaning. It is important to conceptualize cultural violence, particularly when tradition and identity are challenged by modernization and Westernization. Today, some scholars are talking of the violence against nature. The concept of violence against nature is strong in indigenous cultures and in some of the Asian religions, such as Buddhism and Taoism. Violence against the environment is a global problem and pertains to human survival. It is also obvious that a good theory should try to show the relationships between types of violence.

Could we say that some cultures are more prone to violence than others? Galtung lists the six cultural domains which legitimize structural and direct violence as religion, ideology, language, art, and empirical and formal science. He suggests that some religions, particularly the Judaeo-Christian religions, have a strong concept of the "chosen people," which is the source of racism and the negation of other cultures and religions. Many studies have concentrated on the role of ideologies such as fascism, communism, and nationalism in legitimizing violence. Benedict Anderson suggests that modern nationalism has replaced religion as the source of meaning and identity. Myths of nationalism can be powerful sources of violence and destruction. A more modern version, prevalent in many third world societies, is the ideology of the national security state.

Recent anthropological studies have also contributed to our understanding of the role of culture in legitimizing violence. Of significance are those cultures which ascribe demonic significance to other cultures and religions. Essentially, the myths and rituals of everyday religious practice tend to reproduce the demonic characteristics of others. It has been suggested that in many ethnic or identity conflicts the demonic aspects of ritual and religion tend to reproduce the stigmatization of the other (see Bruce Kapferer, below).

Other studies have emphasized the role of scapegoating in role conflicts, where, in extreme situations, cultural scapegoating mechanisms are found to restore societal equilibrium. Scholarly attention has also been focused on the "role of self-fulfilling prophecies" in engendering and reproducing violence. These are situations where scapegoating can be reproduced in massive collective violence against another community.

It is not my intention to explore all the elements of modernity, but to look at some of the elements which tend to reproduce violence. It is precisely modernity which can exacerbate violence, because, as part of the discourse of a bureaucratic, rational, technocratic state, it totalizes the state's wars and its enemies. Myths of origin, linguistic and ethnic differences, traumas and legends, and self-fulfilling prophecies have always existed in traditional societies. Ritualization of violence against the other has existed in many societies. But what gives myths significance is the way in which modernity, with all its paraphernalia, excites the myths to make them real. It is this mediating function between myth and modernity which must be a central concern.

The role of the state

The modernization project has been accompanied by a highly centralized and standardized bureaucratic system whose apotheosis has been the development and articulation of a centralized state. The centralized state and its evolution was the project which was seen as the best vehicle for the evolution of human civilization. The evolution of the state has been the vehicle upon which violence has been mediated between itself and the people, through the evolution of a technocratic/bureaucratic structure which has taken upon itself the monopoly of violence. The evolution of the state and the process of standardization have meant that cultures and languages have been, and continue to be, either eliminated, absorbed or incorporated into the modern project.

What is new is that the process of centralization and state-building has been challenged by a variety of social and ethnic movements. The consolidation of state power in the future is problematic for a variety of reasons, including the following:
– the concept of sovereignty is being gradually eroded;
– the unitary state as a powerful centralizing agency is being challenged by sub-nationalist forces;
– the monopoly of violence is no longer exclusive to the state, and various transnational forces are able to arm, equip, and deliver lethal weapons of terror.

The concept of sovereignty

The modern state system has European origins. Beginning with a small number of states, it has expanded to a plethora of states. This expansion, in itself, has constituted a major global project. The state-building project assumed new vigour after the Cold War with the emergence or re-emergence of many new states. At the same time, there has been – under conditions of modernity – an erosion of the concept of sovereignty. The concept of non-interference in the internal affairs of another state is under considerable strain, while many prerogatives of the state are being challenged domestically and by external actors. Modern communication and the metaphor of the "global village" have helped to advance this process. Furthermore, international institutions – which, in large part, were founded to foster or complement state-building projects – have assumed an autonomy which sometimes leads to the imposition of their will on individual states.

The unitary state

The process of state-building was characterized by strong centralization and bureaucratic management. Often, unitary state structures are controlled by hegemonic élites who marginalize the periphery and other identities. As well, unification or maintaining the unity of the state has often been promoted on the principle of "one language, one nation." The centralized state is challenged by many factors. State formation being an evolutionary process, there are some formations which have achieved a high degree of integration, while a majority of states are less cohesive. This applies to almost all decolonized societies, including the former Soviet Union and parts of Eastern Europe. Often, states are dominated not only through bureaucratic centralization but by hegemonic élites with wide patron/client networks, which exclude other groups. Some of these states may evolve into truly multi-ethnic societies, but the idea of the "melting-pot" as a paradigm for social integration is unlikely to be relevant to all segmented and deeply divided societies.

Most of these types of internal conflict are about the nature of the state and its formation. Whether the conflicts are over the devolution of power, federalism, governance, or the distribution of resources, what is fundamentally at issue is how the state manages its business. Several states are themselves a result of violence and bloodshed. Some states are hegemonic states in that they are based on communal, ethnic, or religious loyalties, where patterns of recruitment to the army or to the bureaucracy are based on ethnic affiliations. Some can be called "defective" states, in that they continue to preside over their own retardation. But, in general, all states are confronted with several challenges, the most significant being the requirement for modernization of their economies within a globalization process which is frenetic and accelerating. Most often, the internal threat to democratic development comes from the military or from ethnic or religious fundamentalist forces. In dealing with these issues, states have become agents of arbitrary violence, perpetuating violence and militarism as a way of resolving conflicts.

The state and the monopoly of violence

An important historical process which brought about changes in forms of violence was the concentration of power in the hands, first, of a few princes more powerful than others and, later, of the modern state. Through its military, police, and security apparatus, the state became the custodian of arms and the protector of civil life. This centralizing logic meant that violence gradually became a state monopoly. According to Max Weber's well-known definition, the state successfully claims the monopoly of the legitimate use of physical force within a given territory. The state's monopoly of violence can be either legitimate or illegitimate.

Today, however, the monopoly of violence no longer rests with the state: it has been eroded, in part, by new transnational actors who are able to sell and distribute lethal weapons to all comers. Non-state actors now have easy access to arms and thus have a greater influence over the direction of conflicts and their perpetuation.

The expanding arms market, the proliferation of weapons, and the diffusion of weapons technology to new actors are further significant reasons why internal conflicts are becoming increasingly unmanageable. In particular, there is a growing transnational network, with links to the drugs trade, which trades in small weapons.

4 The end of war?

The end of the Cold War led some scholars to believe that there would be a decline in inter-state wars. Mueller has argued that there has been a significant shift in the culture and norms governing war and peace in the advanced democracies. Many observers have noted the absence of inter-state wars in the last few years. Mueller argues that a change in norms and culture in the developed world may have a demonstrable effect on the obsolescence of war in the third world. He notes that there have been virtually no wars among the 44 wealthiest countries and that war has taken place almost exclusively within the third world. He has also observed that when countries improve their standard of living, they will find the prospect of war decreasingly attractive because they will have more to lose. Another interesting proposition is that war outside the developed world has tended to take place among new states, not old ones. Many scholars have pointed to the fact that no significant inter-state wars have occurred between democratic regimes.[14] To some, this has suggested that a democratic zone of peace has evolved over the years and that the furtherance of democracy will best ensure peace.

But what about wars between democratic and non-democratic states? Are they not equally ferocious? There is considerable evidence that, in the late 1950s, democracies were about as likely to become involved in war as were other regime. While the thesis that there are no wars between democracies is acceptable, there is nothing in the empirical evidence to suggest that there will not be wars between a democratic country and a non-democratic country.[15] Wars between democratic and so-called non-democratic countries, such as those between the United States and Viet Nam or Panama, the British war against Argentina, or the Allied coalition against Iraq, are evidence of democracies' willingness to engage in inter-state wars.

We may witness a resurgence of inter-state wars in the future. There are several intractable trouble spots where war preparedness is considerable. Notwithstanding the major breakthrough in peace negotiations between Israel and the Palestine Liberation Organization, the Middle East remains a highly volatile and dangerous region. Although there is a ceasefire in the Iran–Iraq war, hostilities may well erupt again. Other instances of war preparedness include the India–Pakistan conflict, the Sahel, and sub-Saharan Africa. Certainly, emerging conflicts may also arise from resource depletion and the need to share rivers, forest reserves, and oil.

As the fears of a nuclear conflagration caused by a superpower confrontation receded, the spectre of nuclear and conventional arms proliferation in Asia and the Middle East grew, thanks, in part, to the West's ongoing willingness to help stock arsenals, as they did with Saddam Hussein's. Deterrence and nuclear terror remain the rationale for the Pakistani, Indian, and Chinese bombs. It is reported that North Korea is attempting to join the nuclear club. The various safeguards and early warning mechanisms are still at a primitive stage. Further, there is a greater demand for long-range ballistic missile technology. Many countries in Asia and the Middle East are seeking to acquire or develop long-range ballistic missiles and many are also acquiring combat aircraft with strike capabilities rivalling the destructiveness of a ballistic missile payload. Disarmament and de-escalation of the arms race in Europe has meant that some of these arms are being sold cheaply to third world governments.[16] The war in the Gulf provoked a surge in demand for conventional and high-technology weapons, particularly in that region. Meanwhile, there has been a tremendous proliferation of small arms, which are difficult to monitor. The drug trade also fuels the traffic in arms and provides resources for the guerrilla and the military.

Armed conflicts and their characteristics

The 1988 *SIPRI* [Stockholm International Peace Research Institute] *Yearbook* identified 33 contemporary major armed conflicts, with over 1,000 casualties each.[17] Thirty-two armed conflicts were recorded for 1989.[18] Despite these indications of a decrease in major armed conflicts, if armed conflicts with less than 1,000 casualties are considered, the number is rising. The total number of ongoing armed conflicts in the world today is staggering. In some locations there are several destructive conflicts going on simultaneously.[19] The 1990 *SIPRI Yearbook* suggested that the number of armed conflicts had increased to about 75, and it is likely that more efficient reporting would show an increase to about 150 conflicts. The incidence of direct violence, as measured by casualty rates, does not, however, provide us with a full picture of the scale of social violence.

Some interesting observations can be made based on the empirical data available. Most of the armed conflicts take place in third world countries. The basic issues in the armed conflicts of 1989 were related to internal matters. Inter-state conflicts are currently on the decline – perhaps only for the moment. With regard to conflict management or resolution, the UN Security Council has rarely been involved. In some cases, the good offices of the UN Secretary-General have prevailed, but most often conflict resolution has been the function of a big regional power. It is likely, however, that the UN and, in particular, the good offices of the Secretary-General will play a more active role in conflict resolution in the future.

In most cases, internal conflicts have been fuelled by sales of arms and military equipment to combatants. Arms have been provided not only by the superpowers but also by some states in the third world.

Apart from arms, there is evidence that chemical weapons are being used by both states and guerrillas.[20] There have been consistent and flagrant violations of human rights and minimal respect for the laws of war. Gross abuses of human rights are evident on the part of both states and guerrilla movements. Civilians account for 74 per cent of official deaths, almost three times as many as military deaths.[21] In most cases, the conflicts have involved cross-border affiliations or networks, where a neighbouring state provides sanctuary as well as arms and training to insurgents. Many of the conflicts listed are identity conflicts, where granting substantial devolution of power or territorial autonomy would probably bring an end to the violence. An analysis of the various types of internal conflict also shows that a majority of them have reached stalemate.[22]

In all cases the conflicts are between the state and particular social and/or ethnic groups. Although these conflicts are characterized as conflicts between two parties, i.e. the state and a particular ethnic group, often there are multiple violent conflicts, involving many parties and issues. It is sometimes difficult to identify relevant actors, and the most articulate, with command over resources and communications, have a higher propensity to advertise their claims. Generally the conflicts are over non-negotiable and intangible demands such as identity, security, and social justice. In some cases, the principal demand is for a separate state or for some form of regional autonomy.

The environment in which conflicts occur is highly non-egalitarian and without a pervasive rationalist discourse. Often these conflicts take place within a multilingual and multicultural environment, where different meanings are attached to the discourse and where communication may be not only between the parties but also within the parties themselves. The objective seems to be to consolidate political power within one's own community. The discourse of conflict, then, is fragmented, disjointed, and multifaceted. Normally the state is ill equipped to deal with violent claims made upon it and tries to resolve the crisis by military means. Rarely does it exhaust non-military means from the range of options available. There is often no solid tradition of governance in the country and little respect for law and order.

I have of course exaggerated the differences, if only to delineate the specificity of the conflict environments we are dealing with, whether in the so-called third world, the former Soviet Union, Eastern Europe, or elsewhere. What is obvious is that protracted social conflicts, when they are highly politicized, are about power and politics.

The concept of non-intervention in internal affairs is crumbling as conflicts within and between states get inextricably interlinked. The war in the Gulf, the disintegration of the Soviet Union, the social conflicts in Central America, the Islamic revivals in Asian and African countries, the destabilization of Southern Africa, the drug-financed rebellions in South America and South-East Asia, the resurgence of ethnicity and nationalism, and the complex pattern of massive refugee movements from South to North are examples that belong to our generation.

Sources of non-state violence

Ethno-populist movements are movements mobilized on the basis of ethnic identity. Normally this mobilization process evokes a myth of origin, a shared identity, and a geographical location. These ethno-populist movements differ from the movements for national liberation which evolved before and after the Second World War and were aimed against a formal oppressive colonial power. They also differ from the class-based movements that were typically a product of the Industrial Revolution and a growing proletariat. Today, class-based insurgent movements, particularly if they were tied to one socialist camp or the other, have entered their death throes, while popular movements, coalitions, networks and other types of creative organizations are emerging. In addition, we must be aware of the new and increasingly violent ethno-populist movements. These organizations are not only based on primordial ties and perceived interests but also seem to share specific characteristics, particularly in their modes of organization, their age composition, the sociological basis of their recruitment, the tactics they adopt, the way they define armed struggle. Some may be linked to drug networks and seem to operate at the borders of criminality.

Another aspect of direct violence which requires serious interdisciplinary study is the use of paramilitary organizations and vigilante groups, élite counter-insurgency or commando units, and death squads used by the state or factions of the military against general political opposition or to suppress claims for self-determination. The extralegal character of these formations and the cover which is provided through indemnity laws create an environment in which these groups can operate.

There are also other perpetrators of violence. Guerrilla terrorism against unarmed civilians constitutes grave and persistent violation of the integrity of civilians, and these acts tend to escalate conflicts.

31

5 Violence and its transformation

Wars do not last forever. They have a beginning, a middle and an end. Wars between states have become less frequent and of shorter duration. Some forms of violence have been eliminated – slavery, feudalism, duelling, religious inquisitions, and so on. These institutions did not disappear spontaneously, but through human action. The kinds of violence we are discussing require similar attention and a range of measures. Perhaps we may learn from the ways medical science has succeeded in eliminating some diseases and is going about overcoming others. Medical science is an accumulation of slow and painstaking research and methods of practice. Controlling and eliminating disease requires many professions and disciplines, approaching the problem from different angles. Epidemiology shows how systematic attention and action can and may eventually make an epidemic manageable. There are also different forms of violence, and it is only through the establishment of a system of norms and the development of accountability to those norms that violence can be diminished.

Human rights accountability

In this century a body of organizations has developed and assumed an international role in the protection of the life and integrity of persons. Some of these organizations predate the Second World War, but most of them had their genesis in the post-war era, when the global community tried to evolve a body of universal rights applicable to all human societies. These include economic and social rights, civil and political rights concerned with the integrity of the person, and cultural rights. A third generation of rights has also evolved which insists on the right to development, the right to peace, and so on. There are, however, different degrees of consensus and emphasis with regard to the universality of rights or to what extent they should be prioritized, i.e., whether some rights should be respected and others ignored.

Governments are signatories to international covenants and conventions and some are special signatories to various protocols, including that on genocide. The fact that governments are signatories to the covenants means that they are accountable not only to their citizens but also to the international community. Human rights, therefore, are everybody's business. Adherence to standards of behaviour has become an international event. This fact has profound implications for the establishment of a body of norms and values which are universally applicable. No longer can a state claim state sovereignty and the right to non-interference in its internal affairs as a subterfuge for persistent gross violations of human rights. The marriage between human rights law and the law of war provides the international community with the leverage and entry point for developing standards of accountability.

The fact that governments are signatories to the various protocols means that their behaviour can be monitored. Monitoring of human rights abuses means that citizens are expected to be well informed about what their governments do. It also provides the basic information for holding governments accountable. In many cases, however, local citizens do not have the means to ensure accountability. Nonetheless, there has been an extraordinary growth in local and national bodies which have taken on the task of human rights surveillance. They are in the front line of human rights protection. These local and national organizations can be numerous, as in the Philippines, or very scarce, as in much of the Middle East. At the international level, several organizations have emerged with mandates to monitor and protect the integrity of persons. They have developed professional capabilities and a high degree of specialization with respect to their mandates, terms of reference, and constituencies. Amnesty International is a case in point.

There are several weakness in the international protection system. They are as follows:

1. **Civil and political rights** (torture, disappearances, extrajudicial killings, censorship, limits on freedom of expression): fairly well covered.
2. **Economic and social rights**: not so well covered.
3. **Collective rights**: least well covered.
4. **Non-state violence**: not covered.

Non-state violence

It has been argued above that substantial standard-setting has been achieved in developing accountability of the state in the protection of the integrity of persons. These norms and standards have evolved over time and institutions have developed a capability in monitoring the obligations and responsibilities of governments.

As regards the responsibilities of non-state actors in the protection of human rights and citizens, however, there is still a long way to go. While it is true that the International Committee of the Red Cross (ICRC) has developed additional protocols to cover armed conflicts of a non-international character, much more needs to be done to ensure adherence to international standards.

Non-state violence can take many forms. It can include selective assassinations, kidnappings, torture, detention, extrajudicial killings, indiscriminate bombings, forced recruitment, compulsory taxes, the use of land mines and booby traps, and the use – more recently developed – of chemical and computerized detonators. Often, non-state groups do not allow for freedom of expression or dissent, do not allow the right of assembly and the participation of other groups. Far too often civilians are held captive to the creed of the guerrilla. The guerrilla also operates death squads, burns dead bodies without inquest, and perpetrates other crimes against human standards.

There are many complex reasons why standard-setting and monitoring processes have not advanced in their efforts to hold such groups accountable. One of the fundamental problems has been that of determining at what point a group becomes an actor in a conflict who should be monitored and held accountable. As far as the ICRC is concerned, any group which is sufficiently large to assume governmental power may have the same obligations and duties as a government. But what about the hundreds of groups which may not be large enough to assume power?

Another recognizable problem is the lack of information available about non-state groups. Non-state organizations may not necessarily have constitutions, mandates, and rules. It is difficult to find the stated aims and goals of such organizations as Hezbollah in Lebanon or Alice Lamwaka in Uganda. If these organizations do not subscribe to mandates, goals and rules, how can common standards be applied to them?

Who is accountable to whom?

Political groups may be aspiring to be future governments or to influence future governments. But what is common to all may be that they feel governments are accountable. Yet, while these groups complain about violations perpetrated by governments, they feel that they themselves are beyond accountability. Governments do often claim, quite legitimately, that the international community is one-sided in its criticisms, when each year their policies come under the scrutiny of various bodies, fact-finding missions issue reports about their behaviour, and different bodies monitor their performance. Meanwhile, few non-state parties are subject to the same scrutiny.

Every effort should be made to monitor and evaluate the role of non-state bodies. The criteria for monitoring can be derived from human rights and humanitarian law. Amnesty International and other relevant human rights bodies have begun to address this issue by providing effective reporting of non-state violations, despite the fact that this type of reporting is far more complicated than monitoring governments. But much remains to be done to develop criteria for accountability and to communicate moral approbation against those who persist in engaging in criminal behaviour. Furthermore, efforts should be stepped up to criminalize such violations as violations against humanity.

Codes of conduct regarding internal armed conflicts

Given the salience and intensity of internal armed combat and the extent to which civilians are victims of civil war, there is clearly a need to apply the laws of war to all sides engaged in combat. A considerable part of the activity of the International Committee of the Red Cross takes place in internal armed conflict situations not regulated by the Geneva Conventions for the Protection of Victims of War.

Some very important work in this area has been initiated by International Alert, particularly Eduardo Mariño, in developing a *Code of Combat Conduct: Minimum Combatant Duties – Minimum People's Rights*.[23] Codes of conduct for all armed combatants have also been under development in El Salvador and Guatemala. In several places, armed groups and governments are engaged in official or unofficial discussions regarding the development of codes of conduct. Another example of an attempt to develop criteria of accountability are the Zones of Peace in the Philippines, a subject dealt with in more detail below.

Mercenaries in armed conflicts

In general, mercenary activities have been closely linked to decolonization. Many African states have been the victims of mercenary aggression. In recent years, an aspect of South Africa's aggression against Angola, Mozambique, and Zimbabwe has been its organizing of mercenary "liberation armies" such as Unita and Renamo. However, mercenary activity has not been restricted to decolonization, and there is reason to believe that it is appearing in new places and in new forms. In 1985, the UN Commission on Human Rights decided to examine mercenary activity as a human rights violation and an impediment to exercising the right to self-determination. The Special Rapporteur drew attention to the changing forms of mercenary activity as a threat to the right to self-determination, security, and the peace of nations. The activities of mercenaries are relevant in a changing global order, where states could resort to encouraging mercenary activity to destabilize regions.

We should examine the role of mercenaries, the changing character of mercenary activity, and its persistence within the framework of ethnic and internal conflicts. To what extent has the UN Convention against mercenary activity been effective, and where does mercenary activity persist?

Death squads, commando units, and vigilantes

Since the mid-1970s, political killings carried out by governments and government-backed forces in violation of the law of war have become the most serious human rights problem in many continents. There seems to be a proliferation and a rise in the influence of paramilitary security structures, whether they are death squads, vigilantes, or paramilitary units trained by the armed forces. The distinctive manifestations of these groups are kidnapping, disappearances, and killings, usually accompanied by mutilation and torture. Given the international surveillance and accountability of governments, extralegal forms are resorted to. Extrajudicial forces are frequently used in class and ethnic conflicts. An empirical survey of these activities and a comparative analysis of the methods and structures involved are needed. The popular notion that military regimes more often resort to extrajudicial forces than so-called democratic regimes may be challenged by such research. We should also focus on this grey area in terms of finding avenues for international standard-setting.

Transfer of arms

There is a considerable literature on the international transfer of arms. Annually, SIPRI publishes information on arms transfers between states. There is, however, growing concern about the increasing number of states involved in the arms trade and the destruction and criminality related to the illicit and unregulated international arms trade. Of particular concern have been the proliferation of small arms and other lethal weapons and the diffusion of arms manufacturing technology to both states and non-state groups and other entities. We need to study the expansion of transnational economic crime and the covert funding of arms transfers, as well as the drugs, arms, and hostage connection, so that more effective monitoring can be implemented.

New transnational actors: Drugs, guerrilla, and the state

The illegal movement of controlled substances, particularly marijuana, cocaine, and heroin, is beginning to influence international politics. The drug trade permeates politics and the military and economic life of significant communities.

To many peasants coca and poppy cultivation provide their sole source of income. Drug trafficking also constitutes a North/South problem. The connections between drugs, arms sales, and the military and insurgents are not restricted to Latin American countries. They are present also in the traditional growing areas of the Golden Triangle of South-East Asia and in the Afghanistan/Pakistan belt. We should obtain a comparative perspective between the traditional growing areas and the new growth poles in other regions. Much can be learned from the research already done on the Golden Triangle. An examination of these linkages could also probe the dependence of ethnic and indigenous producers on drugs as a cash crop and the adequacy of regional and international efforts to find alternatives.

6 Empowerment in different cultures

In the literature and theoretical discussion on conflict resolution more attention should perhaps be focused on conflict transformation. Conflict transformation attempts to empower all the parties to a conflict. This approach recognizes that social conflicts need to be transformed in a less violent way, not because violence cannot achieve limited objectives but because contemporary violence and its manifestations maim and injure all sides, including large numbers of civilians. I would now like to reflect on some approaches we may consider within the comparative experience of violent conflict and suggest that **each specific culture has enough resources** within itself to resolve its own conflicts. The task is to identify those resources meaningfully.

Let us first take the resurgence of religious revivalism and fundamentalism and consider how a religious discourse that could lead to violence may be transformed. Generally, religious fundamentalists tend to capture the space for the religious discourse. They define the terrain of the discourse, the symbols to be used, and who the enemies are. In many societies where religion remains a potent mobilizer of people, the process of criticism and deconstruction has advanced significantly amongst intellectuals; but, unfortunately, this scholarly discourse rarely touches the mainstream religious communities, and it is here that more needs to be done. Perhaps the reason for this is that so-called progressives or modernists have not given enough thought to ways of encouraging the modernization of religion. In some instances they may even have abandoned the terrain altogether. However, it is readily apparent that religious discourse can only be met from within its own traditions.

Another significant aspect of religious fundamentalism is that in many cases the priest still plays a significant role in religious interpretation. Benedict Anderson suggests that with print capitalism the monopoly of religious interpretation was no longer the exclusive privilege of the priesthood. This may be true for Christianity, but can we say the same for other religions? What can we say sociologically about the role of the priest in Sri Lanka, for instance? Generally, Sri Lanka's Buddhist priests are at a crossroads both as individuals and as members of the institution of the priesthood. They have to rely on meagre state stipends for a living and they have little economic means. Religious institutions need to be studied and ways found for their modernization. For example, the Sangha are, as Professor Nathan Katz suggests, "capable of enormous political influence ... Many observers have remarked that were the Sangha to rise forcefully and unequivocally against the recurrent anti-Tamil violence, then it would be stopped. Perhaps, they are the only force in Sri Lanka with the influence to effect such a response."[24]

For countries such as Sri Lanka and others, in which highly influential religious establishments exist, this is very significant. If the Sangha could develop their own approach to reconciliation and a vision of their own role in the national peace process, this would be a major force for transforming the conflict. However, such developments must be rooted in their own tradition and expressed in their own language. It would be acceptable and legitimate only if it came from within Buddhism itself and as an internal response to the crisis.

The second question I would like to address is the question of conflict transformation under conditions of massive violence against civilians. Many countries have experienced armed conflicts which have encouraged civilian passivity because armed combatants define the terrain, and both insurgents and the security forces perpetrate the most horrendous crimes. In the transformation of violence, every effort must be made to recover civilian space and democracy from the armed combatants by insisting on accountability to civilian rule. This is not easy and in some cases may be impossible for those living in such conditions. But there is a growing body of international norms on human rights and monitoring, which is significant, and the international community may play a role in ensuring civilian protection. Ultimately, however, accountability must be ensured and sustained from within the society.

The democratic revolution in the Philippines and the ouster of President Ferdinand Marcos were accomplished largely through non-violent means. No political party played a vanguard role, but a web of popular organizations and networks was able to intervene through militant non-violence. After the overthrow of Marcos and during President Corazon Aquino's period in office, violence continued to be endemic in Philippine society through the activities of armed insurgents, the military, and death squads. As a way of meeting the violence, popular organizations developed innovative methods of expanding civilian governance. In some instances, they declared "peace zones" in selected communities and called upon combatants to respect the areas as peace zones. In several instances, the armed groups learned to respect the civilian space.[25]

Another example is drawn from the experience of violence in Colombia. Colombia is faced with multiple levels of violence, including that perpetrated by drug cartels, insurgents, security forces, and the death squads. Here, with the help of urban intellectuals, peasants were able to declare an entire region a no-war zone. Early in 1989, when I visited the country, I was told of an extraordinary "self-made peace case." In La India, a rural area rich in natural resources but inhabited by poor colonist-peasants, the armed groups (left-wing guerrillas, the army, and paramilitary groups) had the civil population trapped in the crossfire. The peasants had three alternatives after 15 years of fear and deaths: leave their land, join one of the armed groups, or be killed. But in mid-1987 they decided to organize themselves and begin a dialogue with the oppressors. They scheduled a meeting with the guerrillas to explain to them how the community could not bear the hostilities any longer. The talks took about six hours. As a result, the guerrillas promised not to force the community to help them any more. A few days later, the peasants talked to the army and elicited the same agreement from them. With the right-wing death squads, they had informal talks. The three leaders from La India we worked with were assassinated in 1990, but the peace process has continued. Later in 1990, the Right Livelihood Award (the alternative Nobel Prize for peoples' organizations) was given to the peasants of La India.

There are many ways in which a culture of negotiations can be developed within a violent environment. These are but two examples of concerted actions which may transform violence. But these examples do not answer several major questions. One is whether these approaches can be applied to ethnic and nationality conflicts in deeply divided societies. Non-violent approaches have not stood a chance when conflicts begin to have an ethnic dimension. This, I believe, is an area on which peace researchers must focus more attention, so that we can begin to elaborate viable frameworks for the transformation of one of the most intractable and destructive forms of internal conflict.

To conclude, I would suggest that we must evolve a new concept of security which is not restricted to the notion of state security. In situations of violent internal conflict, peoples' security will mean developing countervailing stratagems which link up with popular movements to make violence illegitimate and the violent accountable through the articulation of popular sovereignty. It also means recognizing and nurturing movements towards multi-ethnic, plural societies in which social structures and institutions reflect and guarantee that plurality.

Notes

1. A. Giddens, *The Consequences of Modernity* (London: Blackwell, 1990), p. 1.
2. See M. Featherstone (ed.), *Global Culture, Nationalism, Globalization and Modernity* (London: Sage Publications, 1991).
3. P. Wallensteen, "The Origins of Peace Research," in Wallensteen (ed.), *Peace Research: Achievements and Challenges* (Boulder: Westview Press, 1988), pp. 7–29.
4. M. Melko, *Peace in Our Time* (New York: Paragon House, 1990). See especially chap. 3, "The Remission of Violence," pp. 53–89.
5. A. Schmid, "Twentieth Century Megamurders: Determining the Extent of Democide," based on research by Rudolph J. Rummel, University of Hawaii. *PIOOM Newsletter and Progress Report*, vol. 3, no. 1, Summer 1991.
6. Sources include the UNHCR; US Committee on Refugees, *World Refugee Report 1989*; map entitled "Refugees 1988: Where They're From, Where They've Gone," compiled by Freedom House, in Bruce McColm, "The World's Unwanted," *Wall Street Journal*, 23 September 1989.
7. E. Azar, "Protracted International Conflicts. Ten Propositions," in E. Azar and J.W. Bur-

ton, *International Conflict Resolution, Theory and Practice* (Hemel Hempstead): Wheatsheaf Books, 1986. Also L. Kriesberg et al. (eds.), *Intractable Conflicts and Their Transformation* (Syracuse: Syracuse University Press, 1989).

8. For an extended discussion of these issues see my chapter, "The Disappearing Boundaries Between Internal and External Conflicts," in K. Rupesinghe (ed.), *Internal Conflicts and Governance* (London: Macmillan, 1992), pp. 1–26.

9. T.A. Northrup, "Dynamics of Identity in Personal and Social Conflict," in Kriesberg et al. (eds.), op. cit., p. 65.

10. Quoted in A. Hyman, *Muslim Fundamentalism*, Conflict Studies no. 174, London: Institute for the Study of Conflict, 1985.

11. I.S. Lustick, *For the Land and the Lord: Jewish Fundamentalism in Israel* (New York: Council on Foreign Relations, 1988).

12. T.R. Gurr, "Psychological Factors in Civil Violence," in I.K. Feirabend et al. (eds), *Theories and Research* (New York: Prentice-Hall, 1972), p. 39.

13. Ibid.

14. This hypothesis is well elaborated in R.J. Rummel's "Libertarianism and International Violence," *Journal of Conflict Resolution* vol. 27, no. 1, March 1983.

15. See E. Weede, "Democracy and War Involvement," *Journal of Conflict Resolution* vol. 28, no. 4, December 1984.

16. A. Mack, "In the Third World, Nuclear Dominoes," *International Herald Tribune*, 26 May 1990.

17. *SIPRI Yearbook 1988* (Oxford; Oxford University Press, 1988), pp. 285–301.

18. Ibid.

19. K. Lindgren, G.K. Wilson, P. Wallensteen, and K.-Å. Nordquist, "Major Armed Conflicts in 1989," in *SIPRI Yearbook 1990* (Oxford: Oxford University Press, 1990).

20. There were widespread allegations that Iraq used chemical weapons against the Kurds. Similar allegations were made by the Sri Lankan government *vis-à-vis* the insurgent Liberation Tigers of Tamil Eelam.

21. Data from William Eckhardt, Lent Peace Research Laboratory of St Louis. See *COPRED Peace Chronicle*, Fairfax, VA, April 1990.

22. Rupesinghe, op. cit.

23. "Towards a Comprehensive Code of Conduct," *The Diplomat's Review* vol. II, no. 12, December 1990.

24. N. Katz, "Sri Lankan Monks on Ethnicity and Nationalism," in K.M. de Silva et al. (eds), *Ethnic Conflict in Buddhist Societies: Sri Lanka, Thailand and Burma* (London: Pinter Publishers, 1988), pp. 138–52.

25. E. Garcia, "Empowering People for Peace: The Philippine Experience," in K. Rupesinghe (ed.), *Internal Conflicts and Governance* (London: Macmillan, 1992), pp. 65–80.

2

Rejoinder to the theory of structural violence

Felipe E. MacGregor, S.J., and Marcial Rubio C.

In Johan Galtung's expansion of the boundaries of traditional cosmology to include social cosmology, his theory of structural violence plays a very important role. In 1978, speaking to the New Zealand Law Association, Galtung made one of the many presentations of the subject since his seminal article "Violence, Peace and Peace Research," written in 1969. He said: "Talking about violence is a little like talking about disease in general: one knows one is touching something important, something very complicated, that it is easy to moralize and difficult to come up with a diagnosis, prognosis, not to mention a cure, a therapy, or the best of all: preventive therapy."[1]

Galtung maintains that:

A theory of violence should be victim-oriented, not method-oriented, and the victims we are concerned with are human beings who *suffer*. We shall use a broad definition of violence as *any avoidable* suffering in human beings ... Suffering may not be the best term: a better expression might be avoidable reduction in human realization, leaving open what this might mean in various cultures, in various points in geographical space, in various points in historical time.[2]

Structural violence is "somehow the result of the working of social structures." Galtung says of himself that "being trained as a sociologist, I came to see peace research in the early years as a plea for a structural perspective, for a heavy emphasis on structures, rather than on the act committed (or omitted) by persons or states."

The plea for a structural perspective is consubstantial and ever present in Galtung's work. The theories of W. Benjamin and M. Weber on violence in lawful and illegal domination of people were part of Galtung's intellectual environment. Galtung, faced with Marxism, discovered that it is a power structure. Societies dominated by Marxism are almost the perfect image of the vertical society. Galtung's Latin American experience, travelling and teaching, brings together exposure to the realities of daily life and intellectual efforts to find reasons for those dire realities. When Galtung was teaching in Santiago de Chile, Theotonio Dos Santos and his fellow Brazilian colleagues were exploring the theory and "the structure of dependence." Galtung also considers his visit to India and acquaintance with Gandhi's thought one of the landmarks in his life.

In 1959 the Peace Research Institute, Oslo (PRIO), began its activities. "An effort was made ... to avoid identifying peace research with one single theme of research, e.g. research on arms races, on conflict resolution, on problems of development. Peace research was conceived as an approach rather than a discipline, as committed social science with no respect for any disciplinary or scholastic borderline in social science. The commitment was to a less violent world, violence being conceived of broadly."[3] Galtung, as well as PRIO, is firmly committed to a process rather than to paradigms or basic definitions. "An individual working in the field of peace research would have to be sclerotic or isolated to avoid changes in his own scientific orientation."[4]

In peace research the changes in orientation and identification are from ethnocentric to global and, more importantly, from exploiter to exploited, "from oppressor to oppressed, whether the reference is to nations, peoples or people."[5] This language, difficult to handle by social scientists, has prompted some evasive answers. In particular, structural violence has been considered a metaphor, a myth, or a model. Professor Kenneth Boulding led the way of those who call structural violence a metaphor. Marxists inspired by what Sorel called the myth of socialism consider structural violence a prodrome of class struggle and part of the myth described by Sorel:

Experience shows that the framing of a future, in some indeterminate time, may, when it is done in a certain way, be very effective, and have very few inconveniences; this happens when the anticipations of the future take the form of those myths, which enclose with them, all the strongest inclinations of a people, of a party or of a class, inclinations which recur to the mind with the insistence of instincts in all the circumstances of life; and which give an aspect of complete reality to the hopes of immediate action by which, more easily than by any other method, men can reform their desires, passions, and mental activity. We know, moreover, that these social myths in no way prevent a man profiting by the observations which he makes in the course of his life, and form no obstacle to the pursuit of his normal occupations.[6]

Some attribute to the concept of structural violence the rigidities of mechanical models. Galtung, we think, will admit that structural violence is a model in the sense of a system, a theory of reality. We at the Peruvian Peace Research Association consider structural violence a working hypothesis whose validity can only be probed empirically. We have aimed to do that and have arrived at the following thoughts.

1 On violence in general

Galtung's position

On the subject of violence, Galtung has declared that "violence is present when human beings are being influenced so that their actual somatic and mental realizations are below their potential realizations."[7] We share the following aspects of Galtung's definition:
1. Violence is a phenomenon which reduces a person's potential for performance. A distinction must be made between violence and force, since the former breeds negative results, while this is not necessarily so in the case of the latter. This is an important option, because many people consider that violence may have both positive and negative results.
2. Violence should be objectively measured according to its results, not in a subjective manner. Although the concepts of a person's effective performance and potential performance are not measurable in their true scope, this is not so for certain other aspects, particularly in third world countries plagued by hunger and a lack of adequate health conditions, education, and employment, all of which are statistically verifiable facts. These problems are not so acute in the first world. However, in the third world, they make up a large proportion of human frustration.
3. Therefore, the term "violence" should be treated as a scientifically manageable concept.

The following are our observations on Galtung's definition:
1. It is an exceedingly inclusive concept, since many other elements of reality will eventually reduce a person's effective performance. Natural disasters, unpredictable events, and accidents are good examples of this.[8]

2. In Galtung's text the quantity and quality of violence are irrele-
vant, a view which is ultimately understandable in view of the violence and peace problems in the northern hemisphere, which until
recently had to cope with the constant threat of a nuclear conflict.
In order to apply the concept in Latin America, however, and in
view of a greater variety of social violence, we must include
nuances. Killing and torture are not the same thing, nor can we
compare torture to physical aggression. A constrained democratic
system cannot be the same as a moderate dictatorship, nor can
either of them be the same as a harsh, outright dictatorship. Indifference towards someone else's pain is not the same as rejection
and stern disapproval of those who expose their poverty on the
streets, particularly if this involves a child. Nor is it the same to
think collectively that the best solution for street children is to
confine them or even kill them. These degrees of violence must
be taken into account in order to understand our reality fully.

3. Galtung's concept, in his text, is focused on personal performance,
considered more from the individual viewpoint than from the collective or group viewpoint. This is understandable because the
concept has been developed in the northern hemisphere, where,
in most cases, societies have successfully met group needs. However, in third world countries, we still have a series of needs which
must be resolved on the strictly "statistical" level. Therefore, we
believe that the concept of violence must be an open one, *vis-à-
vis* not only personal performances but also group performances
(understood as the achievements of society as a whole). Despite
this, we must mention that the problem of insufficient group
achievements has been raised by Galtung and has shed more light
on the topic of violence (particularly as regards the concept of
structural violence).

4. Galtung's concept is devised outside of time and space. It can be
applied indiscriminately to any concrete social reality. In order to
study and classify violence better and in order to determine the
relationship between violence and culture, the definition of violence
must include elements and variables enabling it to be rooted within
each concrete reality with two levels of accuracy: one for each society
(or social group), and another, more abstract one, for gender.[9]

5. Galtung does not deal specifically with the aetiology of violence,
although he has indeed developed the influence of socio-economic factors on violence. In order to study the subjects of structural and institutional violence and violence and culture, the very
sources of violence in each instance must be carefully considered.

45

Our definition of violence

Based upon the foregoing, we propose the following definition of violence:

A physical, biological or spiritual pressure, directly or indirectly exercised by a person on someone else, which, when exceeding a certain threshold, reduces or annuls that person's potential for performance, both at an individual and group level, in the society in which this takes place.

The characteristic traits of this definition are as follows:
1. The term "pressure" refers to the use of force, cohesion, or power to a greater extent than is normally admissible on the individual or the group. The term "normally admissible" is debatable, and in order to consider its scope in depth the following, at least, must be taken into account:
   - the acceptable degree of force that may be used within society in individual or social relationships;
   - the legitimacy or, in more general terms, the ethical considerations required to justify applying such degrees of force;
   - the general standards of acceptable pressure in a specific political system;
   - the distinct requirements of a given situation, when the level of force considered necessary may be increased (wartime, periods of economic stress, constitutionally declared emergencies, etc.).
2. The pressure may be "physical" in the strict sense of the term (confinement, binding, blows, etc.); biological (hunger, thirst, malnutrition, etc.); or spiritual (loneliness, anguish, "brainwashing," etc.).
3. Pressure is inflicted by humanity against humanity. This consideration seems useful in the search for paths leading towards pacification, since natural forces can be controlled through different methods (scientific and technological) which are not part of these concepts. Incidentally, Galtung speaks about violence against nature.[10] In order to avoid changing the concept, we must understand that this refers to ecological harm which is also, ultimately, violence against humanity. Force exerted against nature in such a manner as to affect humankind neither directly nor indirectly is not considered as violence in Galtung's concept, nor in ours.
4. the concept of a "threshold" supposes that the pressure exerted exceeds certain levels of resistance prior to generating harmful effects which we recognize as violence. This is important because the

pressure exists although the victim may overcome it by using his or her defences. Moreover, quite often pressure, tolerably exerted, becomes a stimulus with positive results for the victim, and therefore enables the person to perform better.

5. We speak about a "reduction or annulment" of violence to establish a degree of difference in its effects, according to the degree of violence.

6. The potential of performance is relative to each society. In a developed society, it is probable that securing the minimum level of human life (i.e. at the "animal" level of subsistence) is a prerequisite and not an objective to be attained by society considered as a whole. In third world countries this is a goal yet to be achieved.

7. Violence affects an individual's performance and his or her social relations. There are forms of violence which are not apparent when we analyse the individual's opportunities but do appear when studying the group. In other words, certain kinds of violence can be identified only statistically and not by examining individual cases.

8. One of the cornerstones of the definition of violence proposed by Galtung is its consequence: the reduction of the potential for performance. Therefore, not all force is violence, only that which produces this result in human beings.

On structural, institutional, and direct violence

Galtung's concept

Galtung's distinction between personal and structural violence is based upon the actor: is there or is there not an effectively acting subject (person) who produces violence? He dedicates several paragraphs to this issue:

Again it may be asked: can we talk about violence when nobody is committing direct violence, when nobody is acting? This would also be a case of what is referred to above as truncated violence, but again highly meaningful. We shall refer to the type of violence where there is an actor that commits the violence as personal or direct, and to violence where there is no such actor as structural or indirect. In both cases individuals may be killed or mutilated, hit or hurt in both senses of these words, and manipulated by means of stick or carrot strategies. But whereas in the first case these consequences can be traced back to concrete persons as actors, in the second case this is no longer meaningful. There may not be any person who directly harms another person in the structure. The violence is built into the structure and shows up as unequal power and consequently as unequal life chances.

Resources are unevenly distributed, as when income distributions are heavily skewed, literacy/education unevenly distributed, medical services existent in some districts and for some groups only, and so on. Above all, the power to decide over the distribution of resources is unevenly distributed. The situation is aggravated further if the persons low on income are also low on education, low on health, and low on power – as is frequently the case because these rank dimensions tend to be heavily correlated due to the way they are tied together in the social structure.[11]

Galtung adds, later on:

In order not to overwork the word violence we shall sometimes refer to the condition of structural violence as social injustice. The term "exploitation" will not be used, for several reasons. First, it belongs to a political vocabulary and has so many political and emotional overtones that the use of this term will hardly facilitate communication. Second, the term lends itself too easily to expressions involving the verb exploit, which in turn may lead attention away from the structural as opposed to the personal nature of this phenomenon – and even lead to often unfounded accusations about intended structural violence.[12]

He then states that in static societies personal violence is notorious and that structural violence is accepted as a normal fact of life, while in dynamic societies the reverse happens. He also points out that structural violence and personal violence are independent: there are structures in which violence is "person-invariant" and others in which for people violence is "structure-invariant."[13]

Concerning institutional violence he declares:

The term "institutional violence" is frequently used, but we have preferred the term "structural" because very often it is of a more abstract nature and cannot be attributed to one institution in particular. For example, if the police has many prejudiced ideas the term "institutionalized violence" could be appropriately applied, but this is a very concrete case. Violence may be inserted into a structure lacking a police institution ...

Our concept of structural violence

Structural violence, as Galtung would say, contrasts with personal or direct violence. Our concept of the latter is as follows: personal or direct violence is that in which the aggressor can or may be identified. It is face-to-face violence, and is important because the victim can recognize the guilty person through direct confrontation. This is the case with criminal acts, labour conflicts, physical aggression, and the like. Essentially, we embrace Galtung's concept here.

Our concept of structural violence is as follows:

Structural violence happens to a person from and within society's structures, which are shaped, maintained, and eventually transformed with margins of plasticity by human beings, and in many cases this also includes the victims, all of whom are shaped by the same structures.

Structural violence is different from other forms of violence because it comes from the structures and not from people. It is not, therefore, a direct relationship from person to person, but rather a relationship based upon the intermediation of the structures. In structural violence the aggressor is faceless.

Structural violence flows inside social structures and stems out of them into interpersonal relationships. This is a very important issue for the subject of the relationship between violence and culture because, for us, "it flows inside the structures and stems out of them into interpersonal relationships" is a unique expression and not two distinct expressions. That is, structural violence is contained in the very structures of society itself. But what precisely are society's structures? They are people's ways of relating to each other according to accepted rules, to such a degree that these rules become virtually the very essence of human interrelations. They exist in the intersubjectivity of people, and in each person in so far as she or he belongs to the group. That is why we say that structural violence stems from the structures (that is, the rules regulating human behaviour) but is also, simultaneously, within the structures (which make up the individual and the collective psyche). In other words, the relationship between culture and structural violence is very intense; in some cases, we could say, they may even be identical. We shall return to this issue below.

These rules are transmitted and learnt by each and every one of us. Hence, structural violence tends to reproduce itself. Although the rules vary and the structures have a built-in, internal flexibility, they tend constantly to reproduce themselves, with certain adaptations.

An outstanding feature of structural violence is that the victim is also a part of it, in a position of acquiescence or confrontation. We cannot predetermine which of these positions will be taken, because this depends, among other factors, upon the degree to which the victim has internalized the predominant culture or the degree of criticism towards it that he or she has developed. In any case, the victim shares some or all of the rules of the game to which he or she is submitted, and so the victim becomes an objective "accomplice" of these rules.

Poverty and, in particular, broad differences of access to wealth are structural violence, but there are also several other social rules of the game that are also structural violence and should be mentioned.

Examples of structural violence in which poverty is not necessarily involved are:

1. The inefficient administration of justice, which fosters direct violence because the individual tends to take justice into his or her own hands and because in many cases the most effective way for a person to secure justice from the courts is to bribe, is one of the ways of corrupting social peace. Poverty may aggravate these phenomena but they are independent of it. They also occur in societies not stricken by poverty.

2. Authoritarian socialization of children within a family in which we find various expressions of physical mistreatment: machismo; the husband who beats the wife; paternal or maternal absence; miseducation. All these phenomena transform boy or girl children, today's innocent victims, into the executioners of their own children when they replicate these rules. These phenomena, independent of poverty, can become worse when poverty is present.

3. Discrimination is engendered in relation to gender (against females), age, beliefs, religion, race, language, and so on. Of course, there is also marginalization for economic reasons, but the former discriminations are independent of this.

4. "Silent" socialization is the repression of human speech. A child learns how to control his or her impulses in order to adjust quickly to the adult world. Women control talking about their emotions and feelings (sexual and non-sexual). The mass media in many countries reflect the ideas only of a certain social sector and whenever they deal with others they do so only to exhibit those sectors' weak or painful spots and therefore do not express the entire picture. In many countries the exercise of democracy tends to be a "top-down" monologue restricted to electoral campaigns, and electoral promises are systematically neglected once elections are past. As in the former cases, poverty

aggravates many of these features, but does not necessarily condition them.

On institutional violence

Our concept of institutional violence is that institutional violence is that type of structural violence which is found formally or truly embedded in the institutions and is accepted, or at least tolerated, with the complicity of the people.

Institutional violence is, in the first place, a form of structural violence; that is, it is one of its subspecies. Formal or true violence is actually embedded in social institutions: formally, in the case of a positive and expressed acknowledgement of such violence – for example, when armed forces must be trained in skills founded on counter-subversive doctrine, to apply them whenever they find it convenient; or in the formal establishment of repressive secret police corps. True violence occurs when, despite there being no formal acknowledgement, or even in the case of express prohibition, the institutionality cohabits with institutionalized violence. Other cases are organized drug trafficking or subversive groups.

Institutional violence has received considerable acknowledgement in social settings, through accepted principles or facts and in cases when people agree with this violence (e.g. counter-subversion confronting unpopular subversion, in many countries, or cases in which subversive groups have acquired social acknowledgement).

3 On the relationship between violence and culture

Galtung's concept

Galtung establishes a sort of triangle between structural violence, direct violence, and cultural violence. He states that:

Cultural violence can now be added as the third supertype and put in the third corner of a (vicious) triangle as an image. When the triangle is stood on its "direct" and "structural violence" feet, the image invoked is cultural violence as the legitimizer of both. Standing the triangle on its "direct violence" head yields the image of structural and cultural sources of direct violence. Of course, the triangle always remains a triangle – but the image produced is different, and all six positions (three pointing downward, three upward), invoke somewhat different stories, all worth telling.

Despite the symmetries there is a basic difference in the time relation of the three concepts of violence. Direct violence is an event; structural violence is a process with ups and downs; cultural violence is an invariant, a "permanence," remaining essentially the same for long periods, given the slow transformations of basic culture. Put in the useful terms of the French *Annales* school in history; *éventuelle, conjoncturelle, de longue durée.* The three forms of violence enter time differently, somewhat like the difference in earthquake theory between the earthquake as an event, the movement of the tectonic plates as a process and the fault line as a more permanent condition.[14]

His concepts of direct and structural violence are well known to us by now. On cultural violence he further states:

By "cultural violence" we mean those aspects of culture, the symbolic sphere of our existence – exemplified by religion and ideology, language and art, empirical science and formal science (logic, mathematics) – that can be used to justify or legitimate direct or structural violence. Stars, crosses and crescents; flags, anthems and military parades; the ubiquitous portrait of the Leader; inflammatory speeches and posters – all these come to mind ... The features mentioned above are "aspects of culture", not entire cultures. A person encouraging a potential killer, shouting "killing is self-realization," may prove that the English language as such is violent. Entire cultures can hardly be classified as violent; this is one reason for preferring the expression "aspect A of culture C is an example of cultural violence" to cultural stereotypes like "culture C is violent."[15]

There is no truly violent culture, but within culture there are certain aspects which could be used to justify or legitimize structural violence or direct violence. This Galtung calls "cultural violence."

After having reviewed these terms, we understand that Galtung's position means the following:
1. First, there are three different types of violence; direct, structural, and cultural violence.
2. The difference among these three forms of violence resides in their relationship with time: direct violence is a fact; structural violence is a process; and cultural violence is a non-variant in so far as cultural phenomena are modified over long periods.[16]
3. The three forms of violence are closely related to one another and allow for many different combinations (the six possible positions formed by the triangle's rotation).
4. Galtung also expressly states that so-called cultural violence is used to justify or legitimize direct or structural violence, although in the final part of his synthesis he does not mention it.

Our position

We consider that structural violence is made up of social rules of the game which have an economic, social, political, cultural, or ideological content, according to the case, and which are generally accepted by both the beneficiaries and the victims. In other words, it is convenient and correct to distinguish between structural and cultural violence, but we do not consider that this involves phenomena of an excluding taxonomy, because many of the rules of structural violence actually belong to the realm of culture and ideology. This statement supposes that structural and cultural violence are like secant circles.

It is extremely important when working on this subject to distinguish violence from its effects. A swollen lip is the effect of violence inflicted by one person on another during a brawl and is not direct violence in itself. The figures proving widespread poverty are the result of the rules of the game leading to an unequal distribution of wealth in the world, or in a given society, but are not structural violence *per se*. In this case, the rules organizing the unequal distribution of wealth constitute violence.

There are rules of structural violence which are typically cultural; for example, those which we mentioned previously: a society organized for silence, authoritarianism, discriminations, and/or distortions in the socialization process.

We should add to these others which are not strictly cultural but do have a cultural layer. At the economic level we can identify the rule dictating that capital resources must be channelled towards those who can best guarantee them. We can hardly say that this rule, as it stands, is "cultural." It does, however, have a cultural basis, which in the long run is the assumption that "profit must come before need," and it concerns the interests of those involved in a social organization in which the contract and equality of the parties are valid maxims in themselves, despite the fact that social reality may contradict them.

At the social level of many underdeveloped countries we can identify the rule which states that without a professional career a person (especially if male) is worth " $-X$ "; this is evident, for example, in the requirements to gain access to better employment, where the applicant must have a professional qualification. This phenomenon is actually a leftover from an aristocratic culture in which there was scant social mobility. There is no need for it in societies with greater social mobility.

At the level of political organization, there may be structural violence through the rules of the game inherent in a restricted democratic system. However, this would be linked to the cultural principles of marginalization, such as the assumption that "illiterates do not have political awareness and we, therefore, have to establish a special voting method for them"; or "the population is prepared to elect representatives but not to decide on concrete points of policy, therefore the choice of governors must be established but not the mechanisms of complementary direct democracy."[17]

In this manner, the relationships between structural and institutional violence and a culture are varied, whenever we assume as a starting point that which we have proposed: that structural violence comprises the rules of the game leading to certain consequences, and not the consequences themselves. In some cases, the rules of the game are directly cultural. In others they are economic, social, or political, with a cultural substratum.

Galtung is right when he says that some violent aspects of a culture justify direct and structural violence, but we must add that culture in itself is very often structural violence. An issue which merits further mention is that cultural justification of violence is related to the cultural homogeneity desired by each human group.

Culture, of course, is related to violence in general and not only to structural violence. For example, culture influences the determination of "thresholds" which pressure on a person must overcome in order to move that person from being controllable, or even positive, to being negative (that is, into violence).

4 A final methodological digression

We wish to conclude this paper by drawing attention to one aspect of this subject which has been very important to us throughout our studies on structural violence. Owing to the scarcity of empirical studies on the subject of structural violence (and, we could say, on violence in general), we have dealt with the subject through examples. This procedure has two severe methodological disadvantages. Firstly, we are attempting to provide a picture of the entire puzzle with specially chosen examples exhibited in a random fashion. That is, we hope to demonstrate violence in a society through examples. This procedure is an obstacle to reaching generalized conclusions. In the Peruvian Peace Research Association (APEP) we are aware of this circumstance and have undertaken comprehensive studies, which have provided preliminary results. But, evidently, these do not give a clear image of the complete puzzle. It is important that we continue undertaking empirical studies which will lead to increasing and ever-improved generalizations if we are to continue to gain ground in our understanding of this phenomenon.

Secondly, working with examples allows us to see episodes more clearly than social processes. The example of drug trafficking in Peru is significant.[18] Formally, it is penalized and thoroughly repressed. From the viewpoint of social consciousness very few people, if any, agree with drug trafficking and few people actually dream of their family's prospering from drug trafficking. However, over a considerable span of time we toyed with the idea that foreign currency attracted by drug trafficking could be positive for Peru and must therefore be tolerated. (This is no longer the case, since the flow of drugs and drug money disrupts the proper functioning of currency exchange rates and has negative effects on both the government and ordinary citizens.) Furthermore, the toleration of drug trafficking and the industry's cohabitation with national institutions has had a series of consequences related to institutional violence, such as illegal enrichment, corruption, the corrosion of social ethics, and international confrontations. It also produces direct violence by breeding the use of hired assassins to settle accounts with adversaries, by fuelling the accumulation and upkeep of illegal power, and so on. As a result, with a phenomenon such as drug trafficking, episodes of direct violence mix with institutional violence and, when viewed in a larger scope and over a longer period of time, with cultural violence.

This indicates that in order adequately to study violence resulting from drug trafficking, we cannot focus on isolated violent occurrences such as assassinations, economic power, or corruption, but will rather have to study it as a holistic, complex, multifaceted violent phenomenon. Our societies are replete with "cases" which, like drug trafficking, cannot be explained through examples. This leads us to emphasize the need for more empirical studies on violence.

Appendix

General theoretical conclusions of the inquiry into structural violence carried out by the Peruvian Peace studies and Research Association (APEP)

1. Structural violence differs from other forms of violence because it impinges on human beings from within the very structures of society. In other words, the efficient cause of structural violence is different from that of other forms of violence.

2. In structural violence the pressure exerted on human beings derives from the way they relate to one another and from the rules (whether accepted or not) that govern those relations. There appears to be a certain threshold beyond which that pressure has negative consequences for the individual. This is a feature of all violence, not just the structural variety. In fact, a certain tolerable level of physical force does not harm the victim if he or she has the strength to overcome it. The point about structural violence is that aggressive forces and defence capabilities within it are complex and difficult to perceive, and hence not so easy to measure. What is more, the same observation shows us that structural violence (and indeed any other kind of violence) is qualitatively distinct from its harmful effects on the individual. The latter occur only when the violence cannot be confronted successfully. Yet the violence is there – even if its results are still latent – before the threshold is reached in the form of pressure exerted on human beings.

3. Social structures are shaped, maintained, and eventually transformed by human beings in a process of permanent interaction with natural factors. For that reason we can state that structural violence forms part of human pressure on human beings, although in an indirect manner.

4. An important feature of structural violence is that the victim is part of it, whether he or she acquiesces in it or opposes it. In the structures involved, no one component can be explained without reference to the whole. This means that the victims are shaped by the structural violence inherent in the structures but that they themselves also help shape it. Structuralists go further and argue that the structures tend to persist over time and act dynamically, not just reproducing themselves but doing so with a degree of flexibility that allows them to adjust to non-change in spite of the tensions conducive to transformation. Thus, the victims of structural violence probably hold positions and act subject to certain structural laws, tending to maintain the status quo.

5. This is all the more important if, as structuralism also maintains, the central characteristics of the structures are not immediately evident. Structural violence can even result from a combination of apparently positive or neutral elements which only have an undesired effect once they are put together.

6. To the extent that the structures reproduce themselves and persist, they are not static but dynamic (although they do have a tendency to remain closed in on themselves). Thus, when studying structural violence, it is probably true that "cross-sections" at different intervals in time are not as revealing as a combination of static analysis with analysis of processes, hence the importance of historical studies of violence in its various facets within social structures.

7. Structures, in the way in which they operate, undergo permanent tension. When that tension becomes too great, the structures are transformed. They then have to be re-examined completely, because a change in one part causes a redefinition of each of the parts and of the operating rules for the whole.

   This observation requires one to try and work out which tensions arise from within violent structures, their nature and degree. At the same time, the self-regulatory (preservation) mechanisms at work, and those tending towards a reproduction of the tension, must be studied.

8. Some structuralist schools – as well, obviously, as other theoretical viewpoints – maintain that human beings can intervene in the process by which structures are

changed. This modification can be for better or for worse, depending on the quality and quantity of the change carried out and on its significance in the context of the structure.

9. Pacifying societies by getting rid of structural violence presupposes a transformation of structures. However, bearing in mind what we have said above, we have to discern with some care those aspects of a structure that most generate violence, as well as the efficient consequences of annulling or changing them. Not all changes of violent structures necessarily lead to an improvement.

10. There are four important corollaries to the conclusions reached so far:
   - First, structural violence does not consist just of poverty and injustice. These are major factors, but alongside them is a whole set of institutions and social rules that may be crucial to an explanation of structural violence. Nevertheless, it will be necessary to examine the connections between these elements, in order to distinguish those which are central from more peripheral factors.
   - Studies of the effects of structural violence are doubtless an invaluable aid in our attempts to understand it, but they are, precisely, results, not structural violence itself. It follows, for example, that a greater level of poverty need not indicate greater structural violence; conversely, an absence of poverty is not a sign that structural violence does not exist in a given society. Naturally, in poor countries like Peru, poverty combined with injustice is a subject that studies of structural violence ought to tackle, linking it to numerous other factors in order to attain a more complete definition of structural violence.
   - All this underlines the need for interdisciplinary studies of structural violence. No one discipline suffices on its own, while a series of parallel studies would fail to grasp the wealth of structural factors and the different shades of interconnection between them.
   - The main purpose of studying structural violence is to bring peace to society, to search for paths leading to improvements for humanity. This involves finding out the strengths that human beings possess within the structures in which they find themselves, and enabling them to withstand pressures beyond the threshold we referred to earlier.

11. Institutional violence, for its part, may be conceived as that kind of structural violence that people accept, since it is embodied, formally or materially, in institutions and is considered formally or materially acceptable. "Formally," in this context, means that people may not necessarily agree with its content, but nevertheless recognize the appropriateness of its existence. Something is materially acceptable when people agree with its content. Law (regardless of how much we might disagree with the content of laws) becomes a form of institutional violence when it has negative effects. Principles of education that hamper adequate development of the personality might be an example of material institutional violence.

Notes

1. Galtung, 1975a:281.
2. Ibid.
3. Galtung, 1975a:13.
4. Galtung, 1975a:14.

5. Ibid.
6. Sorel, 1961:124–5.
7. Galtung, 1975b.
8. There are, of course, other more or less predictable accidents and disasters, and in many cases the attack of a disease, such as cholera, can be foreseen. In these cases, we probably would be confronting a situation of structural violence, but not because of the natural phenomenon *per se*, rather because of lack of foresight.
9. Galtung himself has managed this in his essay "Cultural Violence" (Galtung, 1990).
10. Galtung, 1990:294.
11. Galtung, 1975b:110–11.
12. Galtung, 1975b:114–15.
13. Galtung, 1975b:123.
14. Galtung, 1990:294.
15. Galtung, 1990:291.
16. In a previous work we have noted that the difference Galtung establishes between direct and structural violence is based upon the variable "identification of the aggressor," in the sense that in direct violence the aggressor can be identified, while in structural violence this is not so. In relation to the new differentiation now encountered, we should ask ourselves whether Galtung has modified his thoughts or now considers that two variables for differentiation are important: identifying the aggressor and the time-related aspects of the phenomena. In other words, they may be complementary variables. This demands a very precise and nuanced redefinition of his own conceptual statements.
17. An anecdote pertinent to this subject concerns the debate on female suffrage during the Peruvian Constitutional Congress of 1933. The conservative sectors (the majority) opposed this idea because they thought women were unable to exercise this right. However, after the discussion, they did agree to give women the vote for municipal elections, because mayors were in charge of regulating and controlling everyday issues, many of which were considered to be within the realm of a housewife's functions. Thus, based upon a cultural issue, a norm was created for the restricted democratic participation of women in municipal elections. Women finally achieved full voting rights in Peru in 1956.
18. APEP has studied Peru as a "case" of structural violence. Some of our conclusions are presented as an appendix to this chapter (see above, pp 55–57). APEP is also studying the matrix of structural violence and its presence in the Andean region (Ecuador, Colombia, Venezuela, Peru, Bolivia, and Chile).

References

Galtung, J. 1975a. *Essays in Peace Research*. Volume I. Copenhagen: Christian Ejlers.

———. 1975b. "Violence, Peace, and Peace Research." In Galtung, 1975a:109–35.

———. 1990. "Cultural Violence," *Journal of Peace Research* vol. 27 no. 3, pp. 291–305.

Sorel, G. 1961. *Reflections on Violence*. London: Collier Books.

3

Remythologizations of power and identity: Nationalism and violence in Sri Lanka

Bruce Kapferer

This essay is about some of the features of the violence that has erupted tragically in Sri Lanka.[1] It concentrates on those events involving Sinhalese, focusing specifically on the 1988 and 1989 violence centring on the Janatha Vimukthi Peramuna (JVP) insurrection. This insurrection must be placed in the context of a total situation of political violence engaging the Sri Lankan government and the Tamil guerrilla movement, which is fighting for Tamil autonomy in the north and east of the island.

The thesis I develop here extends earlier statements of mine (see e.g., Kapferer, 1988, 1989). From the start it must be noted that I am not concerned with giving an explanation of the causes of the violence. The ethnic struggle, which has left few corners of Sri Lanka untouched, extends from a complex of historical processes. The critical ones for understanding the crisis have been widely debated already and debates will continue well into the foreseeable future (see, e.g., Committee for Rational Development, 1984; Tambiah, 1986, 1992; Wilson, 1988; Spencer, 1990). Among the forces to which I, and others in greater detail, have drawn attention are Sri Lanka's colonial history, the particular location of Sri Lanka within processes of capitalist globalization, the internal dynamics of class formation, uneven economic development, increasing poverty, and much else. My interest here is not with causation as such, which is always prob-

59

lematic, not least because of its linear, before-and-after perspective. Recent criticism of so-called "modernist" theoretical perspectives, which tend towards explanations in terms of deterministic processes within closed systems or structures, has asserted the openness of processes and their multidirectionality, in directions which are not necessarily tightly interconnected. This anti-modernist position is close to my own and fits, I think, with historical and cultural processes as they continue to work out. It is a position which underpins the approach to violence I develop here.

First of all, I am concerned with the content and pattern of violence as this is shaped through particular ideological orientations to power and to power as this is organized in relation to ideological conceptions of identity. My discussion is *not* about the *causes* of violence. Rather, it is about the intervention of certain ideological conceptions of identity and polity in what are already violent processes. These violent processes are part of a far greater historical complex which embraces a far more inclusive meaning of violence than those of its most poignant expressions, physical killing. In my expanded meaning of violence is included the violence of class forces which bring the suffering of abject poverty, and the ambition of political command which insists on unwilling submission.[2] I focus on the role of ideological forces in situations which are already violent. I am not concerned with ideology as causation, but with the role of ideology in creating meaning and giving shape to violent processes already in train.

My second, closely related, interest in this essay is with the way violence (here, specifically physical destruction) as an instrument of power and oriented through ideology can become a totalizing force. That is, how violence can come to realize the totalizing aspects of that ideology which becomes harnessed to the process of violence. Sri Lanka exemplifies the dreadful paradox which is the potential of a country and a people caught in such a process. The paradox is one whereby the course of such totalizing violence is the destruction of the very grounds, ideological and existential, upon which it grew.

Ricoeur (1984) has spoken lucidly about the diversity of symbolic discourses in any society and about the nature of the socio-political imaginary or *imaginaire*. His discussion extends an understanding of the broad intellectual context of this essay and I quote it at some length.

Every society ... possesses, or is part of, a socio-political **imaginaire**, that is, an ensemble of symbolic discourses. This **imaginaire** can function as a rupture or a reaffirmation. As reaffirmation, the **imaginaire** operates as an "**ideology**" which can positively repeat and represent the founding discourse of a society, what I call its "foundational" symbols, thus preserving its sense of identity. After all, cultures create themselves by telling stories of their own past. The danger is of course that this reaffirmation can be perverted, usually by monopolistic elites, into a mystifactory discourse which serves to uncritically vindicate or glorify the established political powers. In such instances, the symbols of a community become fixed and fetishized; they serve as lies. Over against this, there exists the **imaginaire** of rupture, a discourse of **utopia** which remains critical of the powers that be out of fidelity to an "elsewhere," to a society that is "not yet." But this utopian discourse is not always positive either. For besides the authentic utopia of critical rupture there can also exist the dangerously schizophrenic utopian discourse which projects a static future without ever producing the conditions of its realization. (Ricoeur, 1984:29–30)

The argument which follows is about the way certain groups in Sri Lanka, the agents of state power and those in radical resistance, imagine ideologically their identity and action. Their imaginary is both of the politically legitimating type and of the utopian kind to which Ricoeur refers. I focus on their dangers as a process of their violent engagement, one which *makes* what is imagined a terrible reality. I stress that I write of ideology as an imaginary. The imagined views, or what I will call mythologizations, which political agents and their followers engage probably never had existence in empirical fact – that is, an existence outside their symbolic representation or discourse. However, to say this is not to deny the force of the imaginary. Quite the contrary: in fact, it is through their imaginations of reality that human beings address and act in the world. This is why the nature of what they imagine ideologically (ideology in my understanding is always the product of the human imagination) should be explored. The imaginary I explore here, and its part in the violent process, is that produced in the discourse of a society which conceives itself to be Buddhist. This raises an issue about the role of religion and Buddhism in contemporary Buddhist states. I discuss the issue broadly as a way of both introducing the Sri Lanka material and clarifying further my approach to ideology in such political contexts.

Buddhist ideologies, nationalism, and violence

It appears paradoxical to many scholars and lay persons alike that religions which eschew violence and stress peace as an ultimate value so often appear to be intimately associated with war and human destruction. Perhaps the paradox is clearest in the case of Buddhism, which gives central place to the doctrine of non-violence (*ahimsa*). Modern Buddhist states evidence considerable violence, usually of an ethnic kind. This is especially so in the tragic situation of Sri Lanka, where a Buddhist nationalism is implicated in the conflict between Sinhalese and Tamils and within the Sinhalese community. Similar intolerance and violence have been documented for Burma and Thailand (Keyes, 1971; Ling, 1979; Tambiah, 1976, 1986).

Diverse explanations are offered. Some are understandings of a universalist kind, others seek a more complex marriage of the universal and the particular. With few exceptions (e.g., Tambiah, 1986; Kapferer, 1988) the dominant position on Sri Lanka is universalist. Broadly, the argument is that the situation is but a specific historical example of widespread processes of nationalism and ethnicity already well documented for Europe. Indeed, we are told that modern nationalism, in which a heightened sense of ethnic identity is a marked feature, is a kind of European "export" (e.g., Spencer, 1990; Nissan, 1989; following Gellner, 1983, and Kedourie, 1960). The particular force of Buddhist nationalism in Sri Lanka is driven within the familiar conditions of colonialism, class conflict, and so on. This historicist and materialist view has little place for ideology except as superstructural reflection or distortion. Nissan (1989) is quite explicit, citing approvingly the somewhat strange statement that "Culture is less a reflection of society than a reflection on history" (Peel, 1987:112). The statement is odd, for I cannot see "culture" as something abstracted from history or, indeed, from society. While I do not reject out of hand the sentiment directing the position – ideology as distortion is a major theme of this discussion – the dualism of the approach reduces the force of ideology to the social and material circumstances of its production and existence. Ideology is left unexamined save as a reflection of its circumstance and becomes "mystification" or "false consciousness" or "inauthentic."[3]

I explore ideology, those imaginary constructions whereby human beings render meaningful the contexts of their experience, as in a way integral with the contexts in which it is produced and applied, yet not a representation of it in the sense of the reductionist positions I have referred to. Ideology does not float on the surface of "reality," nor is it reducible to the social circumstances and material conditions of existence as these may be "objectively" described. For example, many ideologies are the constructions of class political élites. The state

Buddhism of Sri Lanka can be seen as one of this kind. But élite interest is disguised in the content of the ideology, which engages symbolic themes intended to extend beyond narrow sectional interest.
The orientation in construction of such an ideology is simultaneously
motivated in a particular class interest and concerned to deny this
fact. Of central importance to the approach here is the necessity to
examine ideology as an imagined construct in itself. In this sense, it
is symbolic, never a representation of empirical reality (although produced by agents living in such realities), and is at one and the same
time always *more* and *less* than empirical reality.

Later I will refer to the ideology of Buddhist Cosmic Kingship invoked in current nationalist discourse. This is frequently based on ancient and medieval chronicles usually written by Buddhist monks.
These are never mere representations of the realities in which they
were produced. Empirically, as many scholars have shown, the realities were something other than that presented in the chronicles (see
Gunawardena, 1979; Obeyesekere, 1984; Tambiah, 1992). In terms of
political complexity, for instance, the reality of the chronicles was
presented as much less and rather different from what empirical
historians of today conjecture it to have been. The reality of the
chronicles was also much more, probably motivated towards objectives long past recall and never in the texts, and – perhaps more
significant here – constructed through metaphor and symbol, which
had universal cosmological import, rather than through particular historical facticity. The chronicles are imaginary constructions related
to, yet far from identical with, the historically lived worlds outside
them.

Ideologies as imagined constructions establish a relation to their
contexts of application by the fact that they are subjective creative
acts. Human beings inscribe themselves in the very ideological fabric
of their constructions as a function of the creative act in itself; or by
their acceptance of the constructions of others, by their self-recogni-
tion in the ideologies that are constituted around them. Thus ideologies have force as a process of the imaginary working in context and
demand exploration in themselves and not by a reduction to what
they are always more or less than, i.e. the context.[4] Ideologies are
their own context, and it is the processes whereby they break out of
themselves, via the agency of their creators, into the lived world and
are made vital within it that are the concerns of some of this essay.

Scholars working in Burma, Thailand, and Cambodia have directly
engaged the ideological role of Buddhism in processes of intolerance

63

and violence. Reynolds (1978b:175) says that the general legitimating role of Theravada Buddhism in politics "is no longer a matter of serious dispute." In another article (Reynolds, 1978a:105) he states that "in spite of the impact of modern ideas and ideologies, the deeply ingrained sense of cosmological order, and its role as a context within which royal authority has meaning, remains an important factor both in the villages and in Thai national life." Tambiah (1976) demonstrates in the greatest detail for Thailand (but making comparative sorties into the Sri Lanka material) the relevance of Buddhist cosmologies relating to kingship and the state for understanding modern political dynamics. Keyes (1978) addresses the problem of militant Buddhism and specifically that of a monk who advocates violence, a phenomenon also apparent among the Buddhist clergy in present-day Sri Lanka (see Kapferer, 1988:86–7). He opposes the reflectionist approach to Buddhist ideology, which gives it only a marginal role in modern political process rather than an integral role in directing it. Keyes (1978:160) suggests that the violence of some Buddhist practice and rhetoric is the potential or "darker side" of the non-violent and peaceful ideal of official Buddhist civic religion.

My approach, which addresses the role of Buddhist cosmic symbolism in the ideological imagination of power and identity, steers between the courses outlined. It recognizes that the violence in Sri Lanka receives its energy, the fury of its destruction, from the particular social and political fracture and contradictions of a contemporary, post-colonial, technologically-based society. But my orientation resists the simple reduction to such factors. That is, the violence is not merely an expression of class conflict or of class suffering constituted in a third world nation further exacerbated by global political and economic transformations. The violence is certainly fired and fanned through such general processes and many others. What I claim is that the violence receives some of the manner of its content and destructive energy through the imagined constructions of ideology. I focus particularly on the role of Buddhist nationalism in Sri Lanka. Buddhism *per se* is not the object of discussion. Rather, the concern of this analysis is what I call the Buddhism of the state, or Buddhism in its contemporary transformation as the imagined construction of an ideology of power which gives stress to the idea of the Cosmic King. This ideology is in my terms a modern mythologization of reality which gives particular form and direction to the processes involved in its creation.

I emphasize that the contemporary Sri Lankan state is by no means a continuation of the state of ancient times.[5] Sri Lanka's turbulent history has taken diverse directions. The numerous political orders it has thrown up were conditioned in a vortex of social and political movements, fed by diverse ideologies, flowing throughout the South and South-East Asian region. Moreover, many of Sri Lanka's historical political orders were neither replicas nor necessarily reducible to those political forms which dominated the ancient complexes of civilization at Anuradhapura, Polonnaruwa, and Sigiriya. The contemporary Sri Lankan state is no more continuous with these political orders than those political orders were essentially continuous with each other. Any claim to continuity – and such a claim is indeed made by some ideologues of the current Sri Lankan state – is finally discounted by the fact that the contemporary political world of Sri Lanka constitutes a sharp disjunction with periods which historians label as ancient or medieval. The ideology of state power, as well as the instituted bureaucratic structure of the state, of contemporary Sri Lanka is fashioned in the particular historical colonial and post-colonial circumstances of expanding capitalist forces and their technologies. It is in the context of this kind of understanding that ideological statements to the contrary – that the modem state of Sri Lanka and its legitimating ideology of power are founded in the cosmic polities of the "past" – comprise not just an ungrounded fabrication but, in my usage, a mythologization.

Demythologization and its remythologized ideological form

More properly, the ideology of the Sri Lankan state, or the Buddhist nationalism of the state, should be termed a "remythologization" (see Wyschogrod, 1985:27–9; also Ricoeur, 1984), one which is constructed upon a world demythologized in modern capitalist/technical transformations and subjected to ruling "rationalist" ideologies. The mark of the contemporary political state, possibly everywhere and certainly not in Sri Lanka alone, is its legitimation, above all else, as a rational order which commands the bureaucratic and technical apparatuses necessary to the reproduction of the rationalist order of the state. Rationalist demythologization, impelled and effected in the historical circumstances of its generation, establishes a dominant discourse (also, a discourse of dominance) which at once is "literalist" and negates or suppresses the symbolic extensions, meanings, and potentialities of those realities to which it refers. This is so in the interpretation of the significance of constructions about the "past" as, too, of the "present." Rationalist demythologizers tend towards an impoverishment of the symbolic qualities of context. It is especially the case, as I will show, in the ideologies of contemporary state nationalism.

Global realities abound with examples of ideological rationalist demythologizations. Contemporary religious reformism and nationalism, frequently linked, provide rich illustration. In Sri Lanka, the phenomenon widely referred to as the Buddhist Revival is an instance. Buddhism, along with other civilizational religions such as Christianity and Islam, has reformism – motivated in a search for authenticity or orthodoxy – as ideologically foundational and enduringly vital in its dynamic. A continuing urge to "demythologize" is the name of their game. But this expansion obscures my usage of the term "demythologization," which I see as occurring largely through schemes of meaning and interpretation alien or external to that cosmological or symbolic universe some of whose key terms and statements are being asserted.

Buddhism in Sri Lanka (Gunawardena, 1979; Malalgoda, 1976) and elsewhere (Tambiah, 1976) has seen numerous "reformations" or periods of "revitalization," and well before the advent of colonialism and the incorporation of Sri Lanka into worldwide capitalist processes. The shifts and redirections in meaning and practice which were integral to these revitalizations were consistent with, or possibilities of, the wider field of symbolic discourse in which they were embedded. The Buddhist Revival to which I refer grew apace in the conditions of colonial penetration, and most especially in the circumstances of British rule in the nineteenth and twentieth centuries. The interpretations of the Buddha's doctrine and the invention or reinvention of many Buddhist practices in the main period of the Revival refracted the dominant rationalist bureaucratic/technological order of values that had now been established (Obeyesekere, 1979; Gombrich and Obeyesekere, 1989; Roberts, 1982; Kapferer, 1983). Ideologues of the Revival asserted the "scientific" validity of the Buddha's doctrine, attacked the "irrationalism" of Sinhala Buddhist practices like those centring on demons, and were concerned to establish personal habits and routines highly relevant to the new rationalist order. Not only was the demythologization of the Revival a refraction of this order, but also the Revival, through its inventions of practice and transformations of meaning, was vital in further establishing the hegemony of rationalist values and the new bureaucratic/technical order. The Revival was an ideological process which *made* Buddhism rationalist in a contemporary sense and, conversely, made rationalism Buddhist.[6]

The process was one in which the circumstance and action of demythologization simultaneously provoked a remythologization. Such a dynamic could be fundamental in human being, intimately tied to the urgency in humanity as a whole both to establish meaning in experience and to totalize such meaning, to recognize a unity in self and other through the construction of shared frameworks of meaning.[7] Moreover, the engagement of a mythic consciousness, one which routinely resonates with the symbolic themes of death, rebirth, and original unity also, may be universal while it takes specific shape in certain moments of history. This may be so because the existential condition of human being must always be experientially diverse and fragmenting even as it reaches to overcome or to transcend such experience. In these senses, the remythologizations of the Revival, of political nationalists and contemporary ideologues of Buddhist state and nation – mythologizations which include the restorations of supposedly ancient pristine Buddhist rites, the popularization of festivals to mark major events in the life of the Buddha, the celebration of an essential cultural unity imagined to be present in art, belief, and language, and the selection of specific myths of nation and historical events – are particular historically conditioned and directed exfoliations of a universal human tension to mythic consciousness and thought.

I make this observation not in the interest of an ultimately trivial social scientific urgency to make some universally "true" statement about the nature of humanity. Rather, I wish to suggest that the general mythic consciousness of the remythologizations of contemporary nationalism in Sri Lanka is similar to many other human movements of self-affirmation, and not merely those of nationalism but also, for example, to European millennial cults, witch-hunts, and so on. The association has further point in extending a very limited understanding of the passion in the violence in present-day Sri Lanka. There is a religiosity to the violence which takes its form through certain "utopian" elements of the mythic consciousness. These elements are contained in its birth, death, rebirth, or return to the glories of the past thematic, or projection towards a fantasized future.

If there are ideological, even ontological universals apparent in recent or current remythologizations in Sri Lanka, what I stress is the relevance of their distinct features to the present Sri Lankan crisis of violence: albeit features *made* relevant through particular historical and bureaucratic/technological processes of contemporary societies. I opened this discussion with some broad characterizations of the re-mythologizations of state power in Sri Lanka (see also Kapferer, 1988). What I noted was their infusion with dimensions of the demy-thologized structures and procedures against which their mythologies are in ostensible reaction. Thus the literalism of such mythology: the refusal by many of the mythologizers of the manifold symbolic signi-ficance of events drawn from within great cosmological themes, and their tendency to reduce them to rationalist issues of the fact-or-fiction variety. In so doing, they misconstrue or radically distort the meaning (reimagine the imaginary) of the events of myth. In effect, they create mythic falsities out of their facticities. Conversely, the pragmatic and technical reason of contemporary rationalities be-comes "mythicalized"; they are substantialized in the content and structure of the myth through the process of imaginary reconstruc-tion of the significance of myth. In such a remythologizing process, mythic structures are made rigid and assume the rigorous and in-escapable determination of the rationalist procedures engaged in their reconstruction and interpretation.

Furthermore, myths and the structures or vehicles of myth and mythic consciousness – for example, festival and rite – in the remy-thologizations to which I refer, manifest an internal rupture, a separa-tion of "form" from "content." That is, the logic of the rite, the prin-ciples structuring and transforming symbolic action and event in ritual, appear as *inappropriate* to the symbols, actions and events in-cluded within it. Ritual becomes static, affirmational rather than transformational, representational and stressing its dimension as spectacle. This is something which has happened to the Kandy *pera-hera*, once a festival of the king of Kandy and intimately concerned with both the expression and transformational reconstitution of his cosmic power. The *perahera* was appropriated as a spectacle of the British colonial state and has now been reappropriated as a major symbolic statement of the state of Sri Lanka and of its president (Seneviratne, 1978). The separation of form from content is consis-tent with a central feature of remythologization – the dislocation of the mythic in ostensibly demythicized realities. The rupture I note is also generative, with reference to ceremony, festival, and rite, of more fixed and stable divisions between participants, on the one hand, and audience or spectators, on the other.[8]

Critical in remythologization, and in its fetishistic and reified quality, is the totalizing orientation to constrain complex and diverse experience within the dictate of the logic of its form; put another way, to confine the paramount reality of everyday life within a finite sub-universe of meaning, which to a large degree is cut off, maybe completely, from everyday life. That is, the idea of the Buddhist state and of Buddhist kingship and power presented by the agents of state power and resistance is an imaginary produced by them within a recent history, an imaginary which in all likelihood had no existence in any empirically established historical past. It is a finite province of meaning, one discourse or symbolic possibility of meaning among many. However, through the agency of those who produce it, and by their capacity to institutionalize their imaginary and to create the material circumstance for the life of their imaginary, finite province(s) of meaning can become paramount reality. The remythologizations of nationalist discourse that I discuss were motivated in the historical circumstances of the development of bureaucratic and technological rationalism in the circumstances of colonial rule and capitalist development. I stress the historical process of mythological creation. This process is vital in the meaning to the remythologizations.

The so-called Buddhist Revival is a major influence on the remythologizations of contemporary nationalism. The Buddhist Revival is but part of widespread nationalist remythologizations which gathered force throughout all sections of Sri Lankan society from the colonial period onwards. Like all social movements, the remythologization of realities grew in strength in direct proportion to its resistances. These resistances were produced in the particular historical and transformed demythologized world of colonialism and a bureaucratic/technological rationalist order. I refer to the resistances and hostilities born, for example, of class and education. Moreover, the constructions created to overcome them were, in large part, born of the same rationalism. The categories and classifications of ethnicity achieved definition and significance through the demands of a colonial and post-colonial technical bureaucracy. As an intemperate aside, modern anthropological definitions of ethnic identity, boundaries, and groups (e.g. Barth, 1969; Cohen, 1969) are not outside a rationalist/bureaucratic classificatory convention and understanding.

The general point is that in Sri Lankan nationalism, as elsewhere, the dynamic is rationalist and integral to technological society. Further, it generates its resistances in the process of overcoming them – the present ethnic conflict is the example. Such generation of resistance internal to contemporary bureaucratic/technological societies and their ideological constructions, I suggest, energizes and intensifies nationalist distortions of reality and the move to totalizations of a "utopian" past or future, which appear to transcend the differences and ruptures of the present.

Moreover, the fundamental contradictions integral to contemporary nationalist totalizations can contribute to an increased effort to make reality conform to the way it is imagined. And so, by means of the very bureaucratic and technical resources at their disposal, nationalists can, indeed, act upon the very fabric of their worlds and orient them in the direction of their remythologizations. In this process, the remythologizations of reality are made into reality, or can come to have all the force of that reality upon which they reactively reflect. The mythologizers can become as internal to the constructions they weave and spin as it may be their intention to make others the inhabitants of such constructions (see Kapferer, 1988: chap. 4).

The Buddhism of the state and the ideology of power

With reference to the contemporary situation in Sri Lanka, the Sri Lankan state, its agents, and its institutions took shape in the context of nationalist constructions, and they were made internal to its order. What can be called the Buddhism of the state, embodied in the doctrinal utterances of state leaders and in the public spectacle of their religious and ritual practice as Buddhists, draws heavily on the developments of the Revival. The state has progressively elaborated that which was already ideologically vital within its order; increasingly so since 1972, when Buddhism was made the official state religion. This was announced shortly after an escalation in civil unrest and may not be unlinked to it. I refer especially to the armed uprising in 1971 of mainly Sinhalese rural youth, an apparent precursor to the major and far more calamitous Sinhalese revolt of 1989 (Halliday, 1971; Chandraprema, 1991). It would, I think, be inaccurate to conceive of such action by the agents of the state as mere cynical ideological manufacture and manipulation (in the sense that the state and its agents are somehow external to their constructions). In my view the agents of the state are also internal to their constructions, a possibility which both accounts for some of the orientation of their political action and their commitment to it. They are internal, at the very least, for the simple reason that their own subjectivity is involved. Their own conceptions on history, identity, and the circumstance of existence are engaged by virtue of the fact of their very agency in the construction and practice of such ideology. The remythologizations of religion, of history, and of "culture" ingrain dimensions of the practical orientations of their bureaucratic, technical, and rational world.

The Sri Lankan state, of course, is not the only agency of violence in Sri Lanka. But it certainly plays the main role in defining the situation of violence and is central in the violent definitions of others in the wider field of ethnic conflict and Sinhalese civilian resistance. Elsewhere (Kapferer, 1988, 1989), I have described as hierarchical the key logic of the images or ideas which contemporary ideologists of the state have used to legitimate their authority and power. This term relates to a notion of encompassment, whereby the more potent forces or powers are able to order and incorporate within themselves other forces or powers. This capacity to encompass is the principle of hierarchy to which I refer, which also accounts for the essential processive character or dynamic of systems so conceived. Hierarchical orders constituted in such a logic are continually threatened with a "breakdown" or fragmentation in the direction of those forces they incorporate. I stress that this hierarchical logic is a principle of the imaginary, of how processes of power appear as a logic, for example, of texts and ritual practice; *not* how practices of power and the organization of institutions of power may have been worked out on the ground – in reality, as it were.[9] This hierarchical logic is integral to key myths of state and nation concerning their birth and regeneration, involving the exploits of heroic princes and kings as documented in epic religious histories like the *Dipavamsa* and *Mahavamsa*. They embody a theory of Cosmic Kingship which, when applied to the situation of the contemporary sovereign nation state, asserts a unity of nation and state which is inseparable: the nation is the state and vice versa.

Tambiah (1992:172) in a generous critique of my *Legends of People, Myths of State* (Kapferer, 1988) asserts that the concepts of "state" and "nation" took shape in modern European history and develop in the context of notions of bounded, territorial sovereignty. He is perfectly correct in asserting that such concepts were probably not current at the time of the chronicles, and certainly not in their contemporary senses. This adds to my point rather than weakens it.

In contemporary contexts of the "nation-state," a fundamental problem concerns the manner of the unity of the state with the nation. A hierarchical ideology adapted into the context of nation/state dualisms (hierarchical ideology is basically non-dualist) asserts an

essential unity of nation and state, whereby the dominant nation constitutes the state and has power over other collectivities or "nations"
subordinately incorporated into the polity of the dominant state/
nation. This hierarchical unity is not reducible to European or Western ideological forms. Although there are similarities, they nonetheless comprise different ideological "solutions" to the crises of power
of modern nation-states caught in global economic and political processes.[10]

The crises of Sri Lanka are like those of many contemporary nation-states worldwide. They are crises, like those in numerous other
democracies,[11] which revolve around such important human concerns as individual rights, the nature of citizenship, autonomy, and
the like. However, the way these issues are projected, and also the
responses to them, vary, I suggest, in accordance with the terms
of the ideological arguments concerning the nature of "history,"
"culture," "identity," and so on, through which human interests
(democratic or not) are legitimated and pursued.

One area of ideological distinction in the hierarchical logic adapted
from the chronicles into contemporary Sri Lankan nationalism of the
Buddhist state relates to the role of "difference." Difference in hierarchy is a principle of unity. Individuals and groups interact on the
basis of their differences. This is facilitated and sustained through
hierarchization itself, an organization of power whereby differences
are ranked from more to less incorporating or encompassing. The
unity of difference is dependent on the power of the higher to "incorporate" the lower and to "domesticate" the incorporated to the
ideals of the higher. This in no way means that the incorporated
sacrifice identity and assert a fundamental or essential similarity
with the dominator – a marked pattern in Western nationalisms and
ideologies of state. The erasure of difference, which is a feature of
Western ideologies, is not an orientation of hierarchical logic or
ideology.

The contemporary political ideology of the Cosmic State in Sri
Lanka, ingraining a hierarchical logic, is not exclusionist or separatist
or assimilationist[12] as is the case with many Western nationalisms.
These dimensions of Western nationalist ideologies are mechanisms
for annihilating difference or for creating separate communities of
persons who are the same in identity. These ideological processes,
well exemplified in recent Western historical experience (in a variety
of racisms and ethnic exterminations), are apparent in Sri Lanka.
They may be evidence of colonialist influence and of Sri Lanka's par-

ticipation in the conditions and discourses of global political processes in which Western ideological rhetoric seems to be dominant.
No doubt such aspects contribute to the hostilities and violence of
the present situation in Sri Lanka.

However, what I stress is the import of the hierarchical argument
in the ideology of the Cosmic State applied to contemporary context, whereby the integrity of "nation" or "ethnic community" and
"identity" is dependent on the capacity to incorporate and subordinate other identities within the total unity of a Sinhala Buddhist
state. The ideologically informed issue is *not* difference *per se*, but a
specific location of difference in an organization of power. Power (a
particular conception of it) is the overt and central issue of hierarchy
rather than difference. The hierarchical ideology promoted by agents
of the Sri Lankan state, placed into a context of ethnic tension, makes
the powerful incorporation of the ethnic other equally vital to the integrity of both state and the Sinhala "community."

Moreover, I suggest that, through a hierarchical ideological grasping of current processes, the strength or weakness of ethnic community or identity is vitally linked to the incorporative power of the state.
The state is placed at the heart of ethnicity and identity. Should the
agents of state fail in their incorporative power, this simultaneously
signs the fragmentation and loss of integrity of the dominant community or nation whose identity is defined in the unifying power of
the state. This process is, I contend, also potentially one of the person. The integrity of the person is coextensive with the state as it is
mythologically imagined. A failure in the hierarchical incorporative
power of the state, the incapacity to achieve Sinhala dominance,
threatens the integrity of the person as it does that of the state. Living
in such an imagined reality, human beings may be motivated to reassert the power of the state through their own relatively independent
political action. This is the stuff of riots and more casual acts of violence against minorities, which have become an aspect of life in Sri
Lanka.

This potential identity of person and state has much in common
with the hegemonic direction of most contemporary state nationalisms. The condition of the nation as a collectivity of individuals sharing the same identity is also the potential experience of each of the
individuals who comprise the nation. The ideology is one which di-
rects individuals to realize or to restore their own integrity through
the power of the state. However, I underline the distinction of nationalism constructed and mythologized through an ideology of Cosmic

Kingship. The integrity of nation and of person is significantly linked to the hierarchical principle of encompassment or incorporation which conceives of the identities of the encompassed or the incorporated as vital elements, if subordinate elements, of those identities who make up the totality of state and nation. I stress that the mythic religious histories essay a particular approach to power which, I think, is radically distorted in the remythologizations of the contemporary state. The manner of this distortion, one which comes to value power as annihilation and which aligns the assertion of identity with annihilatory capacity, is a theme that I will shortly come to address.

The events of ethnic conflict and destruction over recent years in Sri Lanka organize their present meaning, if not their direction, through the contemporary logic of state nationalism and the Cosmic State that I have outlined. The myths of religious history provided a framework through which the import of events could be articulated and made to cohere meaningfully, often by government leaders and frequently by the population at large. Contemporary political events could be said to have substantialized the constructions of imagined history. The source of their meaning was in the current political context, but these immediate meanings became attached or moulded to a mythic form which was not part of present experience. The experience of the present through the past was a factor which energized this imagined past and made it, in effect, present.[13]

Thus, Tamil guerrilla attacks in the interests of ethnic autonomy sparked violent anti-Tamil rioting, which received the support of agents of the state. The metaphors of the human destruction were occasionally those of powerful hierarchical reincorporation. Thus Tamil victims about to be slaughtered were made to bow in submission before their killers (Kapferer, 1989). The violence itself created a deepening of ethnic division which gave the myths of ethnic identity greater relevance. Moreover, the riots generated the expansion of Tamil resistance. Sinhalese experienced territorial restriction which achieved conscious import, for example, through the well-known story of Prince Dutugemunu's experience of confinement through the subordination of his father's kingdom to that of the Tamil, Elara. The weakness of the Sri Lankan state was made manifest in the India–Sri Lanka Accord of 1987, which involved an Indian military presence. Sinhalese rioted in protest at the loss of their national integrity. There was a heightening of ethnic nationalist consciousness and a growth in internal civilian unrest among the Sinhalese population. Violence was directed against the state and was coordinated by the revolutionary JVP. Its orientation was no less nationalist than the state it opposed. A major direction of its violence was to restore the power and integrity of state and nation, to encompass where the state it opposed had failed. The metaphors of the JVP, as I will show, drew just as strongly from the cosmic myths as did those of the agents of the Sri Lankan government.

A general point is that contemporary events progressively deepened the apparent relevance of a nationalist mythic consciousness. Events, the product of a great diversity of historical forces and experienced very differently according to the way individuals were positioned in their daily realities, were made to conform to the simplicity of a nationalist mythic consciousness. In this process, a mythic consciousness and the logic of its imagined projections becomes more deeply ingrained as part of the everyday grasping of reality and its experience. A nationalist mythic consciousness, through its engagement in the interpretation of events, becomes more than a framework for the comprehension of their significance. It becomes, as it takes greater and greater imaginative hold through political processes which engage it, more and more part of the motivation to action and the production of historical events. This is especially so if the agents of the state or its political opponents, who command the institutions and organizations of power, also engage such a mythic consciousness and, through their action, increasingly come to live it.

Power as annihilation and the distortion of Buddhist value

I have insisted that the cosmic nationalism of the Sri Lankan state is produced as it is embedded in the demythologizing and rationalist processes of a contemporary world. Its ideology is a remythologization of such a world and embodies the forces of contemporary rationalist realities. As the Buddhist Revival articulates "production" and other central values of technological society, Buddhist nationalism, like all modern nationalism, articulates the overarching importance of "power." This is the supreme concern of the state, and in the specific circumstance of the Sri Lankan state it imparts significant contemporary meaning to Buddhist value and ideas of Cosmic Kingship.

In the current context of intra-ethnic and inter-ethnic violence, officers of the state make intense appeals to the key Buddhist value of non-violence. It is an affirmation of the state as controlling the monopoly of legitimate violence. Non-violence is a strong religious value, but I note, in this context, the subordination and use of the value in the interest of the maintenance of the power of the state. Further, there is, in the current situation, an implication that the state embodies the Buddha-ideal of non-violence through, somewhat paradoxically, the appropriation of all violence to itself.

The myths of Cosmic Kingship, especially those at the heart of the nationalism of the Buddhist state, would appear to assert a different message. This is that violence is integral to the hierarchical order of the state and that the violence of this order and its inherent instability – a tension to the violence of fragmentation – can only be transcended by an orientation beyond the political and a living of Buddhist life outside and, perhaps, encompassing the political. In the cosmic myths there is a recognition of the contradiction between violence and non-violence. When Prince Dutugemunu, a hero in the current nationalism of the state, realizes the destruction of his ordering violence he moves outside the political and into a life of Buddhist virtue.

In contemporary Buddhist state nationalism, not only is a bureaucratic/technical rationalism made Buddhist but also the political and a very contemporary vision of state power is made dominant over, and determinant of, religious value. This process leads to a subversion of even that contemporary rationalist meaning inscribed in much present Buddhist value and practice. It also can be a major factor in the destruction of the bureaucratic/technical order of a modern society, engaging key dimensions of that order against itself. Religious value subordinated to power in the remythologizing of the Sri Lankan state gives potential pre-eminence to the idea of power as annihilation. Power as annihilating force is contained in the nationalist myths of Cosmic Kingship in the concept of the demonic. But this annihilating force is valued only in so far as it is ultimately constitutive of a hierarchical order conditioned within, and oriented to, ultimate Buddhist reason and value. Annihilating power in itself is not valued. It is valued only in its capacity to generate hierarchical order, which, further, is possible only because it is oriented to the Buddha and his teaching as the ultimate encompassing principles. Thus the demon is distinguished from the demonic in the myths of history and also in present-day ritual practice, for example, in demon exorcisms and at urban sorcery shrines. Demons are perfect annihilating power, who cannot transcend their own destruction and violence.

The demonic, however, is the power of annihilation which is also generative of its own transcendence. The demonic, like the destructive power of Prince Dutugemunu or that curative force of an exorcist invoking the authority and teaching of the Buddha, rehierarchizes and reincorporates. In this process the demonic itself transforms into a Buddhist beneficence. Sinhalese Buddhist deities, conditioned as they are in the orientation to the Buddha and his teaching, possess annihilating force, but their release of this force transforms them into a higher, reincorporating, totalizing, and benign form.

The argument of the great cosmic myths and of much current ritual practice is one which devalues annihilating power in itself. The message of the myths and their practice is the negation of such annihilating force. The demon, the fragmentation of annihilation alone, is the destructive energy of non-reason, of ignorance, a space of horrible suffering and death, a Void (*sunya*) – the direct antithesis of Buddhist Nothingness (*nirvana*) (Kapferer, 1991:xii). It is a death world, a world from which the Cosmic King, Dutugemunu, in his Buddhist reasoning, shrinks.

In the Buddhism of the contemporary state, power in itself is given value and, in its hierarchizing, ordering capacity, creates the conditions for the dominance of Buddhist value. Buddhism becomes the greater value because the state is powerful, not vice versa. The remythologization of the state opens the way for annihilating force and the capacity to exercise such force to be the condition for the legitimation of power and the totalizing order of the state. This is an absolute inversion and perversion of Buddhist value, whether the context of its meaning is ancient or modern. But such distortion is realized in practice through the structures of resistance established, in part, in reaction to the Buddhist nationalism of the state. The radical resistance of Tamils to the authority of the power of the state, whose own struggle appears to define power as the capacity to annihilate, contributes to the intensification of the self-affirmation of the state and its agents through a discourse of annihilatory violence. Such a discourse can be expected to extend to others, I suggest, who conceive their identity to be dependent on some state hierarchical order. This appears to be the case in the violent resistance to the Sri Lankan state by the populist-Marxist JVP, which came to a head in the last months of 1989 and which, in isolated areas, continues to exist despite a crushing military response.

The state against itself

It is central to this discussion that violence and the discourse of annihilation are neither external to ideology or a mere meaningless product of it. Ideology is inscribed in a discourse of violence, part of which are the physical acts of violence themselves. This is most apparent in recent events.

In August 1989 a poster and graffiti war of words occurred, involving the JVP and the agents of government. Placards appeared on hoardings throughout Colombo and the provinces. One, purportedly placed by the Sri Lankan army, depicted Rohan Wijeweera (the JVP leader, since killed) in demon guise, surrounded by death and skeletons. Wijeweera was presented as saying, in self-devouring demon terms, "Stalin, Mao, and Marx did not kill their followers, but I do for the sake of my Motherland." Another placard addressed to the JVP declared, "Are you (*topi*) patriots? You hide in caves and destroy the property of the island." The opponents of the state are not simply "demonized," which is widespread in general rhetorics of violence, but their demon identity is given particular hierarchical meaning. The pronoun "you" (*topi*) is used in Sinhala to refer to the lowest of beings and supports a rehierarchizing violence appropriate to the remythologizations of state power. Thus the same placard exhorted the general populace to kill the JVP when spotted and to inflict the punishment meted out by the traditional kings upon them. One was suggested. It involves impaling (*ulatiyennava*) the victim on a stake driven through the anus. Government destruction was reported as sometimes following the pattern dealt out by Sinhala kings. Thus I have one (unsubstantiated) account of a group of captured JVP youths being dismembered and their limbs hung from trees (see Knox, 1958:61). This kind of fragmentation fits with the kind of fragmentation which demons threaten in traditional Sinhala exorcisms and which the order of hierarchy established in exorcism ultimately inflicts on demons.

The violence of the state, from the general evidence available, does not in fact appear to follow the letter of its rhetoric. However, such an ideology of hierarchical annihilation should legitimate this kind of violence and may motivate it. Realization of the dangerous quality of the rhetoric probably caused the Sri Lankan government to bring their part in the poster campaign to an end. Commitment to Buddhist values and to contemporary rationalist principles may have been a restraining factor on state action. The sheer violence of the general situation makes the doctrine of non-violence and a rationalism which sees violence as irrational highly problematic, and does lead to renewed effort among many sectors in Sri Lanka, including government, to assert as strongly as possible the paramount importance of Buddhist non-violence and a rational attitude in an effort to halt the carnage. But a modern rationalism is also engaged in the production of violence and is integral in the remythologized discourse of state power and annihilatory reaffirmation. Thus the placard referred to above understands the demonic to be manifest in its attack on property, the foundation of the rational order of the modern state. Incidentally, this meaning deviates from other common understandings of demonic character. In traditional exorcisms, for example, the demon is that which yearns for property and things of the material world, indeed demonstrates an overdetermined desire for and attachment to the material terms of existence.

It is the rationalism distorted and remythologized in state ideology which, to a degree, energizes the hierarchical reaffirmation of state power. I refer to that bureaucratic/technical rationalism which classifies phenomena into abstract taxonomic categories according to gross impersonal indicators and then asserts the grounded reality of these categories. Such bureaucratic rationalism informs the pattern and form of state violence. Thus the military and paramilitary agents of the state recognize fields of resistance through such crude indicators as youth, caste, and village. There is a confusion of the indicator with the social or political category to which it points. So the danger is always present, in this kind of probabilistic universe of meaning, that those bearing the indications will be destroyed along with those who are the declared objects of destruction. Additionally, indicators are subject to multiplication as circumstances shift and new information comes to hand. Violence organized along the lines of bureaucratic rationalities is potentially self-sustaining, as the record of the twentieth century demonstrates. Such bureaucratic/rationalist possibility is impelled, I suggest, in an ideological context where power is linked to the capacity to annihilate, which must drive the agents of the state to seek out resistance in order to affirm the power of the state. The bureaucratic/technical order of the state is not just the means or the instrument of state violence, it becomes itself generative of an expanding situation of violence. The JVP was a major threat to the Sri Lankan state. However, its existence is also a fantasy, an imaginary, impelled in an ideology of power which affirms itself through the annihilation of resistance. Thus, innocent Sinhalese bearing the taxonomic indicators of resistance to the state are affirmed as resisters in their very destruction by the state.

A common technique of annihilation was the burning of the bodies, usually in gasoline-filled tyres, by the agents of the state. This is not to be seen as a pragmatic destruction of evidence. Rather, this kind of action is, in itself, the very *invention of evidence*, the objectification of resistance, as it is also the affirmation of state power. The eradication of all external characteristics of the person that such burning involves can be understood as grimly symbolic of the impersonal form of the bureaucratic rational order that destroys human· beings. However, there are other symbolic possibilities in the manner of human destruction I describe. One aspect of the logic of hierarchy and the Cosmic State is that the powerful state conditions the integrity and wholeness of the person. Cast outside the state, identified as resistant to its order, the individual loses all identity and enters into a process of radical dissolution. The burning of the corpse – often at the roadside in a place which some Sinhalese would recognize as demonic space and appropriate to demonic destruction – is such a radical dissolution.

The JVP resistance involved a discourse of violence which engaged similar cosmic metaphors. However, these metaphors appear to achieve a greater literalness than those committed to the violent action of the state and a closer unity with context and with the identity of those instrumental in the violence. In the brutal killings perpetrated by the JVP at the height of their violence in the latter part of 1989, the bodies of their victims were often dreadfully mutilated. These mutilations were frequently and explicitly the symbolic wounds of divine punishment for wrongdoing. If the victims were figures of local importance or power they were occasionally beheaded, an action which has the hierarchical significance not just of negation but of sacrificial encompassment. Leaders of the JVP identified themselves personally with cosmic kings. Those executed by the JVP sometimes had notes pinned to their bodies signed "Kirti (Kitti) Vijayabahu." The leader who adopted this *nom de guerre* has since been killed by government forces.

Vijayabahu is a heroic king whose story of conquest and unification of Lanka during his long reign is recounted in the chronicle *Culavamsa*. Some of his exploits, as set out in the chronicle, parallel those of Dutugemunu, the hero vital in the mythologization of power of the contemporary Sri Lankan state. Like Dutugemunu, Vijayabahu embarks on his ambition of reunification without parental authority. He is renowned as a conqueror of Tamils. However, Vijayabahu is markedly distinct from Dutugemunu. His reign is characterized by frequent rebellion from his own people, which he quells remorselessly. There is none of Dutugemunu's Buddhist quietude. Vijayabahu captures the heads of his opponents and burns others at the stake. Vijayabahu operates in a world deeply torn in itself and in which external threat comprises the significant background to the internal conflict which dominates his story. Vijayabahu is appropriate to the context of JVP violence.

The JVP manifested the potential inherent in the nationalism of the state, which mythologizes power as annihilation and views such power as ultimate in the creation of a moral order. But if the mythologizations of state power have force through a bureaucratic/technical order and distort its meanings, those of the JVP achieve their potency in the negation of such an order and also in the construction of an order directly counter to that of the Sri Lankan government. This negation and reconstruction is a process which draws those cosmic remythologizations of the JVP into close intimacy with their context. They are made integral to the creation of a culture of terror whioh becomes more than a framework for the organization of meaning through which power is legitimated. The mythologizations, aspects of their logic and orientation, threaten to become integral within the fabric of the reality they are engaged in constructing.

The negation of the bureaucratic order of the state is consistent with much contemporary revolutionary practice. The JVP consciously adopted such practice. But the violent means, the form and content of the violence, was neither a necessary condition of the violence in any universalist sense nor demanded by the revolutionary ends. There is reason to believe that the violent manner of the JVP resistance was a factor in eventually turning the tide against them. While it succeeded in the short term, it also eroded popular support. The resistance of the JVP was popularly fuelled in the conditions of considerable social and economic suffering, especially among the urban and rural poor. It was exacerbated by the Sinhala–Tamil ethnic war. The ground was well prepared, in part by the nationalism of that state against which the JVP reacted. Its totalizing and unifying claims were contradicted both by its failure in the ethnic war and, most importantly, by its foundation in a rational, bureaucratic, technological order which was the demythologizing contradiction of the state ideology of cosmic unity.

In a sense, the negation and reconstruction of reality motivated and instituted by the JVP was a remythologization of a remythologization. It was a remythologization in a more radical vein, directed against those institutions which may have been the source of the power of the state but also, in the mythic consciousness of those who fought the state, were both at the root of their everyday despair and were the source of the failure of those in government to effect their claim of a unity in Sinhala identity and society. I suggest that this adds to an understanding of some of the popular support for the JVP, initially at least.

An important aspect of the dreadful violence of the JVP was its appeal to what were conceived as "traditional" virtues. Some of the people executed were not merely identified as government stooges or as behaving in defiance of JVP authority. They were also presented as offending village morality by seducing young women, thieving, and so on. The killing occasionally followed the course of long-standing village disputes which, as may be expected, focused on questions of cultural value and the breaking of customary convention.

I conducted interviews in 1990 and in 1991 in areas in the Western, Southern and Eastern Provinces affected by the JVP violence. Although many people were still in fear of government reprisal, I gained the impression of considerable approval by villagers and urban poor concerning the moral activities of the JVP. Many felt that the JVP had acted to rectify injustices which the officials of the state were unwilling to rectify. Most people I interviewed felt that the JVP operated against the interests of élites and were not corrupted by bribery.

If the government violence was to some extent motivated, for example, through its remythologizations of a bureaucratic and technological order, the JVP violence found some of its force in the remythologization of "village" society. The violence of the JVP was often highly personal in character, a violence of social relations in contrast to the category violence of the government. A practice of the JVP was to refuse relatives permission to remove for burial the corpses of their executed victims. Not only was the victim demonized and placed outside the ritual conventions of village society, but so too were the relatives.

The expanding dynamic of the JVP violence was driven, like that of the government, as much by the contradictions of its mythologized reality, of the world it tried to reconstitute, as by its need to overcome the resistance posed by the government. Building within the structure of village or localized communities, following the lines of their divisions and conflicts while simultaneously attempting to unify them into an order which resolved such division, the JVP itself became exposed to the conflicts born of the world it tried to control and generated internal resistance to itself through the effort to command and produce unity.[14] The JVP accelerated and possibly intensi-

fied its violence of social relations as a consequence and in direct proportion to the hopeless contradictions it progressively opened up
through its remythologizing action.

I have drawn a contrast between the violence of the JVP and that
of the government. In practice, the contrast is not so neat. The discourse of one influences the other and, in the expanding crisis of control, some of the agents of state reaffirmation adopted the methods of
those whom they opposed.

Theatre of power and death

The pre-colonial state centred around the Divine King has been described as a "theatre state" (Geertz, 1979). In such a polity, power at
the periphery has the principles which motivate and condition power
and its quest displayed in the theatrical ceremonial of the king's court
at the centre. In Geertz's analysis, power gives way to status, to which
power is ultimately oriented and finally subordinated. The theatre of
the court is not one of power but of the transcendent values which
determine it. In contemporary Sri Lanka nationalist remythologizations, engaging the metaphors and logic of the Divine King, are involved in a theatre of power in which, increasingly, the only value is
power itself. Moreover, it is a power which can only define itself in
the overcoming of resistance by annihilating it. The theatre of this
power is among the population as a whole and contributes to its fear
and terror. It converts the population into helpless spectators whose
everyday world is drained of its meanings and is conditioned progressively by the "meanings" carried through the violence itself.

Sri Lanka in recent years has become dangerously poised on the
brink of a death-world which Wyschogrod, referring to European experience of recent history, defines as "an attempt to make whole the
broken cosmos by an imaginative act of radical negation, the destruction of the embedding matrix for all social forms, the life-world ..."
(1985:28). In Sri Lanka this imaginative act is driven through particular remythologizations of power and identity. These remythologizations do not have force in themselves. They become destructive
through the orders and processes of the realities against which they
react. In effect, the remythologizations turn these orders and processes against themselves. Thus the rational/bureaucratic order of the
state becomes the instrument for the destruction of the bureaucratic
order and its rational soul. Similarly, the social relations and ritual
processes which give vitality to everyday worlds in the urban neigh-

bourhood or the village become agencies in the destruction of their vitality and of the entire life-world of their subsistence and regeneration. A life-world becomes a self-consuming world of death and the energy of the former is converted into the energy of the latter.

There is no necessity for remythologizations of identity or of power to follow a destructive course. The mythologizing of reality is general to the human experience and is present in all areas of human endeavour and possibly at all moments of human history. Some qualities of mythologization and of ideologies in general may facilitate their destruction and violence. I refer to their totalizing of experience and understanding and also to the distorting simplicity of their argument, whereby they not only reduce the complexity of historical experience and process, but also typically misconstrue such reality. Again, totalizing is a dimension of most thought and practice of human beings, be it scientific or religious – as, I think, is an orientation to simplification and reduction. Misconstruction has been identified by some as the fundamental creative and vital dynamic of humanity, by no means essentially destructive because it distorts "truth" and defies reason.

The destructive danger of remythologizations is in part their connection to the agencies of political domination and power and their construction or interpretive use by the agents of such power and domination. This is especially the case when the remythologization becomes a force in the organization of political coherence and unity, for the conditions of its existence are those which must continually defeat its project. This is exacerbated through the remythologization of political identity itself, whose agents and agencies are likely to intensify their assertions in the face of increasing resistance to those assertions. Such resistance is generated through, for example, the bureaucratic, rational, and technological orders by means of which the remythologization comes to have force in the definition of routine experience. The resort to violence may be the ultimate way in which remythologizations of the power of the state, linked with others such as the essential unity of culture and ethnic identity, can overcome the resistances which are the making of such remythologizations. It is through violence that a mythic consciousness which is not part of the paramount realities of everyday life, which in my usage of the term "remythologization" is out of place in the meaning structures of everyday life, can inscribe itself as, indeed, the dominant meaning of existence. In this process, whether it be directed by government forces or those which are aligned against them, the life-world can move towards its destruction in the space of death.

Remythologizations, in their process of realization through the agents and agencies of violent power, do form a unity with the worlds of meaning in which, at first, they may have largely been out of place. No remythologization of reality is an act of pure invention or imagination in the sense that it has no antecedents in specific areas of meaningful experience. It does not come from a historical or cultural void. But it is largely a suppressed universe of meaning, one confined and made increasingly less relevant to experience through historical processes whose contexts of meaning and action are counter to those they now effectively suppress. Remythologizations are directed towards revitalizing what is suppressed and, in radically expanding their meaning or relevance into erstwhile antagonistic contexts, both transform the nature of the suppressed meaning – or revitalize it by injecting it with the meanings of the present – and also transform the meanings of realities engaged to the remythologizations. This occurs when metaphors of demon destruction which are part of village exorcism rites are made relevant to political experience in contexts outside the control of exorcism and, further, are directed to human beings (rather than demons) and made to define reality as a whole (Kapferer, 1988). Such meanings become distortions of themselves and their process and, as in contemporary Sri Lanka, become the basis for the expansion of terror, rather than for the release from abject fear. A similar process occurs, for example, in the appropriation of bureaucracy and its rationalism to the service of political remythologizations. Their practice becomes distorted through the remythologization, and, as I have suggested, the very rationalist ideals that could place a limitation on violent action become displaced or redefined so that their organizations of practice become the instruments of disruption and human destruction. The centres of controlling rationalist principle, such as the law, may become radically subverted and, indeed, suspended (Tambiah, 1986).

I have said that there is no necessity for remythologizations of power to be humanly destructive – certainly not on a scale whereby the whole ground of existence becomes self-consuming. Sri Lanka's own move to national assertion and freedom from colonial domination was relatively peaceful. There are numerous assertions of a nationalist value and of ethnic and cultural value in Sri Lanka now which are tolerant, as they are also courageously antagonistic to the recent waves of violence by the government and by those who resist it. But Sri Lanka also demonstrates the particular danger of that remythologization of power conditioned in the contemporary circum-

85

stance of the formation of the modern state, whereby the order of the state, and the order of those who would usurp it, are affirmed through the capacity to annihilate and manifests themselves most clearly in the act of annihilation. Such a vision of power feeds on resistance and is motivated continually to discover and search it out, and even invent it, in an annihilating process of self-affirmation. In this course, war directed externally and also internally threatens to become the condition of power and the forms of political institutionalization of that power.

The situation in which Sri Lanka finds itself is conditioned in widespread post-colonial circumstances of the spread of capitalist market economies, their technologies, and their ideologies and practices of rationalism and bureaucracy. The demythologization of the world and the particular historical experience of this in Sri Lanka are intimately involved in the current crises of identity and power. These general processes, however, also achieve some content and meaning through the ideologies in which they are realized. I have stressed the importance of exploring the argument and logic of such ideologies and the nature of their imaginary, which are or can become the condition of ideological ground. In this discussion, the remythologizations of reality impart, through the organizations of political power, particular definitions and force to widespread processes of global experience. Modes of capitalist market formation and the establishment of bureaucratic/rational orders are implicated drastically in the present situation in Sri Lanka. But, in the historical conditions of the remythologization, capitalist and bureaucratic forms and others of routine existence, those of class, caste, and ritual assume particular meaning and direction which is not necessarily reducible to the general form. Nationalism may have emerged first in the Western imperialist thrust, or capitalism may have flowered in the conditions of Protestant Europe and North America. But these are particular ideological formings, which, as contemporary global processes demonstrate, can be radically distinct in the material and no less material ideological circumstances and orientations of their energies.

Notes

1. The research and writing of this essay has been assisted by a grant from the Harry Frank Guggenheim Foundation. I am grateful to Karen Colvard for her assistance and discussion. Mike Rowlands, Buck Schieffelin, and Andrew Lattas have argued with me over many of the points. I am especially thankful to Stanley Tambiah, who sent me "hot off the press" proofs of his forthcoming book *Buddhism Betrayed? Religion, Politics, and Violence*

in Sri Lanka, which caused me to make some attempt to clarify a few of the directions I have taken in earlier work. A Netherlands Institute for Advanced Studies Fellowship for 1991–2 has given me the opportunity to revise and extend ideas present in earlier drafts of this essay.

2. There are numerous other forms of violence in this expanded sense that could be mentioned. For example, the violence of bureaucratic decisions, which follows rules without consideration for the particular case; or the denial of educational opportunity except to privileged groups, or of employment except to those with the appropriate contacts. Forms of cultural appropriation like the "museumizing" of whole peoples may be another kind of violence. The order of colonial rule even in its most peaceful version can be conceived as violence in the larger sense in which I use the term. Bourdieu has developed the term "symbolic violence" to embrace such larger senses of violence.

   I am well aware that such an expanded meaning of "violence" may be next to useless in the development of "scientific" empirical understanding. No hypotheses could be developed from this catch-all meaning. But this is the point. Violence is in the world, in the structures, orders, and modalities of the routine realities of everyday experience. The conditions of violence, which themselves may be conceived as having violent, dehumanizing, and human-destroying consequences, are greater than any particular or mass event of physical destruction.

3. There are other difficulties with the "modernist" perspectives presented. They are fundamentally grounded in the essentialism that difference is ultimately antithetical to human forms of life. That is, that all social and cultural forms of existence ultimately reduce to the same thing. One of the arguments developed in my *Legends of People, Myths of State* (1988), specifically the section on the Australian nationalist ideology of "egalitarian individualism," is that the racism and intolerance which still persists in Australia is driven in the fundamental denial of difference at root, the assertion of essential sameness, and, except as a surface phenomenon, the denial of cultural forms of difference. Somehow one's acceptance into humanity is dependent on the kind of Disney World assumption that differences are only on the surface. By extension, if one insists on one's difference (that one's difference is more than the culture of ethnic foods and restaurants), then somehow one's humanity is in question. *Legends* was concerned with demonstrating, largely through an inspection of the imaginary of Australian nationalist ideology, that such an antagonistic position on difference is at the root of intolerance. Further, I suggested that many Western social science theories, far from being pristinely objective, are ideologically oriented through an intolerance of the kind of difference to which I am referring. My critique in this sense extended to many "modernist" theoretical perspectives including Durkheimian functionalism, structuralism, vulgar materialism, and individualist interests theories of various kinds.

   My analysis of Buddhist nationalism was similarly concerned to demonstrate how its formation in contemporary historical processes transformed a highly flexible form of symbolic discourse into a relatively static and intolerant one: how, in its formation and revaluation of meaning in present-day circumstances, a Buddhist nationalism became intolerant of difference and, indeed, was able to demonize it.

   It should also be made clear that when I write of fundamental difference I in no way imply that this is a difference in human being external to lived structures of practice. The difference of which I write is the creation of human beings who weave diverse forms of life and come to live them.

4. I stress that I do not treat what I call "imaginary" as independent of context. It is always generated in contexts and, through its application by the very human beings who create it and who act in context, has force in context. But the imaginary is not a reflection of context, for the very reasons I have discussed. It cannot be comprehended by a mere reduction to a world which is treated as a reality independent of the way that world is imagined. Neither can it be explored as if it were some kind of rationalization of the "real" world, a distortion designed to make sense of or obscure some "fact" of life.

87

5. I find it necessary to reassert this point, in the face of persistent misinterpretations of my position, initially established in *Legends of People, Myths of State* (1988). My argument from the start has been concerned with the examination of ideological construction and what I gauged to be its internal "logic." The argument of ideologies, I held, had been neglected, yet it was their very argument which seemed to have sway, not empirical realities. My account of the "state" is, indeed, the state as ideologized in certain chronicles like the *Dipavamsa, Mahavamsa, Culavamsa*, etc., and as it is manifested in the ideologized chronicling of heroes like Vijaya and Dutugemunu. I am certain that the way these heroes are presented has about as much connection with the real world of objective empirical study as Roland of Roncesvalles or the Cid of Burgos. There is no suggestion that the *Mahavamsa*, for example, tells it as it was or is, yet this is what some critics seem to suggest that I say (e.g. Spencer, 1989, 1990). Most recently Tambiah (1992) states that his version of medieval and ancient systems as loosely organized and not rigidly bounded "galactic polities" is closer to the facts than the hierarchical view that I present. I think his view of the galactic polity as a description of reality is spot on. But I described what I saw to be the principles behind incorporative, encompassing, cosmic political progress (embodied in the kingship), as these are imaginatively presented in those chronicles which are the reference points of recent nationalist ideological construction. Further, I indicated that the process of the *Mahavamsa* accounts, for example, is replicated in logical scheme by present-day ritual. Maybe I am wrong in my interpretation – but this needs demonstration in terms of what my argument is. At no point do I suggest that the imaginative constructions of the state in the *Mahavamsa* model empirical reality.

One additional point. Present notions of the state are notions developed in recent history. The reading of the modern state into the *Mahavamsa* is a process of the imaginative construction of contemporary ideology. It is why I write later in this essay of contemporary nationalist ideology as a "remythologization of a remythologization."

6. The term "Buddhist Revival" imparts a far too coherent and monolithic sense to what were very diverse processes of a revaluation of Buddhist ideas that largely occurred in the context of colonial power. Scholars have presented the "Revival" as strongly influenced by Western and Christian ideas and practices. The Revival *made* such practices into Buddhist practices. This may have been the case until fairly recently. However, new directions are evident in what I see as enduring "revitalization" processes. Thus, there is a revaluation of "peasant" ritual practices (often labelled as "not Buddhist" by an earlier wave of urban bourgeois "revivalists"), as, indeed, "authentic" Sinhala Buddhist practice. Such revaluation is related to the emergence into positions of power and status in the national arena of Sinhalese of peasant or lower-class background who were previously excluded by the colonially created and often English-speaking élites. Members of this "new class" were brought up in a milieu in which the rites they now value were common practice. Their revaluation has changed much of their erstwhile significance. Nevertheless, such revaluation by a new, politically powerful class has been influential, I think, in the cultural directions and discourse of recent developments in Sinhala nationalism.

7. The urgency of human beings to totalize, to achieve what they conceive as bounded and coherent universes of meaning and action, does not disagree with an observation that sees the worlds of lived experience and discourse as continually shifting, fragmenting, breaking boundaries, collapsing, etc. It could be said that the enduring tragedy of human being is born in an anxiety to totalize against the experience of its impossibility.

8. The process where rites are made into spectacles can be seen as systematic with the demythologizing processes attendant on colonialism and incorporation within the dynamics of global capitalism. Cohn shows this process in colonial India, and Seneviratne's work on the Kandy *perahera* indicates a very similar development. The point is that in being made a spectacle, rites lose their significance in embracing socially and politically constitutive cosmic processes. The Kandy *perahera* is reduced as an intervention within an overall cosmic process because the processes it ingrains and reacts upon are not the encompassing and

paramount forces in lived realities any more. The Kandy *perahera* presents power that is not as vital in its reconstitution as it may once have been. I am not saying that the making of the rites into spectacles is an entirely new phenomenon.

The idea of spectacle is present in the Sinhala concept of *dakum* (Skt. *darsana*). Thus the *perahera* is an occasion of *dakum* whereby the brilliant power of king and retinue and of gods and their followers are made present. However, the making present of king and deities is also a process of empowering them and also empowering the people who gaze upon their spectacle. This notion of the spectacle is not absent from contemporary performances of the Kandy *perahera*. But, I suggest, the *perahera* is weakened in its constitutive force. The powers of king and onlooker are not formed through the *perahera* but by processes external to it which the *perahera* now represents. This shift in the constitutive power of the *perahera* that makes it spectacle in a representational sense occurs in the context of demythologizing processes.

9. Tambiah (1992:173) prefers his notion of a "galactic polity" with its shifting boundaries and multiple centres of countervailing power to the more centralized and bounded sense contained in the hierarchical image. In my view, Tambiah's galactic polity is the appropriate perspective on actual, empirically explored, historical contexts. My presentation of a hierarchical principle is drawn from that apparent in the contexts of the chronicles and contemporary rite. The highly centralized and bounded context of the contemporary state is, I suggest, a context in which the imagination of the hierarchical process of the chronicles can manifest a potential that they never had in the past.

10. I have contrasted one Western "egalitarian" variant, that of Australian nationalist ideology, with the Sri Lanka "hierarchical" nationalist ideology of the Buddhist cosmic state. Both ideological constructs inhabit political societies that have much in common by virtue of the fact that they took form in contemporary global processes of imperialism and post-imperialism.

11. Tambiah (1986) has documented the recent contraction or demise of democratic institutions and the rights of citizens in Sri Lanka. Much of this is to be attributed to the growth of national disturbance in response to growing Sinhala ethnic nationalism. The crisis of power generated has, in my view, given more and more space to a particular hierarchical imaginary of power which is contributing to a further erosion of democratic rights.

12. In my usage, "assimilation" is distinct from "incorporation." Assimilation refers to the process of losing one identity and assuming another. A process of incorporation is one where one identity is included in the other and not lost. Highly significant in this process is that the character of the identity incorporated is the principle directing its incorporation.

13. I have described what I call here "the logic of hierarchy" an ontology in earlier publications. I use the term ontology to distinguish it analytically from ideology. The former can be conceived as the orientational frame which articulates the contextual meaning of ideology. The ontological frame can, in my usage, organize a great diversity of ideological rhetoric of nationalism. However, because they share an ontology, the way is open for the meanings of nationalism to play, for example, into the ontological ground of village ritual practices. Their ontological commonality establishes a metonymic exchange of meaning. A common ontology yields penetrative power to the ideology of nationalism, enables it to invade other contexts of meaning and to elicit their apparent support, and to distort their import. Ontologies are never closed systems of meaning. Rather they are frames within which innumerable meanings, often highly innovative and original, can develop.

One characteristic of the ontology of ideology is that it can be integral in promoting the illusion that present historical meanings are continuous or reducible to the meanings of the past. This is definitely *not* to say that current meanings of Cosmic Kingship, for example, are extensions from the past. This is an egregious misunderstanding of the argument of *Legends of People, Myths of State*, on which some anthropologists have insisted (Spencer, 1989, 1990; Stirrat, 1992).

Furthermore, my usage of the term ontology does not describe a psychology of being which is grounded in persons somehow prior to their action. Ontology is a logic of action, the organizing principles of practice including the practice in myth. My usage has some connection, for instance, with the engagement of the term *doxa* by Bourdieu.

Ontology, as I employ it, is non-determinant and is not essentialist. The direction of my usage is to historicize the notion, to indicate how radically original orientational frames to being can come into existence. My approach is along the lines of Wyschogrod's (1985:57–64) combination of Cassirer with Kant in her understanding of the shift in the orientation to being attendant on the Holocaust.

14. Government forces, of course, used the conflicts in the social relations of village society to crack the JVP and to gain information on the whereabouts of leaders.

References

Alles, A.C. 1990. *The JVP, 1969–1989*. Colombo: Lake House.

Barth, Fredrik (ed.). 1969. *Ethnic Groups and Boundaries*. London: Allen and Unwin.

Chandraprema, C.A. 1991. *Sri Lanka: The Years of Terror*. Colombo: Lake House.

Cohen, A. 1969. *Custom and Politics in Urban Africa*. London: Routledge.

Committee for Rational Development. 1984. *Sri Lanka: The Ethnic Conflict*. New Delhi: Navrang.

Geertz, C. 1979. *Negara*. Princeton, NJ: Princeton University Press.

Geiger, Wilhelm (trans.). 1953. *Culavamsa*. Colombo: Ceylon Government Information Department.

Gellner, E. 1983. *Nations and Nationalism*. Oxford: Blackwell.

Gombrich, M., and G. Obeyesekere. 1989. *Buddhism Transformed*. Princeton, NJ: Princeton University Press.

Gunawardena, R. 1979. "The People of the Lion: Sinhala Consciousness." In Spencer, 1990.

Halliday, F. 1971. "The Ceylonese Insurrection." *New Left Review* 69.

Jayawardena, K. 1984. "Some Aspects of Class and Ethnic Consciousness in Sri Lanka in the Late Nineteenth and Early Twentieth Centuries." In *Ethnicity and Social Change in Sri Lanka*. Colombo: Social Scientists' Association.

Kapferer, B. 1983. *A Celebration of Demons*. Bloomington, Ind.: Indiana University Press.

———. 1988. *Legends of People, Myths of State*. Washington/London: Smithsonian Institution Press.

———. 1989. "Nationalist Ideology and a Comparative Anthropology." *Ethnos* (Stockholm) 54, III–IV, pp. 161–99.

———. 1991. Preface to 2nd edn, *A Celebration of Demons*. Washington: Smithsonian Institution Press.

Kearney, R. 1984. *Dialogues with Contemporary Continental Thinkers*. Manchester: Manchester University Press.

Kedourie, Elie. 1960. *Nationalism*. London.

Keyes, C.F. 1971. "Buddhism and National Integration in Thailand." *Journal of Asian Studies* vol. 30, no. 3.

———. 1978. "Political Crisis and Militant Buddhism in Contemporary Thailand." In Bardwell Smith (ed.), *Religion and Legitimation of Power in Thailand, Laos and Burma* (Anima Books, 1978), pp. 147–164.

Knox, R. 1958. *An Historical Relation of Ceylon*. Sri Lanka: Maharagama, Tisara Prakasakeyo. First published in London, 1681.

Ling, T. 1979. *Buddhism, Imperialism and War*. London: Allen and Unwin.

Malalgoda, K. 1976. *Buddhism in Sinhalese Society, 1750–1900*. Berkeley: University of California Press.

Nissan, E. 1989. "History in the Making: Anuradhapura and the Sinhala Buddhist Nation." *Social Analysis* 25, pp. 64–77.

Nissan, E., and R.L. Stirrat. 1989. "The Generation of Communal Identities." In Spencer, 1990.

Obeyesekere, G. 1979. "The Vicissitudes of the Sinhala and Buddhist Identity Through Time and Change." In Roberts, 1979.

———. 1984. *The Cult of the Goddess Pattini*. Chicago: Chicago University Press.

Peel, J.D.Y. 1987. "History, Culture and the Comparative Method: A West African Puzzle." In L. Holy (ed.), *Comparative Anthropology*. Oxford: Blackwell.

Reynolds, F.E. 1977. "Civil Religion and National Community in Thailand." *Journal of Asian Studies* vol. 36, no. 2.

———. 1978a. "Sacral Kingship and National Development: The Case of Thailand." In Bardwell Smith (ed.), *Religion and Legitimation of Power in Thailand, Laos and Burma* (Anima Books), pp. 100–10.

———. 1978b. "Ritual and Social Hierarchy: An Aspect of Traditional Religion in Buddhist Laos." In Bardwell Smith (ed.), *Religion and Legitimation of Power in Thailand, Laos and Burma* (Anima Books), pp. 166–74.

Ricoeur, Paul. 1984. "Dialogue with R. Kearney." In Kearney, 1984.

Roberts, M. (ed.). 1979. *Collective Identities, Nationalism, and Protest in Modern Sri Lanka*. Colombo: Marga Institute.

———. 1982. *Caste, Conflict and Elite Formation*. Cambridge: Cambridge University Press.

Seneviratne, H.L. 1978. *Rituals of the Kandyan State*. London: Aldine Press.

Spencer, Jonathan. 1989. "Writing Within: Anthropology, Nationalism, and Culture in Sri Lanka." *Current Anthropology* vol. 31, no. 3 (June).

Spencer, J. (ed.). 1990. *Sri Lanka: History and the Roots of Conflict*. London: Routledge.

Stirrat, R.L. 1992.

Tambiah, S.J. 1976. *World Conqueror and World Renouncer*. Cambridge: Cambridge University Press.

———. 1978.

———. 1986. *Sri Lanka: Ethnic Fratricide and the Dismantling of Democracy*. London: Tauris.

———. 1992. *Buddhism Betrayed? Religion, Politics, and Violence in Sri Lanka*. Chicago: University of Chicago Press.

Taussig, M.M. 1987. *Colonialism, Shamanism and the Wild Man*. Chicago: University of Chicago Press.

Wilson, Jayaratnam A. 1988. *The Break-Up of Sri Lanka*. Honolulu: University of Hawaii Press.

Wyschogrod, Edith. 1985. *Spirit in Ashes: Heidegger and Man-Made Mass Death*. New Haven, CT: Yale University Press.

4

The impact of drug trafficking on Colombian culture

Francisco J. de Roux, S.J.

This paper presents the following hypothesis. Drug trafficking appeared in Colombia at a time when the country faced an institutional vacuum in economic, governmental, social, and ethical matters. This vacuum made evident the existence of a cultural crisis. The most resounding proof of this crisis was the continuous and senseless destruction of human life in a way only comparable to the famous *Época de la Violencia*, or civil war, during the 1950s. Drug trafficking aggravated the cultural crisis, corrupting the state and the political and economic institutions of Colombia, and threatening society. Colombians have been looking for a solution to this situation, in an effort to restructure institutions.

The institutional vacuum

During the last thirty years (1960–1990) a profound misalignment has developed between Colombia's institutions and the education, information, expectations, and needs of Colombians. This gap between institutions and people provided the perfect environment for an unhindered increase in drug trafficking, guerrilla and paramilitary movements, private justice and vendettas, and violations of human rights.

The governmental vacuum

Colombia's territory covers 1,300,000 square kilometres. During the 1970s it became obvious that the government's presence was not felt in more than half of this area. In the Orinoco plains and the jungles of the Amazon, which lie on the borders of Venezuela, Brazil, and Peru; in the jungles in the centre of the country and the Pacific region; and in the high regions of Colombia's three mountain ranges, the government had no authority. In these regions there was an absence of justice, no labour regulations, no social security, too few teachers, and no health services. The local and regional authorities were often highly corrupt and were not accountable to any higher authority. The only real government presence in these distant regions of the country was the army and the police, whose duties mostly consisted of putting down public demonstrations over the lack of water and health services and human rights violations.

Something similar occurred at the beginning the 1980s in the crowded, poor neighbourhoods of Colombia's largest cities: Bogotá, Medellín, Cali, and Baranquilla. At the time, Bogotá had a population of four million, Medellín two million, and Cali and Baranquilla each had one million inhabitants. The popular neighbourhoods of these cities housed hundreds of thousands of people who lacked any effective political representation. They also lacked public services, such as sewerage, rubbish collection, and public transport. The relationship between these areas and the political class was virtually non-existent, except for *clientelismo* during the lead-up to elections, when political candidates would make empty promises to buy residents' votes. During the last century, the two main Colombian political parties, the Liberals and the Conservatives, bought public support in this manner. Neither party has effectively increased the government's presence in the popular neighbourhoods.[1]

As a consequence, the level of political distrust among poor Colombians increased and they were forced to look to themselves for solutions to the inequalities and social insecurity with which they live. During the early 1960s, a left-wing guerrilla movement developed in rural areas of Colombia. Originally the guerrillas aimed to capture enough power to fill the vacuum left by the state. That is, they aimed to provide security to the people in the areas. In large part they were made welcome by the *campesinos* (rural inhabitants). *Campesinos* welcomed the guerrillas because they felt abandoned by the government, which had failed to fulfil its promise of agricultural reform. As part of this reform, in 1961 the government had promised to distribute 10 million hectares of land among rural families over the next ten years. However, in 14 years it managed to free up only 250,000 hectares.

When the cocaine trade arrived in Colombia, these areas – in which the government's presence was least felt – provided the most fertile ground for the cultivation of coca. The drug traffickers financially supported the efforts of the *campesinos* and the indigenous people to set up coca plantations. They also became financially involved in regional politics by supporting local politicians and lobbyists on local concerns. In this way the drug traffickers established mutually beneficial relations with local politicians. In many cases they funded politicians in their campaigns and, in return, the politicians supported proposals which benefited the drug industry. The drug traffickers provided regional employment and recreational facilities, and in some ways took up the state's responsibilities and filled the vacuum the state's absence in these regions had created.

Initially, relations between the drug traffickers, the coca growers, and the guerrillas were good. The guerrillas hired out their services as protectors of the coca plantations, maintaining a degree of social control over the area and putting down any unrest. However, around 1983 relations between the guerrillas and the drug traffickers broke down. The reasons for the break are complex, but one of the reasons was definitely rivalry over control of the area.

The drug traffickers joined forces with the landowners' private armies. The Colombian army saw this union as opportune in its fight against the guerrillas and joined forces with the drug traffickers and private armies. Together they created numerous paramilitary groups. Drug traffickers made money and weapons available; the army provided military training; the landowners provided a territorial base. These groups also had regional political support. The army turned over to the paramilitaries the monopoly of repression in the region. In 1988, the traffickers paid for military specialists from Israel and England to come and train the paramilitaries.

The paramilitary groups were given a free hand and impunity from the law for three and a half years. They were responsible for horrific massacres and group assassinations. Neither the army nor the police tried to curb their violent methods. On numerous occasions members of the army were present at and participated in criminal operations. The fight against the rise of "communist" forces was to succeed at any cost. At this time the government of President Reagan was financing paramilitary groups in Nicaragua, calling them "freedom fighters."

The paramilitary groups "punished" all those towns and *campesinos* suspected of aiding the guerrillas. They soon came to represent a force of destruction among the rural inhabitants, who were their primary victims. The *campesinos* named the use of force against their communities the "dirty war." While it lasted, they lived under a constant reign of terror. Everyone knew the identities of those responsible for the violent acts. However, to denounce the guilty parties was, in effect, to sign your own death warrant. The *campesinos* began to migrate to the nearest towns. Popular protest was said to be guerrilla-organized activity and was followed by sudden and violent raids on the towns that protested. While many areas were occupied by the guerrillas, however, these were not attacked by the paramilitaries. Generally, the guerrillas took refuge in the mountains. Every year between 1988 and 1990, approximately 100 massacres, where five or more people died in atrocious circumstances, went unsolved and unpunished. The Patriotic Union (*La Unión Patriótica*), a political party that grew out of the 1984 peace negotiations with the guerrillas, was practically annihilated by the number of assassinations it sustained. Twelve hundred of its leaders were killed in 40 months.

In January 1989, the paramilitaries assassinated a group of 12 employees of the Justice Department who were completing an investigation in the province of Magdalena Medio. This incident drew the government's attention to the area for the first time. It was followed by other assassinations of journalists and politicians. Later in 1989, Luis Carlos Galán, a presidential candidate, was assassinated. As a result of this act President Virgilio Barco Vargas declared war on the drug traffickers.

The president was only partly right in blaming the drug traffickers. The allocation of blame was in fact far more complex. The state through its neglect, the landowners, the local politicians, the military, and the police all had a hand in the development of the paramilitaries.

The war which followed against the drug traffickers brought the violence, which had previously been confined to the rural areas, to the cities. Bombs were placed in supermarkets and in the streets, and one bomb resulted in the mid-air destruction of an Avianca Boeing

727, killing 107 people. Public opinion turned against the war. This public did not support President Barco's decision to reinvoke the power of extradition of Colombians for trial in American courts. Politicians, landowners, the army, and the police were also divided over the prosecution of the war. Thus, the government's decision highlighted not only the absence of the state's control but also its divisions and weakness in relation to the drug industry.

Following the death of Gilberto Rodríguez Gacha, principal chief of the drug traffickers in the centre of the country, the intensity of the war in the cities was reduced significantly. But the terror which the paramilitary groups had brought to the rural areas remained and the political assassinations continued. Four presidential candidates were assassinated.

The situation changed when President César Gaviria Trujillo took office. The war against the drug traffickers ended. Gaviria preferred a political, rather than a violent, solution to drug trafficking and began to establish channels through which the cartel leaders could negotiate with the government. The Gaviria government officially condemned the paramilitary groups.

The development of terrorism as a means of control, the state's incapability to guarantee basic human rights, and the lack of mechanisms to guarantee fair and equal participation of the people in governing the country, revealed the urgent need for a political change. The solution was the deepening of democracy, expressed in three ways. Firstly, it was expressed in the creation of a new constitution. The constitution was written by 70 elected *constituyentes* in 1991. An interesting aspect of the constituent assembly was its highly representative nature. Secondly, the municipal reforms led to a significant decentralization of power. Lastly, the negotiations between the government and guerrilla groups led to the reincorporation of four of these groups into civilian society. A central issue of the negotiations was increased involvement by these groups in political decisions. This attitude of negotiation on the part of the government brought a pause in the drug war in 1991 and the surrender of many of the cartel members to Colombian justice. Even though international opinion may have judged Colombia's recent position to be weak, it had support from the Colombian people, who no longer had to live in conditions of extreme terror. However, in July 1992, Pablo Escobar, one of the leading members of the Medellín drug cartel, and his companions escaped from prison. The government declared "integral war" against narco-terrorists and guerrilla groups. Terrorism again spread through the country, especially in urban areas. Negotiation initiatives subsequently resumed with the drug cartels, after the death of Escobar in a confrontation with police in December 1993.

The civil society vacuum

The chasm which exists in Colombia between the people and institutions evidenced the non-existence of the kind of implicit social agreement which usually unites a community, region, or nation and guides the actions of its citizens, whatever their differences. Until 1992, Medellín was a significant case to illustrate the situation.

Medellín

Medellín was the Colombian city most seriously affected by drug-related violence. There are two reasons. The first relates to rural–urban migration. Originally, the population of Antioquia, the department in which Medellín is situated, was predominantly *montañera*.[2] Between 1950 and 1980, much of Antioquia's population left small towns and headed for the Aburra valley and the "big smoke" of Medellín. The city trebled in size and population. For many of those who migrated, this was their first contact with technology and the pressures of modern life. This meant relearning how to behave in new social situations and in the workforce. The speed with which they were propelled from their rural existence into the frenetic world of the 1970s, and their inability to reconcile the two, produced an internal conflict in these groups. The young, in particular, rebelled against the religious and traditional teachings of their families, which were proving inadequate for the pressures and realities of this new world.

The second reason relates to social inequality. The number of migrants entering the city grew at a rate far superior to that at which the large industries could create employment. The distribution of income and ownership of property was extremely inequitable. The upper class and the wealthy middle class achieved a standard of living that many would envy, even in the developed world. A growing middle-middle class and massive popular sectors faced greater and greater downward pressure on their standards of living. A large mass of the city's population was unable to find employment. This led to an increasing sense of isolation among the youth.

Into this background of discontent, cocaine appeared like the cure for all ills. To some, cocaine provided a means of economic mobility and all the trappings of the wealthy – motorcycles, stereos, televisions, videos, and clothes – as well as a feeling of belonging (no matter how precariously) to a group with power and the sense of security that implied. To others, the drug provided a means of escape from the pressures and social tensions with which they lived in the poorer neighbourhoods of Medellín. Gangs (*bandas*) developed. These groups of youths sold and consumed cocaine, usually in its most pernicious form, *barzuco* or crack. Most youths joined these gangs with the hope of earning large amounts of money fast. Frequently, their aim was to earn enough money to provide their mothers with luxury household items, such as colour televisions, fridges, and stoves.

Most used the sale of drugs to buy power and security. They purchased expensive and sophisticated weapons and became experts in their use. For these youths, killing became easy. They worked as young assassins (*sicarios*) for the drug traffickers. For these youths, death was an integral part of their existence. They were forced to defend themselves against the police, who were also in certain cases hired killers for the drug traffickers. To young people who had to face death daily from the age of 15 and were unlikely to reach their eighteenth birthday alive, existence could be no more than "the moment." Life could end at any time with a bullet, as it had for so many of their companions.

The authorities were largely blind to the extent of the problems in the poor areas of Medellín. Individual journalists and the news media in general chose to remain silent in the face of growing problems. The number of assassins increased, and the violence was no longer contained to poor areas but spilled over into the whole city.

It was from this chaotic environment that Pablo Escobar rose to be head of the Medellín drug cartel. Escobar was admired and loved by those that lived in the *barrios* of Medellín. He was admired by the young, who recognized the skill and strength required not only to survive but to become a leader in the drug business. He was loved by inhabitants of the poor neighbourhoods because he did not forget them. He returned to provide solutions to many of their problems by building houses and sports and recreational centres, by financing small businesses, and by providing health services.

The continued presence of death and the power and attraction of money have greatly influenced the social development of youths in the poorest areas of Medellín. The war between the government and the drug traffickers – or more precisely between the police and the drug traffickers – was largely fought in the *barrios* of Medellín. It centred on these neighbourhoods because poor youths had been the ones hired to fight for the drug cartels. The violence escalated in 1983 when Rodrigo Lara Bonilla, the Minister of Justice, was assassinated, and it continued to worsen until February 1991. At its peak, as many as 100 policemen were killed in one month. After Escobar's escape from prison in 1992, the violence of the narco-terrorist centred upon Bogotá.

From the depths reached during the period 1980–92, a change in attitude developed in Medellín. It did not always develop in a consistent manner but it continued to advance. 1993 marked the beginning of a new scenario. It is most noticeable among the gang members who worked as *sicarios* but have laid down their arms to search for productive employment. Plans are being made in Medellín to establish socio-economic programmes to rescue the communities in danger. The government has created a new council in Medellín to study ways in which the violence prevalent in the city may be overcome. Medellín business associations have begun initiatives to support the council's efforts.

There has also been a revival of some of the old values and entrepreneurial spirit considered traditional to Antioquia. Small businesses are beginning to appear and the people are organizing themselves into human rights groups. Nevertheless, the situation of youths remains serious. Many of them no longer believe drug trafficking to be a viable way out. Armed groups within the *barrios* have begun to crack down. However, they do not believe in the government either and have become disillusioned with the guerrillas. It will take time for these youths to reincorporate themselves into civil society, and alternatives to life on the streets must be found. The solution to the youngsters' problems will require a "global solution" to the problems which have plagued Colombian society.

Survey of Medellín youth

Youths in Medellín who are not involved with the gangs but live in the *barrios* where they originated have an acute awareness of the violence that surrounds them. They feel that both the cause and the solution to the problems lie within them. Their attitudes towards the situation in which they live, and their methods of overcoming the difficulties it implies for their community and families, are illustrated by the following results of a survey conducted in the schools in the north-east of the city during the second semester of 1991. The youths surveyed have not participated directly in violence. Usually gang members abandon their education after primary school. Nevertheless, 40 per cent of those surveyed stated that violence had touched some of their families. Sixty-one per cent replied that a mass assassination, where five or more people had been killed on the same occasion, had occurred in their neighbourhoods.

The survey was completed by the Corporación Región de Medellín.[3] A total of 115 students was questioned. Of that group, 47 of the students were male and 68 were female. The majority of the students (89 per cent) were aged between 11 and 18 years old. All of those surveyed were currently studying and a small group had finished secondary school.

1 The family

When questioned about the occupation of their fathers, 33 per cent of those surveyed chose not to answer, 28 per cent replied that they worked as labourers, and 20 per cent replied that they were employed in "other occupations." In contrast, only 6 per cent of those surveyed were unable to reply when questioned about the occupation of their mothers. Sixty-six per cent of the students replied that their mothers were employed in the home and 16 per cent replied that they were employed in "other occupations." It seems obvious from these results that it is the mother who occupies the central position in the majority of the students' households. When asked about their parents in general, 94 per cent of those surveyed replied that their mothers were good parents and 59 per cent held a high opinion of their fathers. However, a significant number of the students preferred not to discuss their fathers. When asked who was most important in their families, only 2.6 per cent of those surveyed answered that it was their fathers.

As is the tradition in Antioquia, the majority of the students came from large families. Eighty-one per cent of those surveyed had three or more siblings. They also belonged to families strongly rooted to the culture of the *barrios*. Seventy-five per cent of the students came from families who had lived there more than six years and 54 per cent more than 11 years.

This part of the survey suggests that in a city such as Medellín, where the institutions have lost legitimacy, the sense of community and belonging is also lost. The young, more than any other group in society, feel threatened and unprotected and retreat to their familiar stamping grounds, the *barrios*. It is there that they capture some feeling of belonging and where they recognize some of the characteristics of a community. But ultimately it is their families, and more specifically their mothers, that offer the youth of these *barrios* the greatest degree of security and with whom they identify most.

2 The violence

The students are highly aware of the threats to human life inherent in the environment in which they live. In their opinion the problems that Colombia faces today can be ranked by their degree of seriousness, as follows:

1. Violence   44%
2. Unemployment   21%
3. Drug trafficking   16%
4. Other (including the country's external
   debt, lack of education, and the
   government)   14%
5. drug addiction   4%[4]

In the context of this survey, violence represents the destruction of life. In 1990, more than 24,000 homicides occurred in Colombia. In 1992, about 29,000 homicides occurred. Special attention should be drawn to the fact that on a national level the students felt that drug trafficking and addiction presented less of a problem than either the violence or the rate of unemployment.

In terms of Medellín the students placed the problems in the following order:

1. Violence   50%
2. Unemployment   21%
3. Drug trafficking   11.5%
4. Other (including pollution of the
   environment, the police, abandoned
   children (*gamines*), and the city's image)   18%
5. Drug addiction   6%

It is interesting to note that the students consider that drug trafficking presents less of a problem to Medellín than to the nation. If we group the replies by gender, we find that 22 per cent of the male students considered drug trafficking to be the most serious problem

101

facing Colombia, but only 10 per cent thought it the most serious for Medellín.

Finally, when asked to rank the problems facing their neighbourhood, the students ranked them as follows:

1. Violence   37.5%
2. Drug addiction   23%
3. Other (including lack of recreational
   space, lack of health services, and
   pollution)   18%
4. Unemployment   13%
5. Lack of public services   7%

The most notable feature of the replies received in this section of the survey is that drug addiction is thought to be the greatest threat facing the community by 23 per cent of those students surveyed. Drug addiction is thought to be second only to the violence in seriousness. In contrast, the students ranked drug addiction as only fifth in importance in terms of the city and in terms of the country as a whole. It was thought to be the most important for the country by only 4 per cent and for Medellín by only 6 per cent. It is also interesting to note that the students did not think their neighbourhood was as affected by the violence as the city as a whole or the nation. Perhaps this stems from a desire on the part of the students not to acknowledge how violent their neighbourhood actually is, and to negate the image of their culture portrayed in the mass media as a "culture of violence." It is also surprising how little importance was given by the students to the level of unemployment in their neighbourhood.

The results suggest the following. The residents of violent areas assume that the violence must be greater in neighbouring areas. It would seem that, in the case of Medellín, the violence is associated with the level of unemployment. Finally, drug trafficking is not considered to be a serious problem in the *barrios* because the business belongs to the drug cartels and not to the residents.

3 The *barrio*

The students surveyed live in the most violent area of Medellín. When asked about where they lived, it was obvious from their replies that they would prefer to live in some other part of the city. For the students, the most positive aspects of their neighbourhood are the people and the sports grounds. Almost all of the students, 91 per cent of those surveyed, considered themselves to be religious or to believe in God. However, only seven per cent attended Mass at the

102

parish church. When asked whom they considered to be the most important person(s) in their neighbourhood the students gave the following replies:

1. The parish priest   25%
2. No one in particular   25%
3. Other (including the doctor, neighbour-
   hood watch groups, and community
   action groups)   22%
4. My family   13%

When asked why they thought young people joined the gangs, the students gave the following reasons:

1. Family problems   28%
2. Financial reasons   25%
3. Because of friendships   16.5%
4. They are unemployed   16%
5. Did not know   7%
6. To support a drug habit   4%

A whole series of hypotheses follows from these results. Firstly, young people join gangs as a means of escaping from or solving family problems. More often than not, gang members come from large families in great financial need headed by a young, overburdened, single mother. Secondly, a major reason for joining the gangs is an economic one. This is evident from the high rate of unemployment among the young in these neighbourhoods. This would suggest that a major influence on the development of the "culture of violence" displayed by these gangs is their economic situation. Thirdly, often a youngster joins a gang through a friend. This demonstrates the importance given to friendship, peer group acceptance, solidarity, and the need to belong. Fourthly, and perhaps paradoxically, drug consumption rated low as a suggested reason for entering a gang, even though these gangs are highly involved in the trafficking and use of cocaine.

It is also interesting to note that American pop music plays an important role in gang culture. When asked about the music the gangs listen to, the students answered the following:

1. American ballads   47%
2. Heavy metal music   25%
3. Salsa   15%
4. Other   3%

Ten per cent of the students replied that they did not know. This fascination with American music might suggest that poor youngsters in Latin American cities feel some affinity with other youngsters in

103

American cities who experience similar family and economic problems, and who share the same need to belong to a group, through music.

When asked in what aspects the gangs differed from one another, 40 per cent of the students pointed to their differing levels of violence and aggression, 32 per cent pointed to their differing levels of solidarity with the residents of the neighbourhood, and 10 per cent to their differing degrees of power and other aspects, such as the type of music they listen to and the territory they control.

4 The drug traffickers

When asked their opinions of drug traffickers, the students replied as follows:
1. They are bad.   56%
2. They are neither good nor bad.   16%
3. They are good.   13%
4. No reply   15%

These results show how conscious the students are of the violence caused by drug trafficking.

When asked about the war the government is waging against the drug traffickers, the majority of the students took a negative position. Their replies were as follows:
1. It is bad.   61%
2. It is good.   12%
3. No opinion either way   14%
4. No reply   12%

When asked their opinion of Pablo Escobar, the results were somewhat surprising. They were as follows:
1. He is good.   57%
2. He is bad.   17%
3. He is neither good nor bad.   14%
4. No reply   12%

These last results suggest that the students did not think of Pablo Escobar as a drug trafficker, since drug traffickers are "bad" and he was "good." At least, among the respondents, he fitted into a different class of trafficker, owing to his good deeds among the poor of Medellín. Sixty-six per cent of the male students considered Escobar to be a good man.

The moral standing of Pablo Escobar has been much debated in Colombia, especially after a Catholic priest, Father García Herreros, proclaimed him to be a good man on television. Father García Herreros's comments should be considered in the context in which they were made. His mission was to redeem a sinner. There seems little doubt that he was referring to the benevolence of God and sending a signal to Pablo Escobar of the Church's tradition of forgiveness. However, Pablo Escobar's criminal activities are common knowledge and he is suspected of being involved, directly or indirectly, in numerous assassinations and massacres. Nevertheless, the day that the constituent assembly voted to prohibit the extradition of Colombians for trial in foreign courts, there was a noticeable reduction in the social tension caused by the violence which had surrounded this issue in the past and a commensurate increase in the degree of security felt among the people.

5 Colombia

Finally, it was thought to be not only interesting but important to find out how the youths of these *barrios* see Colombia's situation. As their replies demonstrated earlier, in their opinion the most serious problems are violence, the rate of unemployment, and drug trafficking, in that order. When asked their opinion of the government, it became apparent that the students did not hold the government in much higher esteem than they held the drug traffickers. Their replies were as follows:

1. Bad   59%
2. Good   13%
3. Neither good nor bad   12%
4. No reply   16%

In contrast, when asked their opinion of the guerrillas, a significant number of the students supported them.

The guerrillas are:

1. Bad   41%
2. Good   27%
3. Neither good nor bad   19%
4. No reply   13%

These results would suggest that in the eyes of these youngsters the drug traffickers and the government are "bad" because it is their activities which lie at the root of the violence which so affects their daily lives. The students' low opinion of the government seems to be based on its inability to guarantee social equity, justice, or security to the people. Even worse, in the experience of the students, the government's own agencies, for example the police, have been party to the violence. When asked about the police, the students held the following views:

The police are:
1. Bad   47%
2. Good   16%
3. Neither good nor bad   12%
4. No reply   25%

When asked about the army, the students held the following opinions:

The army is:
1. Good   57%
2. Neither good nor bad   13%
3. Bad   11%
4. No reply   19%

It is worthwhile comparing the students' opinion of the army with their opinion of the police. The marked difference no doubt stems from the fact that the students' community has witnessed and been a victim of police corruption, while the behaviour of the military has been significantly better. What is surprising is that the overall opinion of the military among the students is higher than the opinion they hold of the guerrillas.

In general the students seemed disillusioned by the politicians and the political parties.

The politicians are:
1. Bad   64%
2. Neither good nor bad   8.5%
3. Good   8.5%
4. No reply   19%

Seventy per cent of the students held no political affiliations. The parties with the greatest support among the students were the Liberal party, with 10 per cent support, and the M-19 party, with 9 per cent. (Note that this survey was carried out in 1991. By 1994, M-19 had virtually disappeared.)

When questioned who they considered to be the most important person(s) in Colombia, the students replied as follows:
1. My family   23%
2. Pablo Escobar   21%
3. President Gaviria   20%
4. Higuita (soccer player)   13%
5. Antonio Navarro Wolf (M-19) 6%
6. No one   10%
7. Others   7%

These results highlight the central conclusion drawn from this survey. In a society where authority has lost legitimacy the family be-

comes all-important. Secondly, it is interesting to note that these results are consistent with the general impression that students had of
Escobar as a good and generous man, quite separately from his repu-
tation as a ruthless drug dealer. Even though the students consider
President Gaviria to be important, he was considered less important
than Escobar. Possibly the students consider him to be a good politician even though they do not hold a similar opinion of his government. Generally speaking, the students do not consider politicians to
be very important. The only other politician that figures in this list is
Navarro Wolf, the leader of the M-19 party, and he rates as significantly less important than the soccer player, Higuita.

Finally, when asked what is the best method to rid Colombia of its
most serious problem, the violence, the students gave the following
replies:

1. Dialogue   38%
2. Full employment   9%
3. A sense of unity among the people   9%
4. A good government   6%
5. Do not know   2%
6. No reply   17%
7. Other   19%

A large number of students felt that dialogue was the best method
to achieve peace in Colombia. It is also interesting to note that none
of the students thought that the war between the government and the
drug traffickers – or that between the government and the guerrillas –
would achieve peace. However, bracketed under "other" were replies such as the creation of more self-defence groups; a crackdown
on drug suppliers and drug traffickers; fairer distribution of wealth;
and the existence of more good people in Colombia.

The principal conclusion that can be drawn from the results of the
survey is that the students of Medellín belong to a youthful culture in
an extremely violent environment. Within this culture the students
are able to distinguish clearly between good and bad. They consider
anything that leads to violence, either directly or indirectly, to be bad,
and anything that leads to peace to be good. Furthermore, all institutions and people are judged in these terms, that is, on their contribution towards bringing an end to the violence in Colombia.

A number of other conclusions can also be drawn from these results. Firstly, the students do think of their futures. Despite the difficulties that surround them and their familiarity with death, these
students have not lost hope for the future. They would like to continue studying. Ninety-five per cent of the students enjoyed studying,

while the other 5 per cent were only indifferent towards school. None of the students disliked studying. Seventy-seven per cent of the male students had a clear idea of what they wanted to do when they left school. They wanted to be professionals – for example doctors, lawyers, accountants, or mechanics – or sportsmen, or to join the army. Eighty-six per cent of the female students knew what they wanted to do when they left school. They wanted to be nurses or secretaries, or to join other professions such as architecture, medicine, dentistry, and law. This sense of hope among the students and their desire to achieve something with their lives contrasts with the sense of hopelessness felt by the youths in the gangs.

Secondly, the students are religious. Even though they are not practising Catholics, they do believe in God. It would seem that for them moral behaviour and religious practices are not necessarily connected.

Thirdly, they have a strong sense of moral authority. The students have a deep respect for their mothers. The parish priest is also an important and highly respected individual within the community.

Fourthly, the students do not have high opinions of public institutions, the government, politicians in general, or the police. For the students, the greatest problem facing Colombia is the violence. Many of them think these groups, in particular the police, are responsible for the violence which surrounds them.

Fifthly, a large percentage of the students, 41 per cent, support the guerrillas. That is, they see the guerrilla movement as a positive force in the fight for social change. However, the percentage of students who do not support, or are indifferent to, the guerrillas' actions is equally large, 46 per cent. The remaining 13 per cent preferred not to express an opinion. In some ways it is easy to understand the students' support for the guerrillas if it is remembered that they do not trust the authorities or the government and that they consider the guerrillas as fighters against the corruption and injustice which has led to this mistrust. However, the students do question the guerrillas' methods and their inconsistency with the stated objective of achieving peace in Colombia. The students' support for the army, which aims to suppress guerrilla activity, is significant.

Sixthly, the students recognize that drug trafficking poses a serious threat to peace in Colombia. They realize that this industry has been responsible for a great part of Colombia's violence. The students also recognize the negative effect that the increase in drug addiction among young people has had on their community and the violence it has caused.

They consider unemployment, economic hardship, and the need for solidarity and comradeship as the major reasons for joining a gang.

The economic vacuum

Towards the end of the 1960s the Colombian economy was unable to generate enough jobs to employ fully all those seeking work. The government's efforts to promote the development of import substitution industries consisted of protective subsidies to a few select industries, and produced a highly oligopolistic industrial structure. Attempts at agricultural reform failed to disperse the ownership of rural lands, which remained concentrated in the hands of the few. The precarious development of the urban informal economy and of the rural economy meant that many Colombians were unable to earn a stable or sufficient income. The continual extension of the borders of agricultural production into increasingly remote areas led to the displacement of thousands of people. During the 1970s, close to three million Colombians headed for Venezuela, Ecuador, and the United States in search of better employment opportunities.

These conditions contrasted with the notable increase in human capital. The level of education among Colombia's labour force, even among those unable to find employment, continued to increase. Due to the expansion of the mass media, particularly radio, an ever-increasing proportion of the country had ready access to current information and developments. The expectations of social change continued to increase at a rate which surpassed the ability of Colombia's authorities to respond with the policies necessary to ensure their fulfilment. Political scientists talked of an institutional "fear of the people," which prevented acceptance by the responsible authorities of the participation of the large sectors of Colombian society that wanted to get on the merry-go-round of economic development.

Within this context, three industries developed which functioned outside the established norms of Colombian business. They were emerald mining and the production of marijuana and cocaine. These industries share certain characteristics. Each provides a significant source of employment, absorbing a large portion of the economy's surplus labour. All of them are highly profitable. In all three, business is conducted within an environment of violence.

While these three industries have much in common, there is one significant factor which sets apart the cultivation of coca leaves – market share. While Colombia can claim to be the number one excavator of emeralds in the world and the principal cultivator of cannabis in

Latin America, it ranks only a poor third (behind Peru and Bolivia) in the cultivation of coca. Colombia's virtual monopoly of the cocaine market does not lie in its production of the raw material but rather in its transformation and distribution of the final product. There, however, Colombia's number one status in the international cocaine trafficking community seems beyond dispute. At present, Colombia distributes up to 80 per cent of the cocaine hydrochloride traded in the American and European markets. Within a short period Colombian cocaine traffickers succeeded in generating ten times the foreign earnings produced from the sale of emeralds and five times those produced from the sale of marijuana in world markets.

Colombia's position in the international market for cocaine has been secured through a number of "institutional comparative advantages." The country's economic institutions were such that they did not allow ordinary people to compete equally in the dominant sectors of the economy but permitted the development of whole tiers of industries which, while illegal in nature, provided huge foreign earnings. The industry was allowed to prosper by a banking system which viewed it as a source of funds to invest in legitimate industry and the property market, as well as an important source of foreign exchange to apply to the external debt. For these reasons and others, the cocaine industry was allowed to develop, even though it has been recognized as illegal from its very beginning and has used methods of corruption and intimidation to breach barriers to its growth ever since.

Cocaine trafficking, as a business, is the domain of those who live on the fringes of Colombian society and who for reasons of poverty or social class had or have no other means of economic mobility.

To their admirers, they are Horatio Alger heroes, poor boys who worked their way out of the slums ...

One-time delinquent [the head of the Cali cartel] ... emerged as Don Chepe, a billionaire whose marble citadel looms high above the sugarcane fields of Cali ...

"El Gordo" (the Fat Man), as Santacruz is known, is a legend in New York Latin underworld.[5]

The cultivation of coca leaves in Colombia has always been limited. As a proportion of the total Andean production of coca by the three principal producers, Colombia's share has never accounted for more than a tenth. (Note, however, that in 1993 Colombia's share of total Andean production increased significantly. The country also started producing heroin.) Instead, Colombian traffickers buy coca from the other two countries, already partially refined in the form of cocaine paste, and refine it further to produce cocaine base and cocaine hydrochloride for distribution internationally. It is at this end of the business that the institutional environment in which the Colombians work provides its greatest advantage and helps ensure Colombia's worldwide cocaine monopoly.

The 1980s saw the cocaine trafficking industry in Colombia develop and mature. During this period the Colombian economy showed itself to be the most vigorous in Latin America, achieving an accumulated rate of growth in per capita income of 16.2 per cent. Colombia's experience during the 1980s contrasts most sharply with those of Argentina (−24.3 per cent), Peru (−30.2 per cent) and Nicaragua (−40.8 per cent). Even Chile's rate of growth of per capita income, which most closely rivalled that of Colombia, was lower by seven percentage points. There seems little doubt that the continual supply of narco-dollars (between one and four billion dollars annually) strengthened the Colombian economy. At one stage, the value of cocaine produced in the Andean region pivoted around 12 billion dollars annually.

To what extent the cocaine industry has affected the Colombian economy depends on a number of factors. However, it has been suggested that it accounts for between three and five per cent of Colombia's gross national product and, through the multiplier effect, about 12 per cent of aggregate demand in the economy.

The industry surrounding the trafficking of cocaine was allowed to prosper because of the institutional crisis in Colombia which afforded it certain comparative advantages. Its members developed a hierarchical structure which closely mirrors that found in other legitimate industries, those from which they have been excluded. The large sums generated by their business bought them, if not acceptance, at least a high level of tolerance. Colombia's tolerant attitude allowed the industry continually to improve not only the quality of its production but also its methods of transporting and locating the drug within its target markets. These methods become increasingly sophisticated and the margins of profit ever more able to absorb the costs associated with buying the clear passage of their product or the losses occasioned by seizures of the drug.

Cali's leaders have carefully compartmentalized their organization, so that individual losses do not threaten to bring down the whole enterprise. The Cali management style is cerebral, calculating and guileful ... The Cali families are conservative managers, much like other big corporate heads ... The logistics of importing, storing and delivering the product to wholesalers are handled by dozens of overseas branches, or cells, overseen by home office through daily, often hourly, phone calls ... The traffickers know investigators need four or five days to get a court-ordered wiretap, so they use a phone for two days and discard it ...[6]

Faced with the realities of cocaine trafficking, Colombia's economic policies often lacked consistency. On the one hand, for example, the central bank freely purchased foreign exchange without questioning its origin. Vast sums of money entered the economy through formal channels as receipts earned by Colombians from employment overseas. The great majority was laundered money. Well-established and frequented black markets selling smuggled goods developed in Colombia's major cities. All of these illegal activities, which vary only in degree, were common knowledge and were tolerated; the tolerance was paid for, in large part, by the expansion in aggregate demand which flowed on from these activities.

The idea that the flow-on effects of the cocaine industry, such as increases in employment, expansion in aggregate demand, and a better standard of living for all those employed within or on the fringes of the industry, were positive influenced the behaviour of many Colombians. But the economic bonanza generated by the large foreign receipts which entered Colombia from the sale of cocaine overshadows the significant social side-effects of a business which has had such a corrupting influence on Colombia's institutions.

Gilberto [Rodríguez, the patriarch of Colombia's Cali cartel] describes himself as a "captain of industry and banker" and has the portfolio to prove it. He also has reputable friends who are partners, associates or suppliers in his business ventures, which do much to promote development throughout the Cauca valley.[7]

The modernization of agricultural production left behind large tracts of rural Colombia where the traditional family-based mode of production still predominates. To relieve the economic hardship faced by the families in these areas, the young men often seek employment within the industry as "mules" (cocaine smugglers). Thought of as expendable, these young men are often caught and imprisoned or are killed in their efforts to transport cocaine to the United States and Europe. In the eyes of their families they become heroes. Those who die are revered as saints.

Despite its tolerant acceptance of the earnings from the sale of cocaine, Colombia tried to accommodate the desire of the United States to contain its supply. The relationship between the demand and supply of cocaine and its price offers a prime example of a near-perfect market. There is a very little delay between a change in supply and a change in price. Policies which successfully target the supply of cocaine stimulate an almost immediate increase in its price. Obviously, it is hoped that such a sudden rise in price will produce a commensurate fall in demand. However, because of its addictive nature, the demand for cocaine is virtually inelastic; so the policy does not achieve its desired purpose, but makes the business of selling cocaine appear more lucrative, and the production of cocaine increases. Eventually, the price will adjust downwards, but this adjustment will not threaten the profitability of the business. Part of these profits is reinvested in the industry to extend its net of corruption further. Large sums of money end up in the pockets of the police, customs officials, and the army. Another part pays for the intimidation of judges and the development of private armies. Yet another part will be invested in the development of better methods of transporting the drug without detection and of penetrating target markets with greater speed. The scale of these activities and the level of corruption they produce tend to have a contaminating effect on the whole of the economy.

Thus, the comparative advantages created by the inability of the authorities to respond to the reality of the problem were reinforced. The greater the government's efforts to contain the supply of cocaine, the greater the amount of money made available to the industry to overcome these efforts.

It became obvious that the source of the advantages offered to Colombian drug traffickers lay in the moral decomposition of the state and its institutions in the eyes of the people. These same people realized that it was not the growth of cocaine trafficking which undermined Colombia's institutional and social norms but the reverse. These norms were already in crisis prior to the surge in cocaine trafficking. It was, in fact, this crisis which provided the perfect environment for the industry to prosper. Colombia has chosen to confront the problem by ending the institutional comparative advantages. The government is attacking the problem on both the political and economic fronts. It has begun to construct institutions which correspond more closely to the needs and culture of the people. The new constitution provides a clear example of these efforts. On the economic front, the government has closed the foreign exchange window at the central bank. The economy is becoming progressively more open to public inspection and comment. The government has begun campaigns to promote a legal free market and plans to control the surpluses from drug trafficking and to halt the laundering of drug money in financial markets.

As the comparative advantages are reduced in Colombia, the industry is trying to relocate to other countries. However, the Colombian supply of cocaine remained stable in 1993.

The ethical vacuum

Drug trafficking arrived in Colombia at a time when the country faced a crisis in its values and ethics. This crisis has meant that minimum social norms, which had previously governed society's behaviour as a whole, no longer hold. With respect to ethics, Colombian society entered a period of flux – a moral and ethical vacuum. In great part, the success of the drug industry in taking root in Colombia and in imposing its own values upon society was due to this ethical vacuum. The value of any action came to be measured by the amount of money it generated. The greater the profits, the more highly valued was the action, regardless of the methods used to obtain them. More precisely, the end – making money – came to justify the means. The market became the ultimate arbiter, and where demand existed it was to be satisfied. Even if the government created laws that said otherwise and the police acted to enforce those law, laws were to be broken and the police bribed to satisfy the demands of the market. Drug profits provided the key to power, freedom, and the satisfication of multiple desires.

Drug trafficking, like the external debt, the pollution of rivers, and the felling of forests, provides further proof of the ethics which govern the market and its ability to destroy human life and the environment when external moderating factors are non-existent. Colombian society did not have the moral strength to resist the temptation exerted by a market which provided returns equal to one third of the value of Colombia's gross domestic product. The ethical vacuum in which Colombia existed provided fertile ground for the cocaine industry to develop and prosper.

Colombian society, by tradition, has always been a Catholic society. Even after Colombia declared itself to be an independent nation and no longer a Catholic colony of Spain, it retained its Catholic traditions. Until the early 1960s, more than 95 per cent of Colombia's population were baptized Catholics. In general, moral behaviour remained governed by the teachings of the bishops, which were spread in local churches and by the radio and newspapers. In the last thirty years, however, Colombian society has undergone a rapid process of secularization and separation of the Church from the state. Catholic morality remains very much part of family traditions among the Church's followers, in the schools, and in parochial Colombia. But it no longer guides the behaviour of Colombian society as a whole.

This increase in the autonomy of civil society is necessary for the future development of Colombia. However, it has not been accompanied by the type of change in civil ethics which would suggest the development of a pluralistic society that guarantees and respects the rights of its members.

Colombia's ethical vacuum produced confusion over what was and was not socially acceptable. The sources of moral guidance were no longer clear and there were no longer any checks on the arbitrariness of the bureaucracy and the political class. Business was no longer conducted in a serious and honest manner. The justice system was corrupted and impunity before the law was generalized. People no longer trusted each other's sincerity. The newspapers and television became media of disinformation. Finally, human life lost all value. During the last four years more than 50 people have been assassinated every 24 hours in Colombia. In 1992, an average of 75 persons a day were killed in different types of homicide.

The cocaine industry used to its best advantage the fertile ground Colombia provided for its business. By introducing its own values, the industry cleared the way for its own development without hindrance. Drug traffickers enforced the death penalty on those judges that could not be bribed and on those journalists who remained faithful to the truth. The scale of the industry's actions effectively silenced the moral conscience of Colombian society.

Paradoxically, it was the scale of the drug traffickers' activities which precipitated Colombia's emergence from the ethical vacuum into which it had fallen. The rise of drug trafficking in Colombia provoked a social crisis against which the people had no choice but to react or accept the dire consequences. Today, an awareness of community and a new social ethic has begun to take hold in the rural *campesino* regions and in the *barrios* of Colombia's large cities. This new ethic has been demonstrated in the rise of community movements and in the social pressure to rid the armed forces and the police of corruption. The results of the elections of the constituent assembly demonstrated a clear majority vote against corruption. At

115

the same time, however, Colombia lacks viable alternatives to the cash-rich cocaine industry, which has provided a source of livelihood to numerous *campesinos* and others in the low- to middle-income brackets.

It is important to stress that it was the magnitude of the crisis facing Colombia which prompted the re-evaluation of social values. That is, it was the industry's own extremes which produced such a strong social reaction against the values it had tried to instil and this reaction may signify a menace to the industry itself.

Conclusions

This essay has proposed the following hypothesis. The drug industry arrived in Colombia at a time when the country faced a cultural crisis. This crisis, which dates back at least thirty years but gained firm hold at the beginning of the 1970s, was generated by a social, ethical, and governmental vacuum. It provided the cocaine industry with a number of comparative advantages. The drug traffickers exploited the vacuum which existed, not only to further the development of their industry, but also to impose their own values on society in order to ensure the industry's continued prosperity. They tried to develop an authority parallel to that of the state and accumulated territorial power, created private armies, and provided essential services to their loyal supporters. They also acquired friends among the political class. They filled the economic vacuum by providing thousands of *campesinos* with a cash-rich crop, coca, and by offering employment as middlemen and "mules" to thousands of youths in the crowded *barrios* of the cities. The traffickers created a social network which included all those involved in the industry. It provided them with a sense of community and of comradeship. The network also incorporated the families of those employed in the industry and in the regions loyal to it. Their loyalty and support was repaid with increased employment and improved social conditions. Finally, the traffickers imposed their own norms of behaviour.

Nevertheless, drug trafficking did not provide the solution to the vacuum Colombian society was experiencing but rather magnified it to such an extent that people were forced to react against the intolerable situation which developed. Colombia had become one of the most violent countries in the world. However, Colombian society was not quick to react. As with any social change, it has taken time for the change in attitude to mature into widespread behaviour.

Paradoxically, in response to the violence drug trafficking inflicted upon Colombia and its people, a complex development is in progress which has as its primary aim the prevention of homicide through the elimination of those conditions conducive to its escalation. This social development is visible in the numerous Colombian organizations which promote life and peace, in the festivals and songs whose central theme is peaceful co-existence, in the academic seminars which discuss social ethics and justice, in the development of organizations for the protection of human rights, in the peaceful demonstrations against violence, and in the development of government-sponsored advisory councils on human rights, peace, and ethics.

However, it will not be easy to fulfil this potential. Colombians are no longer willing to accept the double standards of the United States and countries in Europe who too readily cast Colombia in the role of the evil supplier of cocaine but do nothing to contain demand. They no longer believe in the impartiality of American justice, which denies Colombians their liberty, sentencing them to long prison terms for selling drugs, while Americans are pardoned for consuming them.

Nevertheless, Colombians are aware of the weaknesses that their institutions have demonstrated in the past and their susceptibility to external and internal pressures. Drug trafficking, as an industry, has began to move its operations to other countries. However, it still remains strong in several regions, where the police are still willing to look the other way for a sufficiently large sum of money. Colombian justice may still falter in applying the law rigorously to the crimes committed by the drug traffickers. The efforts to construct a new social ethic are still in their early stages, and it will take some time before they come to fruition; but it does seem certain that the efforts will continue. Colombians were so seriously alarmed by the scale of the violence and the destruction of human life that they are now willing to do whatever it takes to obtain peace. However, peace will not come cheaply. The costs of peace include an effective and impartial legal system, social justice, and the protection of the dignity of the life of all Colombians.

Notes

1. CINEP, in its publication *Investigación sobre sociedad y conflicto* (1992–93), analysed this problem. In this publication, what we have called the governmental vacuum is referred to as the weakness of the Colombian state. The control of the state by political parties, namely

the Liberal and Conservative parties, who are more interested in their organizations than in the good of the people, is referred to as the "privatization" of the Colombian state.

2. The word *montañero* refers to the people who migrated to the mountains above Antioquia and cleared the forests to create farmland.

3. The Corporación Región de Medellín is a non-governmental organization which promotes education and democracy. It is developing educational programmes directed at the young and human rights organizations in the communities of Medellín. In association with CINEP, the Corporation has investigated community life in Medellín.

4. One per cent of those students surveyed preferred not to reply.

5. *Time*, 1 July 1991, no. 26, pp. 9–10.

6. Op. cit., pp. 11–12.

7. Op. cit., p. 13.

5

Ethnic violence: The case of Bolivia

Xavier Albó

Introduction

In this paper, through the analysis of the case of Bolivia, we shall deal
with one of the most widespread factors that induce violence in multi-
ethnic societies.

Ethnicity may refer to two factors, both of them equally relevant to
our topic: race and culture. Race has to do with traits that are biologically inherited. For instance, colour. Culture refers to behaviour – such
as language or religion – that is transmitted to the members of a given
social group through the process of socialization or enculturation. If
the emphasis is put on the first factor we are dealing with racism; if it is
put on the second, the problem is ethnocentrism. The typical practical
situation is a combination of both without a clear distinction between
them. In any case, ethnic violence can stem from either one.

In fact, it is quite common that cultural differences are reinterpreted as racial. As a result, differences resulting from behaviour
that could evolve are reinterpreted as inherited, and therefore un-
changeable, traits that will make a given group either superior or inferior in some fateful way. This is the beginning of deeper forms of
discrimination and hence of structural violence.[1]

The link between race and culture is often strengthened because
some invasion and/or conquest is at the root of most multi-ethnic societies. This is certainly the case with Bolivia and other Andean countries.

119

A neocolonial society

The strata of present-day Bolivian society reflect a long history with all its contradictions: (*a*) an original setting with the Tawantinsuyu, a major political accomplishment, in the Western Highlands and many disparate ethnic groups in the Eastern Lowlands; (*b*) a colonial, highly stratified, dual society of Spaniards and Indians since 1532; (*c*) a new racial "social Darwinism" since Independence in 1825; and (*d*) a nationalist *mestizo* model since the Chaco war (1932–5) and its aftermath, the Movimiento Nacional Revolucionario (MNR) revolution (1952) and the agrarian reform (1953). Previous phases do not fully disappear as new ones appear, but keep building up into a more complex situation which combines tradition with modernity, democracy with racism, ethnicity with class, and so on.

The MNR's interdiction of the word *indio*, or "Indian," did not prevent the daily use of the concept associated with this word or that of *campesino* or "peasant." Even now the expression "brute Indian" is very common. This is only one example of many expressions of ethnic prejudice.

Let us describe the details of this recurring situation of ethnic violence in contemporary Bolivia. We are referring to a country with about 7 million people, half of them living in towns and communities with less than 2,000 inhabitants. According to the last national census, taken long ago in 1976, 38 per cent knew the Quechua language, 28 per cent Aymara, and about 2 per cent one of over 20 native languages spoken in the Lowlands. Except in the Lowlands, in all major cities about one half of the population knew Quechua and/or Aymara. The others knew only Spanish, the official language. Spanish is also known, with various levels of competence, by most urban Indian-language speakers and, with lower levels of competence, by younger males in the countryside. In fact, all these figures on Indian languages might be somewhat higher because people tend to camouflage identities that could bring them problems.

Expressions of ethnic violence

The ethnic matrix

Major divisions continually mark and divide Bolivian society. The consequences of such divisions in Bolivia are as serious as those caused by the class struggle. One problem for the researcher is that these are subjective labels. There is no clear-cut objective criterion that may be used to assign any citizen unambiguously to a given ethnic group. Except for extreme cases, people do not "belong" to this or that ethnic group but rather are "imputed" to it by others; or, perhaps, while somebody feels self-identified with a higher level group, other people do not think the same about him or her. Except in very intimate or political situations nobody *is* Indian (or *cholo*, see below). People are *seen* as Indian (or *cholo*) by others.

This situation deserves a closer analysis. Subjective categories and feelings are simultaneously linked to unconscious ideologies, to value systems, and to affection. They are, therefore, powerful instruments towards the building of prejudice. Since in our case these are categories used systematically by society as a result of the history we have sketched above, this also is a powerful instrument to build social and ethnic prejudice, which is one kind of structural violence.

The main categories now in use are the following:

1 Gente decente

There is still a strong pride in being or claiming to be white. However, the term "white," or *criollo*, is now less commonly used as an everyday social/ethnic category than it was years ago. Its current popular equivalent is *gente decente* (decent people) or *refinado* (refined, well-bred). This concept obviously implies that the others are rude or ill-bred, by opposition.

It is possible to consider people with dark skin *gente decente*. After more than four centuries, interbreeding has been so widespread that a strictly racial or biological approach is no longer possible. Somebody can be socially "white" even if he or she is biologically of mixed blood. In this sense the concept does not imply a clear-cut division, at least between white and *mestizo*. But racial connotations are still there. For instance, many people claim to have a pure Spanish or European descent even if this claim conflicts with the colour of their faces. However, now the main connotation is cultural. Being *gente decente* (or white) means adopting the lifestyle of the dominant élite – or example in language, dress, and social links – or even that of North Americans and Europeans.

2 Mestizos and cholos

The group made up of *mestizos* and *cholos* is the least stable of all. Here, indeed, the hidden mechanisms of structural ethnic violence are at work. These are people with an ambiguous cultural status and obvious Indian traces in their appearance.

The word *mestizo* is now less commonly used as a social/ethnic cat-

121

egory, except in formal analysis and mostly by foreign observers. Some authors add that a *mestizo* is a mixed-blood who has already accepted the white lifestyle. Therefore, this is a less objectionable term than *cholo*. Since the 1952 MNR revolution, it has come to be accepted that Bolivian society should be shaped as a *mestizo* society. This thesis implies that Indians and half-Indians are to achieve the goal of becoming culturally white, in the way established by the ruling society.

But what about those who, willing or not, cannot achieve this goal? This question brings us to the derogatory term *cholo*, which deserves closer analysis. Except in certain affectionate contexts, nobody likes to be called *cholo*; it is usually a name given to others, especially by those who feel themselves superior. Its diminutive form, *cholito*, is even more pejorative. Only the feminine forms, *chola* and, especially, *cholita*, are acceptable in certain contexts. Here we will analyse the term in its taboo, but very common, connotations.

Cholo denotes a mixed-blood or full-blood Indian (this biological precision is less relevant now) who has basically left his or her original way of life but kept many elements of it. This very definition shows the ambiguous identity of those belonging to this social/ethnic group: their identity vacillates constantly between two worlds. Somehow they have rejected their Indian world, because it was for them a stigma which blocked their social mobility. However, they cannot fully abandon their origins. These are still part of their life for some reason or other, whether that reason is psychological, economic, or social, or whether – most probably – it combines something of all of these.

The dominant society tends to consider the *cholo* as the scapegoat, and all the sins are attributed to *cholos*. One of the most powerful Bolivian writers, the often-quoted Alcides Arguedas, published a diagnosis of the country in a book called *Pueblo enfermo* ("Sick Country"). Written originally in 1909, it has been continuously reprinted. Whether one subscribes to his views or not, any social scientist sees Arguedas as a necessary reference. Arguedas' chapter on the *cholo* has the following synopsis:

The race heritage. The *"cholo"*. His morality. Twirling and variable. Idolatry to the chiefs. This is the class that dominates the country. His vices: alcoholism. Duplicitous character. He is an inferior type, like the *"roto,"* the *"gaucho,"* and other hybrids. Bolivian history is written and performed by *cholos*. II. The white race. Nobility has become mixed up. Moral qualities of the superior type. (Arguedas, 1979:73)

Another writer of those years has written:

The moral contributions that up to now have extolled the life of Bolivian Indians: austerity, work constancy, frugality ... have not been inherited by the *cholo*. He has neither the courtesy of the Spaniard nor the practical spirit of the Indian. We can confidently state that all the superior moral motives that made these two races great cannot be reflected in the *mestizo*. His psychology is that of a distrustful, suspicious, lazy, lying, irresolute, deceitful, insolent man. Cowardly, lecherous, and idle. Smart to plot some indecorous farce. Loves comfort and personal neatness, though such comfort rests on the most disgusting bad taste. (Pérez Velasco, 1929:17)

Both authors claim that the *cholo* summarizes all social vices. True or not, even now this stereotype is certainly the hidden bias of many and reflects the racism and ethnic prejudice of Bolivian society. For instance, if people of apparent non-Indian origin misbehave, it is still usual to say that "the Indian in him shows up."[2] That these intermediate groups have to live amidst many ambiguities cannot be denied. But, obviously, these ambiguities are not the result of an inherent deficiency, as these writers imply, but rather a direct outcome of the asymmetric ethnic structure of Bolivian society. The social and psychological insecurities attached to these ambiguities are indicators of this kind of structural violence.

One example of this ambiguity is the change of name and the denial of place of origin by people, in a futile attempt to become incorporated into the dominant society without being victims of the discrimination attached to their name and origin. The ambiguity appears when these people begin to talk more frankly (perhaps after a few drinks), or in their sometimes unpredictable behaviour, which combines dependence and aggression toward their superiors. Yet these very people, while claiming, for instance, that they were born in La Paz, remain very eager to participate in annual celebrations in their places of origin, because these are the only places where their urban achievements will receive some public recognition.

Some *cholos* really succeed in their ascent within Bolivian society. In past and recent years, Bolivia has had several rulers and presidential candidates labelled by others as *cholos*. In the light of this phenomenon, it is very possible that one of the reasons for the stubborn attitude of the higher groups against the *cholo* is related to the fact that this very mobile group, full of aspirations, is precisely the one that most closely threatens the absolute domination of entrenched élites.

3 *Indios or campesinos*

At the bottom of the scale we find those who have been called "Indians" since the early colony. Though this name was officially changed into *campesino* in the 1950s, it is still much used colloquially, along with other related expressions such as *hijo/hija* (son/daughter). At this colloquial level, even racial myths, such as the claim that Indians smell like llamas, will sometimes be added. The new concept of *campesino* (peasant), as we saw, retains many of the connotations of the former term "Indian." Thus, a non-Indian farmer living in the midst of Indian communities will probably avoid being called *campesino*, in spite of his socio-economic status of peasant: he will prefer the less loaded term *agricultor* (farmer).[3]

In the last two decades the word "Indian" has come back into use in certain political contexts with a renewed positive sense. But the traditional belittling meaning is very much alive in most daily usages. In spite of lyrical descriptions about the great "bronze race" (Arguedas), in real life Indians have not been treated so well by others, whether they be white, *mestizo* or *cholo*. Even famous defenders of Indians in writing behaved differently in their daily practice. The poet and writer Franz Tamayo is a good example. Tamayo himself had Indian blood from his mother's side and wrote glowingly in favour of the Indians and their future role in the country. However, even now he is remembered by his former workers as a cruel and contemptuous landowner.[4] Something similar can be said about the Peruvian Quechua poet Andrés Alencastre, whose lyrical refinement did not impede him from being very harsh with "his" Indians in the *hacienda*, to the point where he was finally killed by them.

The fact that Indians are considered to be at the lowest social level, both from the ethnic and the class point of view, makes them the most vulnerable within society from any perspective. The basic attitude of others towards them is one of contempt and, hence, of exploitation. It is not necessary to repeat here the many well-known examples of direct and personal violence against Indians. Hundreds of books are filled with relevant cases, mostly from periods previous to the agrarian reforms.[5] We will include only contemporary examples below.

4 *Collas and cambas*

The three categories described above are the main ones for our purpose. Let us add, however, a few words about two other terms with ethnic as well as regional implications in present-day Bolivia: *colla* and *camba*.

Broadly speaking *colla* means somebody, either white or Indian, from the Andean Highlands. A *camba* is somebody, white or Indian, from the Lowlands. But, given the tensions existing between these two main geographical divisions of Bolivia, frequently each term also has ethnic connotations when used by the other group. This occurs more often when white Lowland people refer to Highland peasant migrants of obvious Indian background. Then the expression *colla de mierda* ("shitty *colla*") is the most commonly used. On some occasions, as in San Julián in 1984, this hatred of *cambas* for migrant *collas* has led even to bloodshed (APDHB, 1984). On the other hand, *camba* has another ethnic meaning when used by the same Lowland whites referring to Lowland Indians. In that context, *camba* is comparable to "Indian," with its pejorative implications.

The view from the other side

To complete this general view of present-day ethnic categories in Bolivia, we shall note that the use of ethnically loaded terms is not restricted to people in the upper levels referring to those below them. Ethnically loaded concepts are used also in the opposite direction, usually with other words and nuances.

Almost all indigenous groups tend to call themselves by some name which can be translated as "person" or something similar,[6] whereas they label others with words that sometimes imply that they are less than persons. This labelling refers both to white people and to other ethnic groups. The terms used to refer to white people sometimes have had ambiguous implications of reverence and hate. Andean peoples called the Spaniards *wiraqucha*, which was then the name of one of their most popular divinities. But the term now implies only social distance from bottom to top and is semantically linked to the concept of *q'ara* (literally, "naked," "peeled off"; that is, lacking something that is needed). This last word has been interpreted by a Peruvian Aymara as follows:

We call them *q'ara* (peeled off) because they do not have any thing that is the fruit of their own work. They make a living out of the Aymaras' and others' efforts. We Aymaras believe, see, and say that the *misti q'ara* are people "without blood in their faces"; this is to say that they are the ones who treat their fellow Aymaras in an unhuman way. (Ochoa, 1988:438)

The word *misti* (from *mestizo*), reminds us that for these Quechua and Aymara Indians there is no relevant difference between white, *mestizo*, or even *cholo*. All of them belong to the *q'ara* group. Moreover, it is even possible for an Indian to become a *q'ara* if he leaves the community and behaves like the others.

The Guaraní term *karai* and the Moxo *karaiana*, which are used to refer to white people, had a sacred origin similar to that of *wiraqucha*, but now have also the same pejorative meaning as *q'ara*.

However, in spite of such Indian ethnocentrism concerning whites, the semantic history of words such as *wiraqucha* or *karai* shows that the first appraisal was not one of rejection. When this came, it was in reaction to European ethnocentrism and discrimination. Contemporary Indian groups, which are often accused of being racist by others, counter-argue that the racist ones are the others and add that the real problem is not racism but the pitiful maintenance of a "neocolonial" system. There is considerable truth in this statement. Of course racism and ethnocentrism are contagious diseases, and it is no surprise that they appear also in those groups discriminated against. There are indeed racist nuances in some of the claims and arguments of Indians and peasants when they complain and fight for their liberation. Long ago Paulo Freire reminded us that the primary liberation model for the oppressed is the oppressors. But from there the analysis would go wrong if we conclude – as many people from both the right and left do – that this is hopeless racism or that the final outcome will be a war between races. Nuances are not the central argument, which is that oppression is made easier by its being incorporated in a neocolonial system.[7]

On the other hand, more acculturated Indian groups look upon others in a way not too different from that used by white people toward Indian groups. Such is the case with Aymaras in reference to the remnant of Urus, the Guaraní in reference to the Ayoreode, and so on. Similar perspectives tend to reappear at different levels: Spanish or *cholo* versus Indian, *cholo* or Indian versus white, more acculturated Indian groups versus less acculturated groups.

The mechanics of ethnic violence

In this section we shall show how the presence of this overall ethnic matrix adds salience even to conflicts which emerge from other factors. First we identify two very distinctive keys to ethnicity; then we specify the mechanics of ethnic violence; and, finally, we analyse the ethnic factor in several concrete situations.

Keys to ethnicity

After four and a half centuries of interracial mixture, skin colour is an ingredient of ethnic discrimination but not the crucial factor. At pres-

126

ent, ethnicity is more evident in certain symbols. Symbols are always significant in fixing the boundaries between social groups and even in indicating strata within a given group. Hierarchical institutions, such as the army or the Catholic Church, use them formally and explicitly. But the principle is universal. In less formal cases, such as ours, the kinds of symbol used can vary widely from one situation to another but are always present. Within this variety, dress and language seem to be two of the most relevant symbols for ethnic identification in Bolivia, although they are neither universally present nor unique.

In the Andean region, the most obvious dress difference occurs among women between the two styles locally known as *de vestido* and *de pollera*. Both costumes are of European origin, but the *pollera* skirt is more traditional and, as such, quickly identifies an Andean Indian or *chola*, whereas the *vestido* skirt (or slacks) is the only female dress allowed to the other ethnic groups. There are also special terms for an Indian or *chola* woman who changed her *pollera* to adopt the *vestido* dress. She is called *chota* or *birlocha*, words that imply that she is still a *chola* but is trying to ascend the social ladder (Albó, Greaves, and Sandoval, 1981–6:III, 21–36).

The second main key to ethnicity is language. The basic data on language distribution in Bolivia was provided above (p. 00) as perhaps the only available statistical hint to ethnic distribution. Attitudes to language indicate levels of ethnic loyalty, but also the pressures and constraints of the system against maintenance of culture. On the other hand, language discloses unwanted hidden identities as well. Under pressure from the dominant society, people will try to disguise their origins by many means: dress, last name, language, even facial cream. But these efforts may fail when the person begins to speak. It is not easy to overcome certain accents from the mother tongue when speaking a second language. This well-known fact is often used, for instance, as a source of ethnic jokes loaded with discriminatory connotations, or as part of the gossip by the white élite when some *cholo* or *mestizo* tries to attain upward mobility in economic, social, or political life.[8]

Constraints against ethnic identity

Peasant and Indian organizations summarize their present situation in the slogan, "We are foreigners in our own land." As a matter of fact, they have to behave as foreigners who must adapt to the conditions of a new country to survive in it. This occurs in successive stages and not without psychological conflicts.

127

Loss of ethnic identity

The first hidden aspect of ethnic violence is the existence of social constraints which impel Indians to renounce their identity in order to survive through processes similar to those mentioned above for the *cholos*.

From a cultural point of view the "pure Indian" does not exist any more, after four and a half centuries of permanently asymmetrical contact. Even if Indians maintain their identity as ethnically different from others, they constantly adopt traits from the dominant culture. A general symbolic correlate of this widespread phenomenon is that the borrowing of words from Spanish for incorporation into Quechua, Aymara, Guaraní, or other languages is an ongoing process. This is a tremendously corrosive factor, clearly related to ethnic violence. The possibility, and the advantages, of enrichment of any culture with elements borrowed from others is not the issue here. This happens – and must happen – anywhere in the world. The problem of ethnic violence appears when this exchange becomes structurally unequal: strong and pervasive downwards, weak and selective upwards.

The next step is the loss of full institutional sectors to the dominant ethnic and political groups. This occurred in the early colony with religious and political organizations. The change was not absolute, since many of the original elements remained as a substratum. However, it has not been by chance that most of the original political vocabulary has been lost or reduced to the ceremonial enclosure. And most of the original religious rites and practices, if not lost, are now reduced to the level of "customs," although they are probably practised clandestinely. Since the late nineteenth century, the survival of the community as an institution has been jeopardized again and again by transformation into syndicates, into modern townships, or into isolated and very vulnerable individual parcels of land. Even old community names change, perhaps under the influence of the school, in favour of more "civilized" names with Bolivian patriotic connotations.

The final logical step is the total loss of Indian identity. During the eighteenth century a similar loss affected many local ethnic groups, which became indistinguishable in a mass of low-status "Indians," differentiated at most by their languages. The present risk is that these new identities will also be lost, as has happened already in most areas of highland Colombia, along the Peruvian coast, and in many other parts of the continent. The most jeopardized Indian groups are those who have been "assimilated" into the dominant society, such as those now called *campesinos* in the Highlands and, more notably, those who migrated to the cities. It seems that "Indian," on the one hand, and "modern," "urban," or "professional," on the other, are considered contradictory concepts by the ruling élites.

However, Indians are not just passive victims in all these processes. The dominant racist rhetoric is so strong and persistent that it becomes digested also by many Indians, who begin to feel themselves as "brutes" and "uncivilized." They feel continuously hindered in their attempts to improve, precisely because they are "Indians" (or *campesinos*), and this shocking experience leads them to seek an alternate path, namely to ignore their origins and to try to play the non-Indian role. This is the way for an Indian to begin a "cholification" process, with all the identity and ambiguity problems mentioned above.

Is this the only practical solution left to them? Many politicians, and even social scientists and supporters of Indians, think so, while they might not dare to affirm it openly. More pragmatically, many Indians accept this situation as the only one available. However, the most enlightened leaders among them fight to resist this fate. Some turn the implications of the word "Indian" upside down to transform it into a banner for their claims. Others, mostly in the Andean areas, have come to an interesting compromise: they reject the terms "Indian" and "indigenous" given to them by the oppressors and hence loaded with too many discriminatory connotations. Instead they have adopted the term "original peoples," or even "original nations," as an assertion of their historical identity. Is not this resistance a clear sign that behind the "civilization" discourse there is a misleading instrument of ethnic violence?

Non-formal exclusion

Throughout this process there is no formal discrimination based on explicit rules of ethnic exclusion of the apartheid type. No group is formally rejected. However, society is organized as if everybody belonged to the dominant groups. Every aspect of society is thought of from the perspective of the dominant ethnic minority. Those considered "lower" ethnic groups become the invisible others. Yet these groups are needed by those at the top, as domestic servants, rural workers, peddlers, and other forms of cheap labour. Then oppressive and/or paternalistic relationships develop, in which the subordinated position of non-dominant groups is made and kept very clear. Of course, relations of this kind are never formally written down as social rules, but are taken for granted.

Strictly speaking, upward social mobility is still possible. When this occurs, it becomes ethnic as well as social climbing, since it implies for the individual the renunciation of his or her culture and full identity. Yet, as we have seen, this attempt at renunciation does not always meet with success. Many who try it fail and, as an unwanted consequence, develop psychological contradictions such as those described above as *cholo* traits.

The overall result of this set of relationships is that people belonging to the lower-status ethnic groups regard themselves as "second-class citizens" or even "foreigners in their own land." In daily life, this is only a feeling, but it is one of the more frequently stated complaints of peasant unions and Indian political organizations. This kind of discrimination – which includes everyday social exchanges, non-formal regulations of inter-ethnic behaviour, and some openings for upward ethnic mobility – is closer to what van den Berghe (1967: 25–37) labelled "paternalistic racism," in contrast to the "competitive racism" of some Anglo-Saxon societies. According to van den Berghe it is more commonly found in agrarian, pre-industrial societies.

Contempt and fear

Since the process just mentioned includes violence from above, the attitude of others towards Indians and *campesinos* (and of whites towards *cholos*, as well) is not one of contempt alone. At the deepest level there is also a component of fear, perhaps linked to a sense of guilt. This component might help to explain the apparent contradiction between contempt and lyrical, literary praise of the pure Indian. This fear shows up mainly in periods of crisis. Let us look at the following recurring example.

More than two centuries ago La Paz suffered a six-month siege during the Indian uprising of Tupaj Katari (similar to that of Tupaj Amaru in Peru). The suffering the white residents underwent in the siege of 1781 are not completely forgotten, and this memory emerges from time to time. One occasion was the 1899 Federal War, after which the new liberal mining bourgeoisie of La Paz managed to overthrow the government led by the conservative aristocracy in the city of Sucre. The insurgents were able to win with the support of Aymara communities, whom the liberals lured with the vain promise of stopping the takeover of their communal lands. However, when the Aymaras began to take the promise seriously and continued their own struggle, the two white factions came to a quick agreement, fearing "a war of races."[9] Two centuries later, in 1980, a similar confrontation led to a similar result. In a period of political confusion after a failed military coup, peasants organized a blockade of roads in protest against a new economic package which did not take their needs into account. Immediately, rumours begun to circulate in the wealthier quarters about the imminence of an "Indian siege," and an extensive radio broadcast in Aymara and Quechua (for the first time in history) was quickly made, exhorting Indians to remain calm. Addressing Indians as "brother *campesinos*," these radio programmes revealed the centuries-old fear of Indians held by the non-Indian population.

Can this fear be applied to *cholos* as well? That the white population fears *cholos* is not in doubt, as we mentioned earlier. But the fear of *cholos* towards Indians deserves more discussion. Situations similar to the one described for La Paz are relatively common in the rural *mestizo* towns in relation to the surrounding peasant/Indian communities. The *mestizo/cholo* dwellers of these towns despise and try to exploit Indians more openly than others, who have a more distant relationship with them. This is adequate ground for a complex attitude combining open contempt with hidden fear and guilt. But the same cannot be said of some *cholo* urban groups, who sometimes take the side of Indians in these situations, since their relationship with the higher city strata is very similar.[10]

Some situations of ethnic violence

The principles outlined above apply to many situations that cannot be detailed here. We shall restrict our discussion to a few examples.

The rural/urban relationship

The rural/urban relationship is perhaps the most evident expression of the ethnic gap. Except for a few areas of Bolivia where the rural inhabitants are of European descent, the difference between rural and urban settings is much more than just two styles of geographical distribution in a region. The prominence of agricultural occupations in the countryside does not explain the wideness of the gap either. "Rural" and "urban" appear to describe two almost opposite systems of life. "Citizenship" is primarily linked to the "city." The main offices and services are located there and, except for a few low-level civil servants, all significant *gente decente* are concentrated in the city. When some of them – mostly those who belong to the public service administration – move to the countryside, people (including rural people) question whether they moved there of their own will or were transferred as a form of punishment for some fault. On the other hand, when rural people move to the city one of their main concerns is to become "civilized." The general assumption is that dwelling in the city implies adopting the "city" ways, namely the ways of *gente decente*, or at least making a serious attempt to do so. Most people tend to regard Indian cultures as belonging to backward rural areas.

Naturally this supposition is not true, since the main cities are crowded with rural immigrants, most of them of Aymara, Quechua, or other Indian origin, and they also have significant proportions of city-born people of the same ancestry. However, this assumption explains the stress that these ethnic groups undergo in the city.[11]

Public spaces

Streets, market-places, and other public spaces are very handy locations in which to analyse ethnic relations. In all these places non-Indians look upon Indians in a variety of ways. Usually non-Indians ignore Indians, making them invisible citizens. Only if their presence or behaviour disturbs the life of non-Indians are they spoken to, most probably to receive a scornful order. Although the general social etiquette demands addressing unfamiliar adults with the term *usted* ("you," formal), this rule does not apply to Indians, who are always addressed to as *tú* ("you," informal), as if they were children.

Travel and public transportation is another test area. Only certain hotels and restaurants formally exclude Indians. There is also some ethnic distribution of the means of transportation: trucks are for Indians and aircraft for non-Indians. However, even this is a tendency rather than a rule. If necessary, anyone is prepared to ride on the back of a truck, and the number of *pollera cholas* travelling in aircraft increases from day to day (yet all stewardesses remain white). Other means of transportation, such as buses and trains, are open to anybody and their closed space offers many occasions for ethnic confrontation: *gente decente*, especially women, complain loudly and with annoyance if a *pollera* woman occupies a seat while they have to stand; the ethnic insult is on the tip of the tongue if an Indian's bundle bothers somebody else.

The school

This domain can be defined as the last outpost of "civilization" through the state, specially in the countryside. The Bolivian Ministry of Education is divided into two main branches: urban and rural. This could be a very functional division, given the different needs in either area. However, in practice, it leads to first- and second-class educations. Quality is much lower in the rural division, to the point that the request for a single kind of education becomes one of the more frequently repeated pleas from the peasants' organizations.

However, this is only one side of the problem. Good or bad, rural education lacks any respect for cultural differences. Except in a few quite limited programmes,[12] Indian languages are banned from schools. Agricultural tasks and cycles are not taken into consideration by the school calendar. Rural teachers, including most of those of rural and Indian origin, have to make it clear, through their manners, that they are the "civilized" ones in opposition to the local rural population. They evidently long for a quick transfer to the city, which is where they send their own children to school, distrusting the very educational system of which they are part. The curriculum is designed as though students were fully urban and oriented towards accomplishing a full career at university, ignoring the fact that less than one per cent of students reach university and most, especially girls, drop out of school before finishing their primary grades. The general result of this exposure to the school is, therefore, worse than simply a poor-quality output. The rural school system inseminates a value conflict in the minds of the students, since everything in the classroom fosters the tendency to reject the very culture into which they were born and with which they have to live.

Public offices

Most public offices are established in the cities – the "other group's territory" – where everything functions in the Spanish language and its logical structures. To the typical lack of efficiency of this public bureaucracy should be added its disdain towards "Indian" customers, easily identified by their language and dress. They have to wait hours at the end of the line while other *gente decente* jump the queue. They are addressed in peculiar ways that underline their Indian origin, and too often at the end of the day they are asked to provide a bribe and to come back on a constantly postponed "next day."

Some public offices and officers are worse than others. Particularly unkind are those who make a living out of the enforcement of the law: lawyers, judges, police, and jails, both in the city and in provincial towns. Of course, so-called "consuetudinary law" – the unwritten customary rules of a given culture – is not taken into account in the administration of law. Besides this, if the conflict is between Indian and non-Indian, the decision will most probably go in favour of the latter. In any case, the size of a bribe and the influence of the party involved usually carry more weight than the equitable administration of justice. Hence, rural communities tend to administer justice on their own, at least when communal life is really threatened, as with repeated thefts. Otherwise, rural residents argue, the thief will bribe the officers and quickly be free to continue his misdeeds.

The army

The army is another sensitive case. According to the Bolivian constitution, every male is obliged to undergo military conscription. Actual practice shows that most conscripts are Indians or peasants, or Indian-like low-class urbanites. Others pay to get their documents in order, while avoding actually being conscripted. Therefore, conscription becomes a kind of modern *mita* – the colonial system in which Indians were coerced to work in the Potosí mines, in what, in part, amounted to a rite of passage to community acceptance. Now Indians have to go to the barracks in order to be accepted as full citizens by the state. Indeed, this is the way military service is viewed even within the rural community. To become a real "person" qualified for marriage, young men have to go through conscription. On their return will be the main actors of the fiesta for the *machaq ciudadano* (new citizen), a uniquely rural rite of passage that inserts this discriminatory obligation into the framework of local culture. As a result, *campesino* views of the army are ambiguous: it is a source of harsh treatment, including the possibility of meeting death as cheap "cannon fodder"; but, at the same time, it becomes the school for manhood and the second main gateway (after school) to "civilization." This ambiguity appears also in the changing formal relations between the military institution and peasant organizations. During the 1964–78 military regimes the government succeeded in establishing a "military–peasant pact"; however, since 1978, the disintegration of this pact has been one of the main concerns of peasant organizations, which came to regard the military as their enemy.

The hierarchical structures of both the army and the police also incorporate internal divisions between those who will go through their whole careers as officers, and those who, at most, will be able to ascend to a low grade. Indians are not well accepted as career officers. Not long ago, for instance, a promising student with an Indian surname was offered a scholarship at the Military Academy provided he accepted a small formality: that he officially change his last name. On the other side, the ranks of the police (including the transit police) are filled with "Indians" who, after conscription, enter police services to attain social mobility. Such policemen have been labelled with the discriminatory name of *cachos*, an Indian-language borrowing referring to coca chewing.[13]

Ethnicity, class, and gender

Other important factors that lead to structural violence in Bolivia, and in other countries as well, are the class structure of society and unequal gender relations. We take it for granted that such kinds of structural violence exist. Many of the cases mentioned here have also a class and a gender component. Yet these other kinds of conflict acquire an extra ingredient of violence because they are intermixed with the ethnicity factor.

Let us take first the class factor. Here we have peasants and labourers (such as miners and factory workers), as opposed to their employers and other social groups which take advantage of them. Yet, except in the south-eastern part of the Andean region and in parts of the Lowlands, peasants are also Indians and, therefore, have even lower status. The extra influence of the ethnic factor appears both in its absence and its presence. In places like Vallegrande and Tarija, where peasants are not Indians but have (or are supposed to have) common Spanish descent, there are indeed typical class problems, such as those related to differentiated access to land, prices of agricultural commodities, and labour relations. However, the rural–urban continuum is much more flexible and the transfer from one class to the other easier than in areas where peasants are also Indians. On the other hand, the presence of this intervening variable, "ethnicity," adds an extra obstacle to inter-class relations and makes relations between subgroups within the lower class more difficult. The

135

first point is better known and has been illustrated throughout this paper. The second one needs further comment.

For instance, let us look at the relationship between miners and peasants (Harris and Albó, 1986). Both have a common Andean ancestry and common cultural traits, but miners, while extremely conscious of the exploitation they suffer as workers, feel very proudly that they are already "civilized." In spite of the poverty of their accommodation, mining communities are usually relatively "modern" enclaves in the midst of deprived rural/Indian areas. Miners coming from other places call local people Indians and treat them accordingly. Moreover, their wives sometimes try to supplement their husbands' meagre salaries by trading with peasants in the surrounding area and, as such, are identified by local inhabitants as members of the *q'ara* (or white/*mestizo*) world. Local rural people who become miners reach only the lower ranks within the complex labour structure of the mine and feel obliged to change their dress and language. As a result, local political alliances between peasants and other workers become more difficult. Even if the top leaders from both sides come to an agreement, this is not fulfilled so easily in practice.[14]

In the case of gender the arguments are similar. As we have seen, ethnicity is more apparent among women because of their differences in dress. Language skills in Spanish are also less developed among women. In part, this reflects the machismo or male dominance typical of our societies, even within contemporary Indian cultures. At the same time, the combination of machismo and ethnicity reinforces both. Since women, at least those of the older generation, are more reluctant to change their dress habits and have more language difficulties, husbands and children who try to ascend the social-ethnic scale are eager to hide their wives and mothers from public appearance, except among equals. One of the worst insults in this context is to remind others that somebody's relative is a *pollera* woman. We can easily guess how family and gender relations are damaged in these circumstances.[15]

When women change their dress and language, two things may occur. In a few cases – more easily achieved among the younger, urban generation – they are fully successful and become "whiter than whites" (or more *camba* than *cambas*, if they have migrated to the Lowlands). This reproduces the ethnic conflict, but from the other side of the divide. However, usually these women are not fully successful in their attempt to change and, therefore, become *chotas* (former *cholas*). Small details in their language, dress, hairstyle, or cultural habits betray their origin. Some of these traits may be sustained because of low earnings, if for instance, a woman cannot afford to go to the beauty shop, or maintains the traditional back bundle to keep her hands free for her daily tasks, since she cannot afford a maid. It is apparent from the foregoing that economic constraints are not interpreted with the class key alone, but are also seen through the glass of ethnicity. These low-class *chotas* are disregarded or treated with disdain as Indians or *cholas* frustrated in their ambition.

Domestic service provides the best example of ethnic, gender, and class violence combined.[16] Rural girls brought to the city and to provincial towns for this purpose generally range in age from 10 to 15 years old, but are sometimes even younger. The main structural reason for their becoming domestics is economic: their families cannot provide a living or a future for all their children and the only alternative employment open to young women is this. On the other hand, many employers-to-be seek young rural girls because they are cheaper and readier to obey quietly. There is also an important cultural motivation, since this is the main gateway to "civilization" for women in an even more significant way than the few years of schooling they are able to obtain. Among rural women domestic service fulfils a function similar to that of military service among men and provides a similarly ambiguous combination of illusion and hardship.

Physical and psychological violence against domestic servants is common and stems from various sources: class, ethnicity, gender, and even age. Class exploitation is normal: low salary (sometimes none at all), no social security, job uncertainty, and so on. But ethnic discrimination adds other forms of treatment. If a domestic is lucky and works for a wealthy family, she might be given access to the "maid's bedroom," a small, separate room, perhaps under the stairs; more commonly, she sleeps in the kitchen or in some other corner, probably on the floor, protected only with some plastic or old newspapers and her own blanket. She is not allowed to use the family's bathroom, cannot sit down on their furniture, and has to wash her clothes separately. In many places she has to eat different food or only leftovers and even has to use a separate spoon and dish when eating in the kitchen. Ana María Condori comments:

They think that, being *campesina*, she is filthy dirty [lit.: a pig], and say: don't sit down, don't use that. You'll soil it ... But coming back from my community I used to find everything dirty and the lady [*patrona*] waiting

137

for me anxiously, as if I was the queen of the house. The maid solves every-thing: good meal, clean house, trousers and shirts ironed. Then the lady doesn't have problems with her husband ... Some ladies want only a *pollera* maid because, they say, these are more docile while the *vestido* ones are refined and headstrong. Other ladies prefer the *vestido* maids because, they say, they are cleaner. So the maid, willy-nilly, has to adapt. Not only these ladies but the whole society constrains. Without this discrimination, I be-lieve that most women would be *cholitas*: office secretaries, administrators, accountants, university coeds would be *cholitas*. (Condori et al., 1988:60–61, 110, 113)

Being a young woman, moreover, a *cholita*, living away from her home and relatives, without any counsellor or protector but her mas-ter, is also an easy target for physical and sexual abuse. Complaints about physical abuse, mostly from the lady of the house, are com-mon.[17] Sexual abuse can occur within and outside the house. Becom-ing pregnant is a typical reason for firing a maid, but may also be used by the maid's employers as an argument to keep her inside: she may not be allowed to go out, not even on Sunday, to protect her from peril outside. Or, if the baby bears the family's blood, she cannot leave her job with a baby which belongs also to the family.

This traumatic first job experience is the main, almost the sole, path offered to Indian women to the kind of "civilization" that is sold to them from their early school days. Class, ethnicity, and gender com-bine to perpetuate a violent social structure. For this reason it is said that these women suffer a threefold oppression: as women, as peas-ants, and as Indians.

Conclusions

The ethnic factor inherited from the colonial structure of Bolivian (and Latin American) society is still a central source of social strat-ification and, hence, of structural violence. The issue is not the multi-ethnic and multicultural nature of Bolivian society: this is an important element which must be taken into account in the very con-stitution of the Bolivian nation and state. The problem arises from the unequal status of the various ethnic groups and the subjective prejudices attached to this stratification, which reinforce the whole system. Although the damage this causes is much higher when im-posed from top to bottom, ethnic prejudice also appears from bot-tom to top, mainly as a reaction to the former.

At present, the cultural contents of ethnicity are objectively more significant than the biological or racial ones, but the latter are also present as an ideological component of the ethnic discourse. In recent decades, ethnicity has been disguised by the state as only an economic issue, but under the mask of the now fashionable term "peasant," the ethnic factor remains very much alive and has even become an instrument of grassroots political mobilization. In Bolivia, ethnic violence is not of the apartheid type, but acts in a less formal and sometimes paternalistic way, permeating most situations and domains of society.

Ethnicity cannot be reduced to other factors, such as class stratification. However, ethnicity, class, and gender – among other factors – are correlated variables which reinforce each other, making social change more difficult. More specifically, ethnic prejudice, as well as gender prejudice, adds a subjective, unconscious, and taken-for-granted element to the social and economic struggle. Hence, it helps to make any rational settlement even more difficult. This is why ethnic violence is one important element of structural violence.

Notes

1. We shall not develop here the theoretical aspects of the ethnic factor. We hope, however, that the analysis of the Bolivian case will add useful elements to a broader theoretical discussion.
2. In Spanish, "le sale el indio." Arguedas (1909), writing from Europe, went one step further and stated that Bolivia is a *cholo* society.
3. The following anecdote is taken from an anthropologist's recent field notes: "One morning, while I was talking with a friend in the *mestizo* town of Mizque, her 5-year-old daughter came crying: 'Elisa called me *campesina*.' Her mother replied: 'None of my daughters is *campesina*. Go and tell her that she rather is the *campesina*. Look how dirty she is!'" (Paulson, 1991).
4. See Tamayo (1979), particularly his "Creación de la pedagogía nacional" (pp. 3–107) and Mariano Baptista's Foreword. For overlooking the Hispanic side of Bolivia, Tamayo has been called "racist" by Díez de Medina, the ideologist of the MNR's *mestizo* proposal. On the other hand, pro-Indian writer Fausto Reinaga (1968:133–65) has produced a passionate and forceful essay on the contradictions between Tamayo's theory and his personal practice towards Indians.
5. The first descriptions came from fiction, mainly in the so-called *indigenista* novel. See, for instance, the classical novels *Raza de bronce* by the same Alcides Arguedas, published in 1919 in Bolivia, Jorge Icaza's *Huasipungo* of 1934 in Ecuador, and *Todas las sangres* by José María Arguedas, published in 1968 in Peru, all of which have been regularly reprinted. Later, this indigenous topic was transferred to the social sciences. After the agrarian reforms in the 1950s, the topic was left aside by most non-Indian writers. But the problems continue, as shown by Yapita (1977, 1987) – an urban Aymara – and by most documents of the peasant and Indian organizations.
6. For instance, *runa* means "person" in Quechua, *jaqi* also means "person" in Aymara, *mbya* or *ava* means "man" in Guaraní. See Albó (1980a; 1990:325–50).
7. In the present thinking of most Indian political groups, rather than racism we find rejection of neocolonialism along with some idealized vision of the past. The latter can be interpreted

139

as a rhetorical way of projecting the future, not necessarily as a lack of objectivity. Not all societies project their utopia towards the future as our society does. See the debate on this topic in CIPCA (1991: II, notes 13–15).

8. More details on Quechua can be found in Albó (1974) and, on Aymara, in Yapita (1977) and Albó et al. (1981–6: III, 15–21, 79–141).

9. The conservative underdogs also used ethnic arguments against the emerging liberals in La Paz. They called the latter "Indian coca chewers", who "smelt like llamas". See Condarco (1983).

10. There has been lengthy political discussion within Peru and Bolivia on the possibilities and risks of the *cholo* leadership of a political movement (Quijano, 1980) or, as Aymara political parties like to phrase it, the role of the "Aymara bourgeoisie." See CIPCA (1991: Appendix 1).

11. Strictly speaking, the urban/rural opposition has three points of reference: (*a*) the main cities or *ciudades*; (*b*) the provincial towns or *pueblos*, including nearby landlords; and (*c*) the communities in the countryside proper, or *comunidades*. The resulting divisions are also different in the Andean region and in the Lowlands. Ethnic relations in Andean towns are described by Barstow (1979), Cajka (1979), and Lagos (1988). For traditional white/Indian relations in the Lowlands see Healy (1983) and Albó (1990:269–90, 339–46). The case studies in McEwen (1975) cover both regions. Jones (1980) describes relations in a former Jesuit mission. On the ethnic tensions between *colla* whites and Highland colonists, see APDHB (1984) and Painter (1984).

12. See D'Emilio and Albó (1991). Not all these experiences are respectful of the indigenous culture either. Some, like the Summer Institute of Linguistics, which is at the service of fundamentalist missionaries, tend to use Indian languages as more sophisticated instruments toward "civilization."

13. Similar situations could be analysed in reference to political parties, churches, non-governmental organizations, and so on. However, detailed analysis of these is beyond the scope of this paper.

14. Arias (1991) recalls how in recent years both miners and other urban workers have opposed very strongly and successfully the peasant claim that, being the majority in the country, they have the right to improve their small share within the Central Obrera Boliviana (COB). A peasant leader, who spent many years as a mineworker and had even reached a position of some leadership within the mine, commented to us during the debates at a union congress: "I tell you, at the very bottom of it, miners always look down on us peasants."

15. There is an exception, though. Some *cholas* are more successful in their business precisely because they appear as *cholas*. This helps them to trade goods or sell their food. Under such circumstances the opposite gender conflict may occur. Women become the main breadwinners in the family and, as such, no longer accept being mistreated by their husbands. If conflict arises, such women are readier to abandon the marriage and raise their children alone, or even strike their husbands.

16. See the account of Ana María Condori et al. (1988), for La Paz, and the collective book *¡Basta!* (Stop!) published by the Union of Domestics in Cusco, Peru (Sindicato de Trabajadores del Hogar, 1982) for particular case studies.

17. This could have a multiple explanation: the lady's reaction to her husband's machismo; jealousy; need to make her higher status clear both from a class and an ethnic perspective, especially if the maid's employers belong to intermediate social strata where there is upward mobility.

References

Albó, Xavier. 1971. "Marginalidad y grupos raciales en los Andes (Ecuador, Perú y Bolivia)." Santiago de Chile, paper presented to DESAL.

––––––. 1974. *Los mil rostros del quechua*. Lima: Instituto de Estudios Peruanos. Spanish adaptation of doctoral dissertation *Social constraints on Cochabamba Quechua*, Ithaca, NY: Cornell University, 1971.

––––––. 1980a. "Khitïpxtansa. ¿Quiénes somos? Identidad localista, étnica y clasista en los aymaras de hoy." *América Indígena* (Mexico) 39.3:477–527, French version in Necker, 1982:159–209.

––––––. 1980b. *Lengua y sociedad en Bolivia*. La Paz: Instituto Nacional de Estadística.

––––––. 1984. "Bases étnicas y sociales para la participación aymara." In Calderón and Dandler, 1984:401–44.

––––––. 1990. *Los guaraní-Chiriguano. III: La comunidad hoy*. La Paz: CIPCA (Centro de Investigación y Promoción del Campesinado).

Albó, Xavier, Thomas Greaves, and Godofredo Sandoval. 1981–6. *Chukiyawu, la cara aymara de La Paz*, 4 vols.: vol. I, 1981; vol. II, 1982; vol. III, 1983; vol IV, 1986. La Paz: CIPCA.

Albó, Xavier, and Josep M. Barnadas. 1990. *La cara india y campesina de nuestra historia*. La Paz: CIPCA–UNITAS.

APCOB. 1983. "Historia de los encuentros de los indígenas del Oriente boliviano." Santa Cruz: APCOB (Apoyo al Campesinado del Oriente Boliviano).

APDHB. 1984. *San Julián, bloqueos campesinos y camioneros: Testimonio de la lucha de un pueblo*. Cochabamba: Asamblea Permanente de Derechos Humanos de Bolivia.

Arguedas, Alcides. 1979. *Pueblo enfermo*. La Paz: Isla. (1st edn, Barcelona, 1909.)

––––––. 1976. *Raza de bronce*. Buenos Aires: Losada. (1st edn, 1919.)

Arguedas, José María. 1970. *Todas las sangres*. Buenos Aires: Losada. (1st edn, 1968.)

Arias, Iván. 1991. "COB: La hoz frente al martillo." *Cuarto Intermedio* 21:78–102.

Anrup, Roland. 1990. *El taita y el toro*. Stockholm: Nalkas Boken.

Barstow, Jean R. 1979. "An Aymara Class Structure: Town and Community in Carabuco." Unpublished Ph.D. dissertation in anthropology, University of Chicago.

Burgos, Hugo. 1970. *Relaciones interétnicas en Riobamba*. Mexico: Instituto Indigenista Interamericano.

Cajka, Frank. 1979. "Peasant Commercialization in the *Serranías* of Cochabamba, Bolivia." Unpublished Ph.D. dissertation in anthropology, University of Michigan.

Calderón, Fermando, and Jorge Dandler (eds). 1984. *Bolivia: La fuerza histórica del campesinado*. Cochabamba: CERES. Published also by UNRISO, Geneva, 1986.

CIPCA. 1991. *Por una Bolivia diferente: Aportes a un proyecto histórico popular*. La Paz: CIPCA.

Condarco, Ramiro. 1983. *Zárate, el 'temible' Willca*. La Paz: n.p. (2nd, revised edn; 1st edn, 1966.)

Condori, Ana María, Ineke Dibbits, and Elizabeth Peredo. 1988. *Nayan uñatatawi. Mi despertar*. La Paz: HISBOL/TAHIPAMU (Historia Social Boliviano/Taller de Historia para la Mujer).

D'Emilio, Lucia, and Xavier Albó. 1991. "Las lenguas en la educación formal y no formal en Bolivia." *Arinsana* (Caracas) no. 21. A shorter, English version appears in *Prospects* (UNESCO) 20.1, 1990:321–9.

Echevarría, Evelio. 1986. *La novela social de Bolivia*. La Paz: Gisbert.

Harris, Olivia, and Xavier Albó. 1986. *Monteras y guardatojos: Relaciones entre mineros y campesinos en el Norte de Potosí*. La Paz: CIPCA.

141

Healy, Kevin. 1983. *Caciques y patrones: Una experiencia de desarrollo rural en el sur de Bolivia*. La Paz–Cochabamba: CERES.

Hollweg, M.G. 1977. *El mito racial y el hombre boliviano*. Santa Cruz.

Icaza, Jorge. 1953. *Huasipungo*. Buenos Aires: Losada. (1st edn, 1934.)

Jones, James. 1980. "Conflict between Whites and Indians on the Llanos de Moxos, Beni Department." Unpublished Ph.D. dissertation in anthropology, University of Florida, Gainesville.

Klein, Herbert. 1982. *Bolivia: The Evolution of a Multi-Ethnic Society*. New York: Cambridge University Press.

Lagos, Maria Laura. 1988. "Pathways to Autonomy, Roads to Power: Peasant-Elite in Cochabamba (Bolivia) 1900–1985." Unpublished PhD dissertation in anthropology, Columbia University, New York.

Levine, Robert M. 1980. *Race and Ethnic Relations in Latin America and the Caribbean. An Historical Dictionary and Bibliography*. Metuchen, NJ, and London: Scarecrow Press.

McEwen, William (ed.). 1975. *Changing Rural Society. A Study of Communities in Bolivia*. New York: Research Institute for the Study of Man, Oxford University Press.

Mörner, Magnus. 1967. *Race Mixture in the History of Latin America*. Boston: Little, Brown.

Necker, Louis (ed.). 1982. *De l'empreinte a l'emprise. Identités andines et logiques paysannes*. Presses Universitaires de France, Paris and Institut Universitaire d'Études du Développement, Geneva.

Ochoa, Victor. 1988. "Misti q'ara." In X. Albó (ed.), *Raíces de América: El mundo aymara* (Madrid: UNESCO–Alianza Editorial), pp. 437–9.

Painter, Michael. 1984. "Ethnicity and Social Class Formation in the Bolivian Lowlands." Occasional paper, Institute of Development Anthropology, Clark University, New York.

Paulson, Susan. 1991. "Cómo convidar mejor con la Pachamama. Recetas modernas para ritos tradicionales." Paper presented at III Coloquio Internacional del Grupo de Trabajo de Historia y Antropología Andina. Cochabamba: CLACSO–Centro Bartolomé Las Casas.

Pérez Velasco, Daniel. 1929. *La mentalidad chola en Bolivia*. La Paz: La Patria.

Quijano, Aníbal. 1980. *Dominación y cultura. Lo cholo y el conflicto cultural en el Perú*. Lima: Mosca Azul.

Reinaga, Fausto. 1968. *El indio y los escritores de América*. La Paz: Partido Indio de Bolivia.

———. 1969. *La revolución india*. La Paz: Partido Indio de Bolivia.

Reyeros, Rafael. 1949. *El pongueaje: La servidumbre personal de los indios bolivianos*. La Paz: Universo. (2nd, expanded edn: *Historia social del indio boliviano*, La Paz, 1963.)

Reynaga, Ramiro. 1972. *Ideología y raza en América Latina*. La Paz: Futuro Bolivia.

Sindicato de Trabajadores del Hogar. 1982. *¡Basta! Testimonios*. Centro Bartolomé Las Casas, Cusco.

Tamayo, Franz. 1979. *Obra escogida*. Selected, with prologue and chronology, by Mariano Baptista Gumucio. Caracas: Ayacucho.

Van den Berghe, Pierre L. 1967. *Race and Racism. A Comparative Perspective*. New York: Wiley and Sons.

Villavicencio, Gladys. 1973. *Relaciones interétnicas en Otavalo: ¿Una nacionalidad india en formación?* Mexico: Instituto Indigenista Interamericano.

Wankar (Ramiro Reynaga). 1978. *Tawantinsuyu. Cinco siglos de guerra Qheswaymara contra España*. La Paz: Mink'a.

Yapita, Juan de Dios. 1977. *Discriminación lingüística y conflicto social*. La Paz: Museo de Etnografía y Folklore.

———. 1987. "Algunas observaciones de la relación campo-ciudad." *Notas y Noticias Lingüísticas de Bolivia* 1.6:7–13, INEL (Instituto Nacional de Estudios Lingüísticos).

6

Violence and conflict resolution in Uganda

Edward Khiddu-Makubuya

This paper highlights the various major factors relating to the violence and conflict in Uganda endemic from pre-colonial times to the present. It aims to explain these trends of violence and conflict, identifying responses to them and mapping out possible approaches to creative management of these trends. The overarching goal is thus optimum political stability and constructive engagement within the polity.

1 The concepts of violence and conflict

Although concepts mirroring social reality can hardly have rigid meanings (Weldon, 1953), one can, nonetheless, assign to them working, contextual, or operational meanings. Violence and conflict are two such terms.

L.A. Coser (1956:8) defines social conflict as a struggle over values and claims to secure status, power, and resources, in which the aims of the opponents are to neutralize, injure, or eliminate their rivals. This concept essentially focuses on *horizontal* relations involving contestants more or less on the same plane. However, conflict may also include *vertical* relations – the struggle between individuals and groups versus the state. Here the goal may be substantive participation in the values of human dignity, including power, wealth, enlightenment, skill, well-being, affection, respect, and rectitude. When this struggle becomes forceful or coercive, the concept of violence enters into the picture – not as an end in itself, but as a means in the struggle.

Political violence, says K.W. Grundy (1971), means physical attacks upon persons or property associated with the political or civil order. But this addresses only violence against the system – a perspective understandable in studying guerrilla struggle. Given the dynamic nature of the social context of violence, however, an exclusive focus on violence against the system could easily generate misleading insights. R. Khan (1981) sees violence as the exercise of physical force so as to inflict injury on or cause damage to persons and property; action or conduct characterized by such attacks; treatment or usage tending to cause bodily injury or forcibly interfering with personal freedom. J.Q. Wilson (1968) distinguishes between individual and collective violence. Individual violence includes murders, suicides, assaults, wife-beating, and child-beating, while collective violence includes riots, civil insurrections, internal wars, and the violent reaction of regimes to these phenomena. T.R. Gurr classifies violence against the system into three basic categories: turmoil, conspiracy, and internal war (for more specific detail, see Gurr, 1970).

Individual violence is an important facet of social life in Uganda (see Mushanga, 1974). But I shall restrict myself in this paper to collective violence, necessarily ignoring the interface between individual and collective violence. Grundy and Khan emphasize the "directness" of violence (i.e. physical attacks). Here I shall add two other facets of the phenomena: *structural violence* and *silent violence*. In all modern social systems, citizens must deal with an all-powerful state which holds sway over them. Maximal state power is a major plank in the concept of *structural violence*. The maximal state has, hitherto, entailed asymmetries in the distribution of power and other values of human dignity. Inequality and exploitation are part of the general formula for structural violence. To this must be added that the socio-political structure, through such asymmetries, may lead to actual deaths, reduced life expectancy, and general suffering and misery. I use the term *silent violence* to refer to phenomena which seriously undermine the life and well-being of large parts of the population. This category would thus include famine and epidemics. Other categories of violence could be added – economic violence, cultural violence, intellectual violence, and so on (Mertens, 1981) – but I feel they can conveniently be subsumed under the working categories already articulated above.

2 Basic facts and historical background

Land-locked Uganda has a surface area of 91,343 square miles (236,860 square kilometres). Its population of 16.6 million people (1991) has the following ethnic composition: Bantu 65.7 per cent; Nilotic 13.9 per cent; Nilo-Hamitic 12.7 per cent; Sudanic 6 per cent; others 1.7 per cent. Of this population, 31 per cent follow traditional religions, 33 per cent are Roman Catholics, 30 per cent are Protestants, and 6 per cent are Muslims (Uganda Government, n.d., 1982; *New Vision* [Kampala], 25.6.91).

Colonial Uganda

Uganda became a British protectorate in 1893–4. Prior to that date, the two major types of political system in Uganda had been centralized (kingdoms) and decentralized, or stateless, systems (Evans-Pritchard and Fortes, 1940). Conflicts, traditional rivalries, and hostilities were common among and between some of the indigenous communities – for example, Acholi versus Lango, or Buganda versus Bunyoro. (See Apter, 1961; Gingyera-Pinycwa, 1976; Ingham, 1958; Jones, 1962; Karugire, 1980; Kasfir, 1976; Kanyeihamba, 1975; Morris and Read, 1966; Wellbourn, 1965.)

The process of British colonization was accomplished by the use of a mercenary army and other instruments of coercion. True, the British did extract agreements from several paramount chiefs, lending a semblance of peaceful acquiescence to the process. But large parts of Uganda had to be colonized by coercion and active militarism, using a combination of the mercenary army and local recruits. This is particularly true of the colonial conquest of what are now parts of eastern, northern, and north-western Uganda (Tandon, 1989; Agami, 1985). The entire colonial period – from 1894 to 9 October 1962 – was characterized by both latent and active conflicts and violence.[1]

I am quite aware of the usual nice distinctions between colonies, protectorates, and territories; also, that the British pursued a policy of "indirect rule" in Uganda (Hailey, 1938; Lugard, 1922; Morris and Read, 1966). Indeed, the British were invited to Uganda by one of the native rulers of the time. All the same, the very inception of the process of colonization in Uganda was authoritarian, as was colonial statehood. The colonial setup negated democracy in respect of the native peoples of Uganda. Indirect rule preserved many subnational institutions, thus effectively undermining the early devel-

146

opment of genuine national institutions. Moreover, it was applied to ensure colonial domination of indigenous peoples, without granting corresponding responsibility. There was no bill of rights for the natives. Freedom of expression was greatly curtailed through the use of the law of seditious libel; freedom of assembly and association was curbed through deportation and rustification for political activists.[2]

On the eve of independence, the British hurriedly attempted to implant the Westminster model of parliamentary democracy in Uganda, largely under pressure from Ugandan nationalist politicians. Certainly it was in Britain's own interest. Indeed, the "independence struggle" was really a metaphor in the Ugandan context. Independence came about through negotiations by élites rather than through popular struggle.

Post-independence constitutional struggles

The Ugandan independence constitution of 1962 was an obvious compromise among regional, institutional, and ethnic groups. As Mazrui and Engholm (1969) have indicated, the two facts which profoundly affected the nature of Ugandan politics in the first four years after independence were a *latent violence* and a *vigorous constitutionalism* as a style of political contest. The possibility of political violence was linked to such factors as the high degree of autonomy enjoyed by the Buganda kingdom, the "lost countries" issue, relations between the Baganda and other ethnic groups, and tensions in the party system. The 1962 independence constitution practically carried the seeds of its own destruction. It provided for a titular/ceremonial president but also for an executive prime minister, for both federalism and unitarism at the same time. The kingdom areas enjoyed federal status, whereas the central government had limited constitutional authority, while the rest of the country consisted of unitary districts.

And yet the independence constitution worked surprisingly well to begin with. To some extent, the years 1962–1966 were years of innocence in the political system in Uganda. All the included parties and groups, as well as the government, seriously attempted to operationalize the rule of law. On the whole there was stability and tranquillity, despite a few isolated incidents of violence.[3] Otherwise, human rights were effectively protected. Life, liberty and security of the person, property, and so on, were essentially protected and respected, and conflict and violence were generally contained.

However, in 1966, a major watershed in the history of human rights

147

and violence in Uganda was reached. The Ugandan army bombarded the palace of the Buganda king, who was also then the president of Uganda. The then prime minister, Dr A.M. Obote, suspended the 1962 constitution, dismissed the president and the vice-president, and imposed a state of emergency in the southern part of the country (Buganda). The government subsequently promulgated the Constitution of Uganda (15th April, 1966). Members of Parliament found draft copies in their pigeon-holes in Parliamentary Building and were constrained to approve and adopt the document without much debate or reading: hence the appellation "pigeon-hole constitution."

This abrogation of the 1962 constitution was challenged before the High Court of Uganda, which ruled that the illegal seizure of power by one section of the existing government in violation of the independence constitution amounted to a revolution in law. The illegal manoeuvre was a law-creating fact. The independence constitution had been effectively abrogated, the new regime was by and large effective, and a new legal order had been established. Thus, as far as the Uganda judiciary is concerned, violence is seen as one of the legitimate modes of acquiring state power.

The events of 1966 were accompanied by a regionwide "pacification exercise" mounted by the Ugandan army throughout Buganda, involving the killing of innocent people, illegal detention, and various forms of torture. The state of emergency imposed in Buganda continued until 1971.

When the government enacted the Constitution of the Republic of Uganda (1967), this meant a major step in the entrenchment and legitimization of authoritarianism in Uganda. The new constitution abolished the semi-federal structures and set up a unitary structure all over Uganda; abolished the institution of kingdoms; established an executive rather than a ceremonial presidency, centralizing and concentrating governmental power in the executive; and deemed the National Assembly, whose term had expired, to have been re-elected for another five-year term. There are significant features pertinent to human rights and the 1967 constitution. That constitution formally carried a comprehensive bill of rights practically similar to that embodied in the 1962 constitution. However, the 1967 constitution introduced the concept of government immunity for violations of human rights and the consequences of violence by the regime, thus barring any judicial remedy or relief against government to victims of murder, torture, imprisonment, or damage to property which any agents of government might have perpetrated during the violent events of

1966 (Uganda Government, 1967, Article 123). A major instrument of regime violence during this period was the Public Order and Security Act of 1967, which provided for preventive detention and imposition of restrictions on the movement of persons in the interests of public order, public security, and defence. Between 1967 and 1970, many alleged opponents of the government were imprisoned simply by being served with detention orders under this act. The legislation put a seal on regime violence by providing that "No order made under this Act shall be questioned in any court." Moreover, the continuation of the state of emergency in Buganda provided a blanket cover under which people were imprisoned and harassed with impunity.

The period 1966 to 1971 saw the emergence and active operation of a paramilitary organization called the General Service Department. Many citizens have complained that it was instrumental in the torture, harassment, and persecution of real and imaginary opponents of the government at the time. Violence manifested itself in other forms between 1966 and 1971. Armed robbers with sophisticated modern weapons and fast-moving vehicles terrorized, particularly, the southern part of the country. It was suspected that these armed robbers were not just private entrepreneurs but agents of the state taking advantage of their positions and the weak discipline of the regime.

The Amin regime

In December 1969, there was an attempt on the life of President Obote. Curfew and a state of emergency were immediately declared, and all political parties except the then ruling Uganda People's Congress (UPC) were proscribed. On 25 January 1971, the Ugandan army, led by its commander, General Idi Amin Dada, toppled the Obote government in a bloody coup. The immediate aftermath was intertribal fighting within the army, in which thousands of soldiers and officers of the Acholi and Langi tribes (presumed to be partisans of the deposed president) were summarily and brutally executed.

The military remained in power until April 1979, wreaking maximum violence on all sectors of both public and private life in Uganda. The military regime did not formally suspend the constitutional bill of rights; in substance, however, it abrogated it altogether. On the whole, soldiers and other government agents had power of life and death over their fellow Ugandans. Punishment, including death, could be and was imposed on people for many, many things besides distinct breaches of the law. Each and every principle of the rule of law was gravely violated. The ordinary courts of the land still existed, but only as a legal fiction. The Chief of Justice of Uganda was abducted by state agents from his chambers at the High Court and murdered. Other judicial officers were tortured and harassed. The issue of an independent judiciary arose only as a remote theoretical possibility.

The equality rights guaranteed under the constitution became dead letters. Inequality and ascription on the basis of tribe, religion, and race became the order of the day: here one may recall the expulsion of 80,000 Asians from Uganda in 1972 at three months' notice. (See Twaddle, 1975; Plender, 1972:19; Nanyenya, 1974:100; Uganda Government, 1972a.)

The regime of Idi Amin Dada deployed a wide array of auxiliary paramilitary agencies, which served as primary instruments in the violation of human rights and the perpetuation of terror and violence (Khiddu-Makubuya, 1989). In September 1972, a force of Ugandan fighters invaded Uganda from Tanzania with a view to toppling the Amin regime. The invaders captured a few towns in the south of the country but were soon defeated. Thereafter, the Amin regime stepped up its violence against opponents, suspected and actual. Many were arbitrarily executed. It is estimated that up to 500,000 people were arbitrarily executed or disappeared over the eight years of the Amin regime (1971–1979). (See Gwyn, 1977; International Commission of Jurists, 1977; Kamau and Cameron, 1979; Listowell, 1973; Mamdani, 1983; Martin, 1974; Mazrui, 1975; Melady, 1977; Sempangi, 1979.)

The aftermath of Amin

In April 1979, a combined force of the Tanzanian army and Ugandan fighters overthrew the Amin government and successfully overran the capital, Kampala. This followed years of preparation and hard work by Ugandan exiles. The physical and human costs were immense (Avirgan and Honey, 1982; see also Matthews and Mushi, 1981; UNLF, 1979; Atubo, 1979). With the overrunning of Kampala came widespread looting for the first time in the history of Uganda. All law, morality, and authority appeared to have been instantly suspended. Crowds of people pilfered and wrecked commercial premises, government offices, and private residences; properties were burnt or otherwise destroyed. Similar incidents occurred with the "liberation" of a few other towns.

No systematic study of this phenomenon of looting has yet been done in the context of Uganda. We may note that it occurred in reaction to pockets of affluence amidst widespread poverty, in a sour atmosphere in which it was felt that this affluence was gained at the expense of ordinary people. It happened in the few days following the collapse of an unpopular regime and before the new regime could gain effective control; and it also involved deaths and injuries among the looters, and between the looters and the police or army, whose instructions at the time have never been made clear. No legal action was taken against the looters, but the immediate post-Amin government appealed for the return of property looted from government offices and got a limited positive response.

Religious conflict also manifested itself in violent form in 1979 shortly after the removal of the Amin regime. Idi Amin happened to be a Muslim, and to some extent his government tended, ascriptively, to favour Muslims, to the annoyance of other religious groups. Some Muslims were also alleged to have taken advantage of the regime to amass fortunes, and to have participated in the regime's violence. In Busjenyi, Western Uganda, the fall of Amin set off anti-Muslim feelings and violence which resulted in the wanton and brutal murder of about 60 Muslims by an angry mob, the uprooting and expulsion of many more, and the general harassment of Muslims in that area. Nobody was ever prosecuted for these acts (Kiyimba, undated; Wamy, 1991).

The Uganda National Liberation Front (UNLF) set up a government in Uganda headed by Professor Y.K. Lule as president. However, violence did not necessarily abate with the overthrow of Amin's military regime. Rather, the takeover of the entire country brought more violence with it. In particular, the Uganda National Liberation Army (UNLA), which took over as the government army, wreaked vengeance in the West Nile region, where Amin was believed to have been born. By some arbitrary association, many felt that West Nile people had benefited militarily, materially, and politically in the years 1971–1979; hence the brutal and destructive vengeance which the UNLA meted out in the region after Amin's overthrow (Minority Rights Group, 1989).

President Lule lasted in power for only 68 days. After some internal conflict within the UNLF, he was removed from power in June 1979 (Nabudere, 1980). Lule's ouster was accompanied by pro-Lule protest demonstrations in Kampala, with protesters chanting "No Lule, no work." The army was called out and several deaths and injuries were reported. Lule was replaced by President G.L. Binaisa. However, there was hardly any abatement in internal violence during 1979–80. A large contingent of the Tanzania Peoples Defence Force (TPDF) remained in Uganda while the UNLA was also in place. Tension over how authority was to be shared between the two led to violent incidents. Moreover, Binaisa was not universally popular within the UNLF. His period of rule was characterized by politically motivated violence and acts of urban terrorism, which the government was unable to control or check. Many held that this violence was being perpetrated by various groups *within* the government in order to undermine and discredit the Binaisa government and its political plans. This regime was itself overthrown in May 1980 – by the very UNLA of which Binaisa was supposed to be the commander-in-chief – and replaced by a government of the Military Commission under the chairmanship of Paulo Muwanga of the UNLF, still under the overall umbrella of the UNLF.

The return of Obote

In December 1980, Uganda held its first general elections since independence. The campaigns leading up to the elections were partially characterized by violence and intimidation; some candidates were violently prevented from even processing or presenting their nomination papers. A few shooting incidents were reported, and one candidate was abducted and murdered shortly before the elections (Bwengye, 1985; Commonwealth Secretariat, 1980). In the end, the Ugandan Peoples Congress (UPC) was declared the winner; it formed a new government headed by President Obote. The election was immediately denounced as a fraud by several influential groups within and outside Uganda.

The years 1981–1985 saw the second Obote government deeply locked in protracted civil war with several fighting groups, especially the National Resistance Movement (NRM). The period also saw massive violations of human rights, notably in connection with the wartorn districts of Luwero, Mpigi, and Mubende, popularly known as "the Luwero Triangle." In the midst of this intense civil war, the government accepted and put in place an International Monetary Fund (IMF) structural adjustment programme, under which the country's fixed exchange rate was abandoned and the Ugandan shilling freely floated against the dollar, with a simultaneous steep devaluation. Scarce hard currency was made available to the highest bidders through weekly auctions. At the same time, government expenditure on social services was drastically reduced and policies instigated towards privatization of those services. The government also took a drastic step to reverse Amin's "economic war," in which he had expelled 80,000 Asians and allocated their businesses to Africans. The allocations of the former Asian properties to Africans were nullified in 1982 and their former Asian owners were thenceforth welcome to reclaim and repossess them.

The period 1982–1983 also saw another manifestation of social conflict and violence in Uganda. Historic ties between Uganda and neighbouring Rwanda, as well as ethnic conflict in Rwanda, had resulted in many generations of Rwandese becoming residents and later citizens of Uganda – as itinerant labourers, alien refugees, foreign traders, spouses of Ugandans, and the like. In late 1982, some Mbarara District officials, with the apparent blessing of some authorities in the UPC government, whipped up a wave of public antipathy towards these Rwanda residents and had them driven to the Uganda/Rwanda border and right into Rwanda (Minority Rights Group, 1989; Clay, 1984; Winter, 1983). Families were uprooted; their homes, cattle, and household goods were looted; their properties were taken over by their tormentors. Violent deaths were also reported. Eventually Uganda, Rwanda, and the United Nations High Commissioner for Refugees (UNHCR) worked out a scheme for systematically identifying which of the displaced persons were Ugandans and which were Rwandese, for the purposes of permanent settlement. This arrangement did not satisfy all elements in the Rwandese community in Uganda, and violence erupted on 1 October 1990 with the Uganda-based invasion of Rwanda by the Rwandese Patriotic Front, initially with the view of self-repatriation of Rwandese exiles back to Rwanda (Watson, 1991).

In July 1985, the Obote government was overthrown by the UNLA and replaced by a government headed by a Military Council under the chairmanship of General Tito Okello Lutwa but composed of representatives of various fighting groups. The July 1985 military coup was accompanied by another looting spree in Kampala. From July to December 1985, peace talks were held in Nairobi between the Military Council and the NRM in an attempt to end hostilities. Meanwhile, violence and violations of human rights continued unabated within Uganda. A peace agreement was signed on 17 December 1985 but was never implemented.

The NRM government

On 25–6 January 1986, the Military Council government was removed by the NRM army after heavy and protracted fighting. The NRM set up its own government. Many Ugandans now hoped that this would end the violence and attrition that had gone on unabated since 1966. At the time of writing the NRM has been in power for more than five years, and assessments of its performance range from the very positive and approving (Nsibambi, 1991) to total condemnation (Otai, 1991). A more realistic evaluation will admit that the NRM has had a mixed record – certainly more positive than negative, but still mixed. Elements to be taken into account in this evaluation include the following:

(i) The armed-cum-political struggle
The NRM has waged an active armed-cum-political struggle in an essentially rural setting among peasants. This has been buttressed by attempts at political conscientization and enlightenment.

(ii) The ten-point programme of the NRM
This, in outline form, is as follows:
1. Democracy;
2. Security;
3. Consolidation of national unity and elimination of all forms of sectarianism;
4. Defending and consolidating national independence;
5. Building an independent, integrated, and self-sustaining national economy;
6. Restoration and improvement of social services and the rehabilitation of war-ravaged areas;
7. Elimination of corruption and misuse of powers;
8. Redressing errors that have resulted in the dislocation of sections of the population and improvement of others;
9. Cooperation with other African countries in defending human and democratic rights elsewhere in Africa;
10. Following the economic strategy of developing a mixed economy. (See Museveni, 1986.)

This programme strongly underlines the need to marginalize regime violence and to restore respect for human rights, and outlines some practical steps to achieve these aims.

(iii) *The NRA Code of Conduct*

For the first time in the history of Uganda, the official army is to be subjected to a strict and people-centred Code of Conduct – a major step indeed (see Uganda Government, 1986).

(iv) *Cessation of state-inspired murder and terror*

The NRM has so far managed to silence most of the guns of Kampala and also to marginalize state-inspired murder and terror. The real challenge is to ensure that those two developments become permanent features of life in Uganda. War situations are by definition complicated and there may be a need to resort to the provisions of the Geneva Conventions 1949 and the Protocols Additional to the Geneva Conventions of 1977 before a realistic assessment can be made. It is clear, however, that the NRM administration has not endorsed or condoned breaches of the rule of law and violations by government troops.

(v) *Resistance Councils and Committees*

The establishment of Resistance Councils (RCs), from the grass roots through districts to the national level, has significant implications for the control of violence, the rule of law, and the promotion of human rights. Re-empowering ordinary people through the RC system should give them more control over their own affairs and destiny, and marginalize regime violence and violations of human rights (Oloka-Onyango, 1989).

(vi) *Human rights commission*

In 1986, the NRM set up a Commission of Inquiry into Violations of Human Rights of the 1962–1986 period. The Commission has been taking evidence in public since December 1986, and human rights watchers everywhere are awaiting the commissioner's report with great interest. Meanwhile, the very setting up of such a Commission raises the hope that the offices of the powerful and the influential may, in the long run, be subjected to public scrutiny.

(vii) *The Inspector-General of Government*

Established by Statute no. 2 of 1988, the Inspector-General of Government (IGG) is generally charged with protecting and promoting human rights and the rule of law in Uganda and eliminating and fostering the elimination of corruption and abuse by public offices.

There have been long-standing calls for government to establish such an office (see Mubiru-Musoke, 1971; Khiddu-Makubuya, 1984). It is expected that the IGG will have enough properly trained staff and that the office will open grass-roots branches to make its services more widely available. The need for an adequate budget and facilities cannot be emphasized too strongly.

(viii) Control of the intelligence community

With Statute no. 10 of 1987, for the first time in the history of Uganda, the intelligence community was given a statutory basis. It is now officially known who controls the intelligence community, and the extent of their powers has also been spelt out (see also Khiddu-Makubuya, 1989).

(ix) Ministry of constitutional affairs/Uganda constitutional commission

The setting up of these institutions gives the people of Uganda an opportunity to re-examine the entire constitutional history of the country and to come up with a more perfect constitutional framework for the promotion and protection of the rule of law and human rights. The process of writing a new constitution has opened a new avenue for political participation in Uganda, generating a wide-ranging national debate on the country's history and future. This is, by all counts, a very positive development. Let us hope that this process will generate an effective constitutional formula for the management of conflict and violence.

(x) The gender issue

All sorts of social, marriage, and religious customs have barred women from active participation in public life in Uganda. In 1964, the government was constrained to set up a Commission of Inquiry into marriage, divorce and the status of women (Uganda Government, 1965), but very little was ever done to implement its recommendations. Women and children have been at the front line of direct suffering, malnutrition, and death as victims of conflict and violence in Uganda. (On this issue, see Obbo, 1980, 1989; Tadria, 1987; Uganda Government, 1985; UNICEF, 1989.)

The NRM has taken bold steps to address the gender issue. The NRA is the first army in the history of Uganda to accord women a fair and substantive opportunity to participate directly in military affairs. The system of Resistance Councils and Committees also takes particular interest in women's participation. The law now requires that every district must be represented in the interim parliament called the National Resistance Council (NRC) by a woman elected by the District Resistance Council. Also, for the first time in Uganda, a cabinet portfolio called "Ministry of Women in Development" has been set up with a view to articulating the special interests and needs of women and to work towards their practical realization.

With the 1990/91 academic year, Makerere University embarked on a system of affirmative action in favour of women by conceding to women applicants a bonus of 1.5 points at the time of admission, where necessary. The scheme, which has already enabled an extra 100 women to be admitted, generated wide controversy.

It is expected that, unlike past constitutions, the new Ugandan constitution currently being drafted will carry substantive provisions that fundamentally address the gender issue.

(xi) The return of Asians

As noted, the second Obote government enacted the Expropriated Properties Act of 1982, authorizing expelled Asians to return to Uganda and reclaim their former properties. Despite some opposition and controversy, the NRM administration – for human rights and economic reasons – continued this policy.

(xii) IMF structural adjustment programme

The NRM administration has accepted and put in place a wide-ranging structural adjustment programme as stipulated by the IMF. This includes massive devaluation of the Ugandan shilling; strict control of credit; cutting government expenditure on social services; liberalization of the trade and monetary regime; putting a cap on wages and salaries; removal of commodity subsidies; programmed privatization; and broadening the tax base (Ministry of Finance, 1990; Uganda Government, 1991).

(xiii) The Karamoja issue

Karamoja, Uganda's north-eastern region, is populated by nomadic pastoralists and cattle herders. The region suffers from attenuating extremes of heat and heavy rain. The British left this region to a bizarre form of "benign neglect," allegedly in order to attract tourists. The indigenous people of Karamoja have remained untouched by many positive elements of modern civilization. Ugandans living in districts bordering on Karamoja complain of the insecurity and violence perpetrated upon them by the Karamojong's traditional cattle rustling (Dyson-Hudson, 1966; Welch, 1969; Uganda Government, 1970). During the Amin era, the Karamojong took advantage of the general chaos to overrun military installations and acquire modern arms and ammunition, which they currently use in cattle rustling. This has greatly raised the stakes of the Karamoja issue, and made it urgent in view of the increasing human toll.

Under point 8 of the NRM's ten-point programme, the government committed itself to "redressing errors that have resulted into the dislocation of sections of the population and improvement of others." In pursuit of this, the government has also set up the Karamoja Development Agency, with a mandate to spearhead the urgent development of Karamoja. This statute clearly shows that the Karamoja issue is involved and complicated. It represents a valiant attempt to deal with a long-standing and complicated issue, although its long-term success remains as yet unproven.

These positive developments are major achievements which should not be minimized, given the poor historical human rights record of practically all pre-NRM governments, as well as the perpetual violence. They show that the NRM is committed to and serious about human rights. However, it is also a fact that aspects of conflict and violence have persisted. Highly disturbing is the anti-NRM armed rebellion in some parts of the north and east of Uganda, accompanied by unexpectedly large-scale violence. Admittedly, war situations are complicated and one should not make glib or dogmatic assessments of them, but all elements in the NRA should at least have upheld and/or strictly adhered to the NRA's operational Code of Conduct (see also Busuttil et al., 1991).

Government has persistently affirmed its belief in the freedom of the press. Despite the substantial freedom enjoyed by the Ugandan press, the tough line and occasional action taken against some journalists have been cause for concern.

The structural adjustment programme deprioritized education, as a consequence of which Makerere University students' vital allowances were eliminated in the name of cost-sharing. In December 1990, the police opened fire on a crowd of striking students, killing two and injuring several others.

Internal conflict and disharmony has been a perennial feature within Uganda's Muslim community, mainly involving disputes over doctrines and leadership. In 1991, clashes between one faction and the riot police led to the violent death of four policemen and one civilian and the arrest of more than 400 alleged Muslim rioters (Wamy, 1991).

While famine has occasionally afflicted some parts of Uganda (e.g. Karamoja), the outstanding example of silent violence, which has now reached epidemic proportions, is the occurrence of Acquired Immuno-Deficiency Syndrome – otherwise known as AIDS or, in Uganda, "Slim." Some 1.5 million people are afflicted in Uganda, with grave consequences for the nation. Uganda has mounted a national AIDS Control Programme emphasizing the need to publicize the facts about AIDS and the behavioural modification that is necessary to check its spread. The deterioration in health services and other infrastructure over the years and the moral collapse which has occurred as a consequence of violent conflict have almost certainly aggravated the spread and incidence of AIDS in Uganda.

In conclusion, then, we note that conflicts of all types have been a social fact throughout the historical development of Uganda. These conflicts have been accompanied by practically all forms of violence – regime, anti-system, tribal, political, economic, religious, and others. Nearly every class of Ugandan society has been touched by this process, and there is hardly a single part of the country which has not reverberated with some form of conflict or violence. Clearly, then, these phenomena and processes call for some explanation. The next section attempts to address this question.

3 Towards explaining conflict and violence in Uganda

As K. Rupesinghe has pointed out: "There is no general theory of internal conflicts applicable to all situations. There are difficulties in conceptualising an internal conflict, particularly as every conflict has its own historical setting, interacting with external factors in a particular configuration. We are here dealing with a situation where the past not only has a bearing on the present, but where it is also difficult to distinguish between external and internal root causes" (Rupesinghe, 1989:1). Nor would I claim to present an explanation of the Uganda situation in terms of a general theory of conflict and violence. Nevertheless, the quantity, the quality, and the geographical spread of the problem of violent conflict in Uganda suggest various questions about the nature and viability of the Ugandan state, the nature of the political, social, economic, cultural, and religious differences, and the coherence or otherwise of civil society (Kannyo,

1986/87). The full-scale development of a coherent analytical and explanatory framework of violent conflict in Uganda cannot be undertaken within the limitations of this article. Let me indicate, however, some of the fundamental factors that such a framework should have in focus.

The colonial legacy

The colonial state had no roots among the indigenous people of what is now Uganda. It was a structure imposed upon them by force and trickery. In the process, the colonial authorities had to resort to violence and to draconian and authoritarian legalism to compel compliance. Today's post-independence state in Uganda is hardly more rooted among the people than was the colonial one: basically, it has continued to be an external structure artificially and forcibly imposed upon the people from above. The post-independence state inherited and embraced the colonial instruments of violence and found it imperative to use them to subjugate and terrorize the people.

Ethnicity

It may well be that "all internal conflicts cannot be merely ethnic in character" (Rupesinghe, 1989:2). Yet ethnicity and ethnic identity must be reckoned with as a factor in the sectarian and factional orientation of the public life of Uganda. Pre-colonial ethnic cleavages were deepened by the colonial system of indirect rule. Some Nilotic and Sudanic peoples of northern Uganda were deemed to be the "martial" tribes and were therefore preferred for service in the army and the police, as opposed to the allegedly "stubborn" and "aristocratic" southern Bantu peoples, who were deemed better suited for offices and commerce. The collaboration of the Baganda people with the colonialists as chiefs and colonial agents laid a foundation for long-term hatred between the Baganda and the rest. The army remained predominantly Nilotic and Sudanic until 1986, when, for historical reasons, the tables were turned; the present army has its core personnel from the Bantu and Nilo-Hamitic peoples.

Religion

Religion has also led to divisions along clearly marked lines. The colonial state began with widespread religious wars involving traditional believers, Catholics, Protestants, and Muslims. The Democratic Party was founded in 1954, *inter alia*, to fight discrimination against Catholics in Uganda's public life. The other major political party, the Uganda People's Congress (UPC), draws most of its support and sympathy from the Protestant community. The violent harassment and killing of some Muslims in the wake of the defeat of the Amin regime was arbitrary but certainly left long-lasting scars on society (Wellbourn, 1965).

Different levels of development

The reasons for Uganda's uneven and unequal geographical spread of development, economic activities, modernization, and receptivity to change and innovation are partly historical. For example, while the colonialists encouraged cash crop production in central and southern Uganda, they tended to keep some parts of northern Uganda as a labour reserve. Likewise, Karamoja was deliberately preserved in its undeveloped form, allegedly in order to attract tourists. These historically conditioned differences coexist with differences in social visions and world views, which generate a social atmosphere full of superiority and inferiority complexes, feelings of neglect, grudges, and anxiety – all of which provide fertile grounds for violent conflict. It has been argued that the armed insurgency recurring in parts of northern Uganda since 1986 is a reaction to many years of "benign neglect" by successive governments (Gingyera-Pinycwa, 1989).

Poverty

Uganda has been called "the Pearl of Africa." Yet it is one of the least developed countries in the world. Poverty has been both cause and effect of structural violence in Uganda. Governments with violent tendencies have not lacked supporters, henchmen, and operatives whose lowest common denominator is socio-economic opportunism and desire for economic gain. Promises and expectations of money, employment, and a good life have lured people to serve in notorious instruments of violence – the army, the police, and, especially, the paramilitary agencies. Many poor and deprived people have jumped on the bandwagon of violence in the hope of obtaining political and economic justice. The looting of Kampala twice in a decade cannot be entirely dissociated from the phenomenon of mass poverty and economic frustration. Poverty has persisted and, in some respects, increased even though Uganda accepted and implemented a structural adjustment programme dictated by the IMF.

Poor leadership

Post-independence Uganda has not been generally blessed with competent or capable leaders. There have been problems of lack of vision, inferiority complex, susceptibility to flattery and sycophancy. Some leaders have been victims of political myopia, narrow-mindedness, a lack of imagination and creativity. Some have viewed and conducted themselves as tribal chieftains (Banugire, 1985). Moreover, some leaders have firmly believed in violence as an instrument of policy, spearheading the use of instruments of coercion and violence.

This has been partly because of the way in which most leaders have come to power. Between 1962 and 1986 Uganda was ruled by a total of ten governments, only two of which were the result of some form of general elections. Thus, most leaders in government have hardly enjoyed even the minimum legitimacy necessary to run principled government. For their political survival they have had to depend, not on popular support, but on the support of the notoriously violent military and paramilitary agencies. In these circumstances, leaders felt forced to give these agencies free rein, to ensure their own political survival.

Foreign interests and the external debt burden

Following the Berlin Conference of 1884, the British exercised colonial authority in Uganda for 60 years, largely in their own interest. They left in place an externally oriented economy whose linchpins were the production of primary products – coffee, tea, cotton, copper – and the import of manufactured goods largely from Britain. This neocolonial economy has been a major springboard for the entrenchment of other foreign interests and a major factor in the structural violence under which Ugandans have suffered. Uganda's artificially prescribed international boundaries have divided communities, leaving parts of them in Kenya, Rwanda, Sudan, and Zaire. Ambivalence and divided loyalties in these divided communities are social facts with which Uganda has had to live. Their impact on violent conflict in Uganda cannot be ruled out. Moreover, foreign interests have supplied arms and other instruments of violence, as well as intervening directly in conflicts in Uganda (Avirgan and Honey, 1982; Nabudere, 1988).

Post-independence Uganda has accumulated an enormous external debt, which has grown from US$138 million in 1970 to US$1,116 million by 1987 (World Bank, 1989; Lindgren and Wallensteen, 1989). In addition, servicing these loans costs Uganda US$200 million a year. This debt burden is a major hindrance to the effective resolution of both direct and structural violence in Uganda.

Militarism

By militarism we do not mean the mere presence of the military. Rather, as the World Council of Churches states, "Militarism is a result of a process whereby military values, ideology and patterns of behaviour achieve a dominating influence over the political, social, economic and foreign affairs of the state." (For further clarifications, see Tandon, 1989.)

Every change in government through *coup d'état* has resulted in the dismantling of the defeated army, whose personnel have gone into hiding or exile with their weapons. Also, because of the porous nature of Uganda's international boundaries and the foreign connection already alluded to, arms and ammunition tend to find their way easily into the country. Whether militarism is cause or effect, or both, of violent conflict, it is a factor in Uganda's public life which cannot be ignored.

The state and political development

Uganda is as yet politically underdeveloped, with a generally low level of political consciousness. This in turn has led to high levels of credulity and naïvety in matters political among the populace. There have been no credible avenues for systematic articulation of social interests. There are no national political organizations for dealing with violent conflict or for translating the lessons of history into practical politics. Parliament has often been overwhelmed and, indeed, occasionally shut down by the forces of violence. The system of Resistance Councils and Committees may well prove vital in this respect. But it is still new and its practical efficacy is yet to be developed. The conditions outlined above have not yet facilitated the emergence of a very strong civil society. (See also Dahl, 1976; Huntington, 1968; Nsibambi, 1986/87; Ruzindana, 1990.)

4 Responses to violent conflict

Three basic sets of responses to violence and conflict in Uganda may be summarized as follows:

Responses by government and the political system

(i) *Executive/administrative measures*, e.g.: propaganda; administrative, judicial, and quasi-judicial inquiries; states of emergency and deportations; pardon and amnesty.
(ii) *Political measures*: conferences and peace talks; coalition-building and power sharing.
(iii) *Legislative responses*: deportation and emergency law (sedition, treason, terrorism, etc.).
(iv) *Judicial process*: sedition prosecutions for sedition and treason.
(v) *Violence*: the police, army, paramilitary forces.
(vi) *Special responses* have included the creation of separate internal administrative units to accommodate minority nationality aspirations, also the special intervention and development programme for Karamoja.

Responses to violence stemming from the regime and system

(i) *Judicial remedies* sought in Uganda courts by individuals victims of regime violence.
(ii) *Petitions to the executive* put forward by individuals and groups.
(iii) *Silent protest*: a go-slow approach in the public workplace, corruption, indifference, and inattention to duty, as well as outright sabotage.
(iv) *Exile and asylum abroad*: with almost every change of regime, Ugandans have fled from the violence and sought asylum elsewhere.
(v) *Popular violence*: in the form of sectoral popular strikes, student unrest and strikes, and armed rebellion against the system.

Religious groups

A serious ecumenical movement involving Catholics, Protestants, and the Orthodox Church has been under way since the late 1970s. However, these overtures for religious peaceful coexistence have not yet embraced the practitioners of traditional African religion or the Muslims.

The question of responses to violence requires more systematic research and exploration. We need further inquiry into the nature and workings of these responses, methods, and measures.

5 What is to be done

Several themes need to be taken up to in order to provide a vision of the future of Uganda and to contribute to its design.

The nature of Ugandan society

Quite apart from being poor and underdeveloped, contemporary Ugandan society is also deeply divided. Both governments and their opponents have unnecessary recourse to violence, and the social order regularly breaks down, generating frustration and militancy in the society. Ethnicity, religious bigotry, economic inequalities, foreign manipulation, political oppression, and militarism have left deep social scars in Ugandan society and have undermined the development of a national consensus, nationalism, and patriotism. It would be too optimistic to consider that these negative elements will somehow not be factors to contend with in the future as well.

The need for more precise knowledge

Only 25 years ago, Uganda was still described as "the Pearl of Africa" and as a model of the socio-economic stability which British imperialism had benevolently bequeathed to that continent. Various theories attempting to explain violence in society (e.g. Khan, 1981) cannot satisfactorily explain the occurrence of violent conflict in Uganda: further study and research is needed. Multi-methodological and interdisciplinary approaches are likely to yield better results, and priority areas would include:
- Ugandan societies and cultures;
- élites in Uganda;
- government;
- origins and causes of violence, its processes and a refinement of its consequences;

- gender issues in violence;
- the design of a working peace system.

The functions of violence

It has been claimed that political violence is a normal phenomenon, part of the self-adjusting conflict situation (Gurr, 1970); it is more-over a liberating force, freeing colonized natives from their inferior-ity complex and giving them much-needed confidence (Fanon, 1963). According to Senghaas (1981:100), "social and political violence, para-doxical as this may sound, very often turn out to be the only means of social communication." Furthermore, Coser (1956) finds that so-cial conflict contributes to the maintenance of group boundaries and prevents the withdrawal of group members. I have not empirically tested Coser's propositions in the context of Uganda. To the extent that virtually every part of Uganda and every stratum of its society has been affected by violence, which has entailed great human suf-fering and grave economic loss, the Uganda polity may have learnt something. And the possibility of any group's seeking to withdraw from Uganda currently seems rather far-fetched. The maintenance of group boundaries and their reinforcement through conflict is hardly a possible contribution in Uganda, however, since it is these boundaries which promote social conflict and violence and under-mine the development of national consciousness and a common iden-tity.

In any event, violence and conflict in Uganda have entailed very high political, human, economic, and social costs which have offset any alleged positive value. The attendant massive violations of all forms and types of human rights have greatly undermined the people and the country, cutting the very roots on which a viable national society could have been established. The phenomenon of violent conflict has coincided with negative performance in the economy and practically all other areas. The economy, agricultural produc-tion, and the entire infrastructure have suffered. (See Common-wealth Secretariat, 1979; Mamdani, 1983.)

The fact that aspects of violent conflict have occurred under practi-cally all Ugandan regimes means that a society in which violence and conflict are either eliminated or kept within manageable proportions is a continuous struggle. There must be eternal vigilance if substan-tive, optimum peace is to be achieved. Violence is a social problem, so solutions to it must also be devised socially. (See also Dodge and

Raundalen, 1987; Gurr, 1970; Kannyo, 1986/87; Kasozi, 1989.) I wish to put forward several tentative proposals which might be taken into account in any future programme to marginalize the culture of violence and to promote peace, national integration, and social progress in Uganda.

Policy proposals for the future

(i) *Political and economic settlement*
The proper management of the process of power on the basis of nationalism and democracy will have to be a major theme for the future. A process of orderly succession to government and state power needs to be instituted, eliminating conquest as a mode of accession to power. The political system will have to balance the requirements of a strong central government with the interest of local competence. The system of overcentralization and concentration of power in central government has not brought the national unity which it was supposed to engender. Rather, it has been a major factor in the establishment of political repression, violence, and counter-violence. A policy of nationalism and social integration needs to be instituted, with emphasis on what tends to unite rather than divide the population. Political repression needs to be marginalized, and the system of political leadership should be scrutinized with a view to ensuring regular access to leadership by qualified and capable élites, rather than the negative recruitment of élites. We need processes of generating optimum élite consensus, rather than continuing with the system of factional élites.

The political settlement must focus on the constitution as a mediator of conflict. A democratic, nationalist, and development-oriented constitution must be put in place, with an emphasis on realistic separation of executive, judicial, and legislative powers; on popular participation at all levels; and on general justiciability of all major political issues.

The constitution should incorporate a comprehensive bill of rights which would make human rights the subject of state guarantee. One author has observed that the current constitutional debate has unleashed a great urge for increased participation and "has also brought to the fore the fact that human rights cannot be the subject of state guarantee; that unless vested directly in the people, an elaborate Bill of Rights or a sophisticated bureaucratic mechanism will not provide the requisite safety and security against their infringement"

(Oloka-Onyango, 1991). However, it would be very dangerous to take the view that human rights cannot be the subject of state guarantee. We need to return to the fundamentals of the social contract of either the Lockean or Hobbesian type. Any suggestion that human rights cannot be the subject of state guarantee amounts to absolving the state from its primary responsibility to protect, promote, and operationalize human rights. The state's failure to guarantee the rights of all has been a major factor in fomenting violent conflict in Uganda.

Historically, the focus in Uganda has hitherto been on civil and political rights. Life, liberty, and the security of the person must continue to be protected because Uganda's experience has shown that these rights cannot be assumed. The massive exceptions and qualifications usually attached to a bill of rights will have to be eliminated for better protection of civil and political rights.

It is high time for the material concept of human rights enshrined in the constitution to be expanded to include economic, social, and cultural rights: the right to good health, housing, education, and social security, the rights of women, children, the aged, and the disabled. The new bill of rights must make a substantive contribution to the development of Uganda as a stable community and polity. It must address itself to the need to redress historical imbalances in society and economy. It must thus incorporate a right to development and an equitable spread of development activity throughout Uganda. The bill must also guarantee the people's right to peace and a clean environment. Basic duties of citizens must also be viewed as part of the framework of human rights – including the duty of those under orders to disobey orders which patently violate human rights.

The political and other interests of *minorities* in Uganda must be reasonably accommodated. The politics of victor/vanquished and winner-take-all must be eliminated.

The constitutional definition of discrimination should specifically refer to differential treatment purely on account of *sex*. This is deemed necessary in order to incorporate women's energy effectively into the mainstream of development. The positive steps so far taken by the NRM administration on the gender issue should serve as points of departure for a more comprehensive and system-wide programme for the elimination of all forms of discrimination against women. Special provisions must also be included for the protection of the life and personal integrity of women in times of violent crisis.

In the *economic* settlement, care must be taken to correct historically uneven development while still forging ahead. Necessary economic sacrifices must be democratically agreed upon. The structural adjustment programme clearly needs periodic and democratic review, and the special economic needs of the pastoralists of Uganda will have to be accommodated. An egalitarian and just economic settlement will resolve one aspect of structural violence – economic marginalization and exploitation. It should also remove the urge to resort to force in order to reverse economic injustices.

(ii) The military

How to safeguard the constitution against *coup d'état* is a major practical issue which must be addressed. Does it make sense to write constitutional provisions against irregular takeover? Or should the constitution invest specific groups (e.g. the army, the workers, the students) with the power to take over government?

The Kampala Conference on Internal Conflict in Uganda (1987) made the following interesting recommendations on the military:

1.1. That the problems of internal conflict in Uganda can never be truly settled by a military solution. Uganda's problems are essentially political, social and economic; and military solutions are considered deceptive and temporary. A situation of half victors/half vanquished will not last. We have to consider how to build a nation out of a diversity of cultures, nationalities, regions etc.

...

4.11. That all citizens should be exposed to military training. The size of the army should be reduced to a small professional one. Local security should be augmented by people's militia and there should be some form of national service, entailing life and participation in villages and areas different from one's own home area. (Rupesinghe, 1989:295, 300.)

Furthermore, at the Växjo University Seminar on Democracy and Human Rights in Africa, it was suggested that Uganda should abolish the military altogether. Given the Ugandan situation as already exposed in this paper, the total abolition of the military would seem more likely to exacerbate violence than end it. However, if the people of Uganda should democratically decide to do away with the military there is no good reason why anyone should interfere with their decision. Barring any such decision, I tend to prefer the idea of a small professional army with equal opportunities for men and women from practically all Ugandan tribes. At the same time, every able-bodied Ugandan should be trained in and exposed to military science, to avoid the historical monopoly of military skills which has been abused in the past. The military must always be under democratic civilian control.

It is vital to train and fully equip an adequate civilian police force to deal with internal security. Since 1966, the army has become increasingly and unreasonably drawn into internal policing. Uganda needs to pay adequate attention to the refurbishing of the civilian police, with a view to removing the army from internal security and internal policing.

On the whole, the nation should adopt and pursue a philosophy of anti-militarism as part of the national ethos. The elevation of military solutions and values to the pinnacle of society must be eliminated.

(iii) Socio-cultural settlement

Uganda is a country of many cultures and traditions. Positive elements in each culture need to be identified and encouraged, with cultural pluralism and some cultural autonomy made part of the socio-cultural settlement. Religious bigotry must be eliminated and replaced by cultural tolerance. Indigenous Ugandan culture should be encouraged and taught in the formal school system. People should generally be sensitized to the whole range of gender issues, and reasonable minority cultures should be protected rather than assaulted or suppressed.

(iv) Education

The process of education needs to be restructured so that it may contribute more directly to nation-building, peaceful resolution of social conflict, and non-violence. Firstly, there is no good reason why *all* children in Uganda still do not have free and compulsory basic education for the first seven years of the national education system.

Secondly, Ugandans need systematic political education at all levels. Above all, they need to know more about one another's ways of life, and culture. Ignorance among Ugandans about the different cultures in their own country cannot be ruled out as factors in generating mutual suspicions, social stereotypes, hostility, and violent conflict.

Thirdly, women's access to education needs to be given special attention if women are to be fully enfranchised and their roles extended from the kitchen and the garden to formal employment, the professions, public service, and, above all, national politics.

Fourthly, human rights education is a must. People need to be exposed to the history of struggles for human rights, locally, nationally, and globally. People need to know the substance of the national bill of rights, the regional and international bill of human rights, and the mechanisms available for the enforcement of human rights. Widespread ignorance in the field of human rights has been exploited by unprincipled past regimes to oppress and tyrannize Ugandans. Fifthly, it is imperative that peace and humanitarian education be offered both informally and formally at all levels. Such education is certainly among the long-term medicines against conflict and violence in Uganda. By peace education I am thinking of all the systematic processes of enlightenment on the avoidance of conflict and war (negative peace) and on actual processes of stability and their use to advance positive human interaction and development (positive peace).

Uganda has acceded to the Geneva Conventions and made them part of its national law through the enactment of the Geneva Convention Act (CAP. 323: Laws of Uganda, 1964). Yet in some of the violent conflicts that have occurred in Uganda, the conduct of the combatants revealed that they either knew nothing about the Geneva Conventions or, indeed, totally ignored their obligations thereunder. Of course, one hopes that there will be only a few and isolated violent conflicts in future: still, it is important that people get sufficient exposure to the contents of the Geneva Conventions as well as to general humanitarian law.

(v) The language issue

Uganda is also a land of several languages and dialects. English is the official language, but it can be effectively used only by the educated minority. Kiswahili was once declared a "national" language (in 1971–1979), but apart from being the language of the armed forces, it is really not a national language in Uganda. For historical reasons, Luganda is widely spoken in several parts of the country. However, it is the mother tongue of the Baganda, who are not necessarily popular with the other ethnic groups. Any move towards elevating it above the other indigenous languages might provoke violent reaction from the other ethnic groups. Luo, Runyakitara, Ateso, and Lugbara are also possible contenders for national language. The development of a coherent national language policy has encountered numerous problems.

There are many arguments why a preferred indigenous language should be declared the national language of Uganda (see Mukama, 1989). All the same, as problematic as English may be, it should remain the official language of Uganda for the foreseeable future. Meanwhile, in the true spirit of cultural pluralism, each community should be at liberty, with or without government support, to develop its own mother tongue.

(vi) Foreign relations

Uganda's approach to foreign relations needs to be restructured so as to move away from the formal/routine approach to an instrumental approach. The foreign policy process needs to be democratized and also to have a programme orientation. The question of resisting imperialism, foreign domination, and manipulation must be seriously addressed. Structural adjustment needs to be subjected to regular democratic review. While Uganda cannot avoid participating in the global economy, the question of selective delinking must be seriously considered. Uganda's international debt burden also requires some democratic and popular input.

Ugandans should be free to seek international remedies for the negative consequences of violence – for example, before the African Commission on Human and Peoples' Rights under OAU auspices, or the Human Rights Committee and Commission on Human Rights under UN auspices. This has become particularly urgent in view of the recent tendency for the forces of violence to overcome and overwhelm all internal arrangements for resolution of conflict.

(vii) *Judicial remedies*

An independent judiciary is a basic requirement if conflicts are to be resolved without resort to violence. Beyond this, however, the procedures for presenting human rights and constitutional cases need to be streamlined and simplified in order for people to have ready access to the courts. And let me repeat: all manner of political, human rights, constitutional, and conflict-related issues must be justiciable before Ugandan courts.

(viii) *A national ethos of dialogue, compromise, and tolerance*

A national ethos of dialogue, compromise, and tolerance must be generated and nurtured. If conflict has had a positive consequence on Ugandans, surely it must be the realization and actual experience that violence breeds counter-violence, that irredentism and obtuseness breed violence, that persistent government militarism will soon lead to private militarism. Despite the ready availability of arms in Uganda, all politically relevant strata of society must begin to learn to talk before shooting. As mentioned above, the national ethos must have anti-militarism as one of its major planks. To this must be added a national consensus to accept one another and to work together. The sooner the different groups learn to accept others and work together, the sooner will durable peace develop in Uganda. The preferred national ethos will be dialogic and reconciliatory. After 90 years of practically involuntary and circumstantial interaction, Ugandans will naturally have numerous grudges and complaints against one another, but carrying these forward is unlikely to assist anyone. The future must lie in dialogue and reconciliation. In particular, we must begin with those things which tend to unite the people of Uganda. Hence, fora like the Joint Christian Council, which promotes interfaith dialogue among Christian religions, need to be encouraged to broaden to cover all major religions. Other local, regional, and national fora for political, social, economic, cultural, and other bridge-building need to be designed. In these ways, we can begin to build a less violent, more peaceful Uganda.

Notes

1. The many conflicts and uprisings during this period are well documented. For further details see Faupel (1965), Hansen (1984), Thomas (1951), Adimola (1948), Agami (1985), Uganda Government (1945 and 1949), Uganda Government (1960), Bazira (1982), Kasfir (1970), Kasfir (1972), Mushanga (1974), Syahuka (1991), Uganda Government (1962), Kavuma (1979), Low (1971), Muteesa (1967), Pratt and Low (1960).
2. On the former, see *R. v. Y.K. Pailo and 2 others* [1922] 2 *Uganda Law Reports* 98; *The Publishers of Munyonyozi* v. *Lukiiko Court* [1923] 3 *Uganda Law Reports* 124; *R. v. Luima and Tabula* [1949] 16 E.A.C.A. 128; *Masembe and Tabula* v. *R.* [1936–1951] 6 *Uganda Law Reports* 195, and Scotton (1970). On the curtailment of freedom of assembly and association, see, e.g. Binaisa (1959).
3. In particular, three deserve further comment: (1) The Nakulabye Incident (1964) in suburban Kampala, where police shot into a rioting crowd; (2) the 1964 incident at St Mary's College, Kisubi, where an army truck was involved; (3) the 1964 Ndaiga Incident, involving the resettlement scheme in the wake of the "lost countries." See Mazrui and Engholm (1969) and Semakula-Kiwanuka (1974:111).

References

Adimola, A.B. 1948. "The Romogi Rebellion 1911–12." *Uganda Journal* 12.

Agami, J.B. 1985. *Facts about Lado*. Arua: Institute of Sudanic Studies/ISS, 15 May.

Apter, D. 1961. *The Political Kingdom in Uganda*. Princeton, NJ: Princeton University Press.

Atubo, O. 1979. *Why? The Uganda National Liberation Front. I: The Gospel of Liberation*. Tanzania: Moshi.

Avirgan, T., and M. Honey. 1982. *War in Uganda*. Dar es Salaam: Tanzania Publishing House.

Banugire, F.R. 1985. "Class Struggle, Clan Politics and the Magendo Economy." In *Proceedings of the Fourth Mawazo Workshop: "Which Way Africa,"* Makerere University, Kampala, 26–28 April.

Bazira, A. 1982. *Rwenzururu: Twenty Years of Bitterness*. Kampala: Makerere University Printery.

Busuttil, J.J., et al. 1991. *Uganda at Cross-Roads: A Report on Current Human Rights Conditions*. New York: Association of the Bar of the City of New York, July.

Bwengye, F.A.W. 1985. *The Agony of Uganda: From Idi Amin to Obote*. London/New York: Regency Press.

Clay, Jason W. 1984. *The Eviction of Banyarwanda: The Story Behind the Refugee Crisis in Southwest Uganda*. Cambridge, MA: Cultural Survival.

Commonwealth Secretariat. 1979. *The Rehabilitation of the Economy of Uganda*. London: Commonwealth Secretariat.

———. 1980. *Uganda Elections December 1980*. London: Commonwealth Secretariat.

Coser, L.A. 1956. *The Functions of Social Conflict*. London: Kegan Paul.

Dahl, R.A. 1976. *Modern Political Analysis*. Englewood Cliffs, NJ: Prentice-Hall.

Dodge, C.P., and M. Raundalen. 1987. *War, Violence and Children in Uganda*. Oslo: Norwegian University Press.

Domenach, J.M., et al. 1981. *Violence and Its Causes*. Paris: UNESCO.

Dyson-Hudson, N. 1966. *Karimojong Politics*. Oxford: Oxford University Press.

Evans-Pritchard, E.E., and M. Fortes. 1940. *African Political Systems*. Oxford: Oxford University Press.

Fanon, F. 1963. *The Wretched of the Earth*. London: Penguin.

Faupel, J.F. 1965. *African Holocaust: The Story of Uganda Martyrs*. London: Geoffrey Chapman.

Gingyera-Pinycwa, A.G.G. 1976. *Issues in Pre-Independence Politics in Uganda*. Nairobi: East African Literature Bureau.

———. 1989. "Is There a Northern Question?" In Rupesinghe, 1989.

Grundy, K.W. 1971. *Guerrilla Struggles in Africa*. New York: Grossman.

Gurr, T.R. 1970. *Why Men Rebel*. Princeton, NJ: Princeton University Press.

Gwyn, D. 1977. *Idi Amin: Deathlight of Africa*. London: Little, Brown.

Hailey, W.M. 1938. *An African Survey*. London and New York: Oxford University Press.

Huntington, S.P. 1968. *Political Order in Changing Societies*. New Haven, CT: Yale University Press.

Ingham, K. 1958. *The Making of Modern Uganda*. London: Allen & Unwin.

International Commission of Jurists. 1977. *Uganda and Human Rights: Reports to the UN Commission on Human Rights*. Geneva: International Commission of Jurists.

Jones, T.J. 1962. *Political Parties in Uganda 1949–1962*. London: Athlone Press.

Kamau, J., and A. Cameron. 1979. *Lust to Kill: The Rise and Fall of Idi Amin*. London: Corgi Books.

Kannyo, E. 1986/87. "Political and Civic Violence in Uganda 1971–1986. Elements of the Research Agenda," *Ufahamu* vol. 15, no. 3 (Winter).

Kanyeihamba, G.W. 1975. *Constitutional Law and Government in Uganda*. Nairobi: East African Literature Bureau.

Karugire, S.R. 1980. *A Political History of Uganda*. London: Heinemann Educational.

Kasfir, N. 1970. "Toro District: Society and Politics." *Mawazo* (Makerere University) 2/3, June.

———. 1972. "Cultural Sub Nationalism in Uganda." In V.A. Olorunsola, *The Politics of Cultural Sub Nationalism in Uganda*. New York: Anchor Books/Doubleday.

———. 1976. *The Shrinking Political Arena*. Berkeley: University of California Press.

Kasozi, A.B.K. 1989. "Impact of Violence in Uganda Society 1966–Present." Paper presented to workshop on Uganda at Lyngby Landbrugsskole, Copenhagen, 20–23 September.

Kavuma, P. 1979. *Crisis in Buganda 1953–1955: The Story of the Exile and Return of the Kabaka Muteesa II*. London: Rex Collins.

Khan, R. 1981. "Violence and Socio-Economic Development," in Domenach et al., 1981.

Khiddu-Makubuya, E. 1984. "Ombudsman for Uganda," *Uganda Law Society Review* vol. 1, no. 1.

———. 1989. "Paramilitarism and Human Rights in Uganda." In Rupesinghe, 1989.

Kiyimba, Abasi. Undated. *Is the 1979 Muslim Blood-Bath in Busjenyi History? A Review of the Genocide that was Called Liberation*. Kampala.

Lindgren, G., and P. Wallensteen. 1989. "External Debt and Internal Conflict in the

Third World." In *Third World Dimensions in Conflict Resolution*. Uppsala University, Department of Peace and Conflict Research.

Listowell, J. 1973. *Amin*. Dublin: Irish University Press.

Low, D.A. 1971. *The Mind of Buganda: Documents of the Modern History of an African Kingdom*. London: Heinemann Educational.

Lugard, F.J.D. 1922. *Dual Mandate in British Tropical Africa*. Edinburgh and London: Wm. Blackwood & Sons.

Mamdani, M. 1983. *Imperialism and Fascism in Uganda*. Dar es Salaam: Heinemann/Tanzania Publishing House.

Martin, D. 1974. *General Amin*. London: Faber.

Matthews, K., and S.S. Mushi. 1981. *Foreign Policy of Tanzania 1961–1981: A Reader*. Dar es Salaam: Tanzania Publishing House.

Mazrui, A.A., and G.P. Engholm. 1969. "Violent Constitutionalism in Uganda," in A.A. Mazrui, *Violence and Thought*. London: Longman Green.

Mazrui, A.A. 1975. *Soldiers and Kinsmen in Uganda*. Beverley Hills, CA.: Sage Publications.

Melady, T. and M. 1977. *Idi Amin: Hitler in Africa*. Kansas City: Sheed Andrews & McMeel.

Mertens, E.G.P. 1981. "Institutional Violence, Democratic Violence and Repression." In Domenach, 1981.

Ministry of Finance (Uganda). 1990. *Papers Presented at Uganda Government Seminar on the Economy since 1986* (held 12–17 December 1989 at Uganda International Conference Centre, Kampala). Kampala: Ministry of Education/Chartered Institute of Bankers, June.

Minority Rights Group. 1989. *Uganda: Minority Rights Group Report No. 66*. London: Minority Rights Group.

Morris, H.F., and J.S. Read. 1966. *Uganda: The Development of Its Laws and the Constitution*. London: Stevens & Sons.

Mubiru-Musoke, C. 1971. "Uganda Needs an Ombudsman," *Makerere Law Journal* vol. 1, no. 1.

Mukama, R. 1989. "The Linguistic Dimension of Ethnic Conflict." In Rupesinghe, 1989.

Museveni, Y.K. 1986. *Selected Articles on the Uganda Resistance War*. Kampala: NRM Publications.

Mushanga, Tibamanya Mwene, E.G. 1974. *Criminal Homicide in Uganda*. Nairobi: East African Literature Bureau.

Muteesa, Sir Edward. 1967. *Desecration of My Kingdom*. London: Constable.

Nabudere, D.W. 1980. *Imperialism and Revolution in Uganda*. Dar es Salaam: Onyx Press/Tanzania Publishing House.

———. 1988. "External and Internal Factors in Uganda's Continuing Crisis." In H.B. Hansen and M. Twaddle, *Uganda Now*. London: James Currey.

Nanyenya, P.T.K. 1974. "A Case Study of the Law Relating to the Expulsion of Asians and Nationalization of Alien Property: The Case of Uganda." *Uganda Law Focus*, September.

Nsibambi, A.R. 1986/87. "Corruption in Uganda." *Ufahamu* vol. 15, no. 3 (Winter).

———. 1991. "Major Causes of Violations of Human Rights in Uganda." Paper presented to the Seminar on Human Rights and Democracy in East Africa, Växjo University, Växjo, 24–26 August.

Obbo, C. 1980. *African Women in Towns*. London: Zed Press.

———. 1989. "Women, Children and the 'Living Wage'." In H.B. Hansen and M.

Twaddle, *Changing Uganda* (London: James Currey/Kampala: Fountain Press/ Athens, OH: Ohio U.P./Nairobi: Heinemann Kenya), pp. 98–112.

Oloka-Onyango, J. 1989. "Law and 'Grassroots Democracy' and the National Resistance Movement in Uganda." *International Journal of the Sociology of Law* 17.

———. 1991. "Human Rights and the Democratic Question in Uganda." Paper presented at the Uganda Law Society Symposium on the Rule of Law, Justice and Human Rights in Uganda, Kampala, July 18–19, 1991.

Otai, P. 1991. "Arrogance of Power: Uganda Under the National Resistance Movement/Army." Paper delivered to Växjo University Seminar, 24–26 August.

Plender, R. 1972. "The Uganda Crisis and the Right of Expulsion in International Law." *Review of the International Commission of Jurists* 9.

Pratt, R.C., and D.A. Low. 1960. *Buganda and British Overrule*. Oxford University Press.

Rupesinghe, K. 1989. *Conflict Resolution in Uganda*. London: James Currey/Oslo: PRIO/Athens, OH: Ohio State U.P.

Ruzindana, A. 1990. "Corruption and Mismanagement in Government." In Sempangi, 1979.

Scotton, J.F. 1970. "Judicial Independence and Political Expression – Two Colonial Legacies." *East African Law Journal* 6/1 (March), pp. 1–19.

Semakula-Kiwanuka, M. 1974. "The Diplomacy of Lost Counties and Its Impact on the Foreign Relations of Buganda, Bunyoro and the Rest of Uganda 1960–1964." *Mawazo* (Makerere University) 4/2.

Sempangi, K. 1979. *Reign of Terror, Reign of Love*. Glendale, CA: Regal Books.

Senghaas, D. 1981. "The Specific Contribution of Peace Research to the Analysis of the Causes of Social Violence: Transdisciplinarity." In Domenach et al., 1981.

Syahuka, M. 1991. *The Rwenzururu Movement and the Democratic Struggle*. Kampala: Centre for Basic Research.

Tadria, H. 1987. "Changes and Continuities in the Position of Women in Uganda." In P.D. Wiebe and C.P. Dodge: *Beyond Crisis: Development Issues in Uganda*. Kampala: Makerere Institute of Social Research.

Tandon, Y. 1989. *Militarism and Peace Education in Africa*. Nairobi: African Association for Literacy and Adult Education.

Thomas, H.B. 1951. *The Story of Uganda*. Oxford University Press.

Twaddle, M. 1975. *Expulsion of a Minority*. London: Athlone Press.

Uganda Government. 1945. *Report of the Commission of Inquiry into the Disturbances which Occurred in Uganda During January 1945* (N.H.P. Whitley, Commissioner). Entebbe: Government Printer.

———. 1949. *Report of the Commission of Inquiry into the Disturbances in Uganda during April 1949* (D. Kingdon, Commissioner). Entebbe: Government Printer.

———. 1960. *Report of the Commission of Inquiry into the Disturbances in the Eastern Province 1960*. Entebbe: Government Printer.

———. 1962a. *The Uganda Independence Constitution 1962*. Entebbe: Government Printer.

———. 1962b. Mr Justice J. Jones, *The Report of the Commission of Inquiry into the Recent Disturbances Among the Bamba and Bakonjo People of Toro*. Entebbe: Government Printer.

———. 1965. *Report of the Commission on Marriage, Divorce and Status of Women in Uganda*, under the Chairmanship of Hon. W.W. Kalema MP. Entebbe: Government Printer.

————. 1966. *The Constitution of Uganda (15th April, 1966).* Entebbe: Government Printer.

————. 1967. *The Constitution of the Republic of Uganda, 1967.* Entebbe: Government Printer.

————. 1970. Ministry of Planning and Economic Development. *Design of Development for Karamoja District 1970–1971.* Entebbe: Government Printer.

————. 1971. Mr Justice J. Jones, *Commission of Inquiry into Allegations Made by the Late Daudi Ochieng on 4th February 1966. Evidence and Findings.* Kampala: Ministry of Internal Affairs/Uganda Publishing House.

————. 1972a. Immigration (Cancellation of Entry Permits and Certificates of Residence) Decree 1972 (Decree No. 17 of 1972). Entebbe: Government Printer.

————. 1972b. Mr Justice J. Jones, *Report of the Commission of Inquiry into the Missing Americans Messrs Stroh and Siedle, held at the Conference Room, Parliament House, Kampala,* and *Government White Paper on the Report of the Commission of Inquiry.* Entebbe: Government Printer.

————. 1975. Mr Justice M. Saied, C.J., *Report of the Commission of Inquiry into the Disappearances of Persons in Uganda since 25th January 1971.* Kampala, June.

————. 1979. Uganda Liberation Front, *Basic Documents of the UNLF.* Kampala.

————. 1980. *Report of the Electoral Commission, 1980.* Entebbe: Government Printer.

————. 1982. Census Office, Ministry of Planning and Economic Development, *Report of the 1980 Population Census,* vol. I.

————. 1985. *Uganda Country Paper. UN Decade for Women to Nairobi World Conference,* July. Entebbe: Government Printer.

————. 1986. Code of Conduct of the National Resistance Army, appended to Legal Notice no. 1 of 1986 and Legal Notice no. 6 of 1986. Entebbe: Government Printer.

————. 1991. *Budget Speech 1991/92* by Dr C.W.C.B. Kiyonga, Minister of Finance. Entebbe: Government Printer.

————. n.d. Uganda Protectorate Statistics Branch, Ministry of Economic Affairs, *Uganda Census 1959: African Population.* Entebbe: Government Printer.

Uganda National Liberation Front (UNLF). 1979. *Basic Documents of the UNLF.* Kampala.

UNICEF. 1989. *Children and Women in Uganda: A Situation Analysis.* Kampala: UNICEF.

Wamy, 1991. *Another Blow to Islam and Muslims.* Wamy, Nairobi.

Watson, C. 1991. *Exile from Rwanda: Background to an Invasion.* Washington, DC: US Committee on Refugees.

Welch, C.P. 1969. "Pastoralists and Administrators in Conflict: A Study of Karamoja District 1897–1968." M.A. thesis, University of East Africa.

Weldon, T.D. 1953. *The Vocabulary of Politics.* Harmondsworth: Penguin.

Wellbourn, F.B. 1965. *Religion and Politics in Uganda, 1952–1962.* Nairobi: East African Publishing House.

Wilson, J.Q. 1968. "Violence." In D. Bell, *Towards the Year 2000: Work in Progress.* Boston: Beacon Press.

Winter, R. 1983. *Refugees in Uganda and Rwanda: The Banyarwandan Tragedy.* Washington, DC; US Committee on Refugees.

World Bank. 1989. *Sub-Saharan Africa: From Crisis to Sustainable Growth: A Long Term Perspective Study.* Washington, DC: World Bank.

7

Violence and the welfare state: The case of Venezuela as an oil country

Luis Pedro España N.

The last time Venezuela made headlines in the international press on some issue other than oil was early in 1989, with the spontaneous rioting and the subsequent looting of business establishments in the principal cities of the nation. A reporter for *Die Stuttgarter Zeitung* spent those days on the streets of Caracas and interviewing experts on the causes of this unusual outburst of violence. He discovered that a country that international press agencies regarded as boring could suddenly capture worldwide interest in a moment of social upheaval rare in the Caribbean.

For the 25 years preceding the upheaval, Venezuela's population had had no idea of what was meant by suspension of constitutional rights, state of exception, or the breakdown of life's daily routines – and even less of the anxiety and tension produced by the explosion of explicit violence. Since the restoration of democracy in 1958, and, more recently, with the oil "boom" during the 1970s, Venezuela had been seen as a small, rich country, free of major economic problems thanks to its energy resources, and without those linguistic, religious, and racial conflicts that usually resolve themselves through violence. From the mid-1940s on, that picture of a rich country without problems was the image of Venezuela accepted abroad. It did have a basis in fact: in 1939 Venezuela had a per capita income 26 per cent higher than Latin America in general. Ten years later it was 70 per cent higher, and by 1980 it was 80 per cent above the Latin American average.[1] By 1976 Venezuela had the highest per capita income in Latin America, enjoyed a strong democratic political system, presented indices of strikes and work stoppages that were the envy of many developed countries, and conducted its international relations in a context of cooperation and understanding.

Although the nation was as yet far from overcoming the consequences of underdevelopment – characterized by widespread poverty and extremes of social inequality – its social indices were still among the best in comparison with other countries of equal or greater economic development in the area. Thus, in the mid-1970s, Venezuela occupied second place among Latin American nations with regard to percentage of population in urban areas, third place as regards ratio of population per doctor, fifth place in provision of hospital beds, seventh in literacy and life expectancy, and tenth in consumption of calories and proteins.[2]

While Venezuela showed considerable gains in the context of Latin America, the copious flow of income from oil suggested a level of prosperity much better than that enjoyed by most of the population. Nevertheless, the dominant political discourse, public consciousness, and the general experience of upward social mobility all seemed to indicate that it was only a question of time before social and economic growth reached every sector of society. Such expectations, reasonably held by the great majority of the nation's sectors, and a political system that guaranteed the inclusion of all major social interests permitted 30 years of solid peace under a democratic system.

Even with the windfall of the 1973–1981 annual oil income of 12 billion dollars for a population of 14 million, the crisis of the 1980s dislocated much of the solid base that had kept Venezuela free from the conflicts undergone by other countries of the continent. In every area of activity – economically, with the debt crisis and the drop in oil income; politically, with the breakdown of normal channels for settling differences of interest; and socially, with the abrupt lowering of living standards – expectations of progress and well-being which had been constantly nourished since the first years of democracy progressively gave way to disappointment and uncertainty. Since that time, Venezuelan society has been subjected to serious changes, readjustments, and reformulations of what had been the initial democratic political project. In the course of adapting to necessities quite distinct from those envisaged when oil appeared during the first third of this century, social conflicts and tensions have emerged, often

179

seeking outlet in non-institutional ways that contribute to the growth of social violence in Venezuela. This process is still, perhaps, in its initial stages, and its outcome is difficult to predict. It leads us to a discussion of the problem of violence in Venezuela and the reasons for its recent emergence just when we thought that the country's long history of open violence was a thing of the past.

From *montoneras* to the public monopoly of violence

The history of the Venezuelan republic, for the most part, shows a country plagued by successive wars and their resolutions. In addition to the generally pauperized condition of the nation in the early nineteenth century, the dissolution of the colonial institutions and order meant for the new independent republic of 1830 a long period of political violence dominated by warlords (*caudillos*) who, with their rebel armies (*montoneras*), endangered succeeding legitimate governments. If we consider that the consolidation of the republican state – in the Weberian sense of the state as monopolizer of violence – was achieved only at the end of the nineteenth century, it is no surprise that the use of direct violence was the normal means of deciding who would be in power. The impossibility of the central government's being able to exercise control over the non-metropolitan areas meant that the new political order which succeeded the colonial order was weak and piecemeal, beholden to the loyalty of local chieftains and dependent for its continuity on its capacity to defeat by arms the revolts of these chieftains who broke alliances and marched against Caracas.[3]

Thus, in nineteenth-century Venezuela, the only known mechanism for succession in power was armed revolution and palace plots. It was only with the real unification of the nation and the institutionalization of violence as the exclusive right of the state that violence no longer formed part of the country's daily routine. The gradual shaping of the nation, partly through force of arms and partly through the establishment of economic and political mechanisms that transferred power from local bosses to central channels, made it possible for violence in Venezuela to cease being in this hands of private actors. According to Juan Vicente Gómez, the last of the *caudillos* (1908–1935): "Venezuela ceased being a dry piece of leather that when stepped on here pops up there." However, this does not mean that political violence disappeared. The despotic state, as a first version of the modern instrument for monopolizing violence, knows no limits in the use of violence, and its total control prevents the citizenry from calculating when and why violence may be used against them.

However, in spite of the absence of limits on the state's power and on the use of its prerogatives, and the absence of any guarantee that it will not employ excessive force against opponents, the public monopoly of violence remains the basic condition for a nation's pacification. This is so because, as the order which comes from the state's monopoly of violence becomes institutionalized, this monopoly tends to set its own norms, become predictable, and even achieve formal legalization, thus effectively putting limits on the violence of the state. The state's monopoly on violence, eliminating its private use with impunity, occurred in Venezuela before oil began to dominate the country's economic relations. When the nation was unified effectively, toward the end of the nineteenth century, the state did not yet depend on the economic power coming from oil in order to assume a monopoly of violence. On the contrary, it was because the state had already achieved control of the nation that the government was able, at the start of oil-related activity, to share in the business and enjoy the resources which made it the distributor of the country's principal wealth, with a common goal that was to characterize contemporary Venezuelan history: the modernization of the country.

Overcoming the principal cause of political violence, the *caudillismo*, brought about the conditions for crystallizing the objective of the Venezuelan ideologists of the late nineteenth and early twentieth centuries. Modernization, which for these ideologists meant the passage from "barbaric" to "civilized" society, would signify the overcoming of other less direct forms of violence which kept the nation from advancing and its people on the edge of subsistence. The process of civilization was simply the gradual transformation of the prevailing "backward" society and its subsistence economy into a modern society with a manufacturing economy, capable of transforming the physical world and changing people's ways of thinking, acting, and speaking through education. This desire to transform the semi-feudal social relations of the country was to form the new century's main project, also changing the structural forms of violence in Venezuela.

Underground "manna" and the promise of modernization

The Castro–Gómez period (1898–1935) saw the end of the local warlords and the divided political system which produced the extreme violence and social breakdown that characterized nineteenth-century Venezuela. While it was Cipriano Castro (1898–1908) who defeated the last of the important local warlords and established himself as supreme head of government, it was during the 28 years of Juan Vicente Gómez's regime that the central power of the state was firmly consolidated. In the same period, the project of transforming Venezuela would take on the positivist ideals of "order and progress." Order was guaranteed by the figure of the dictator running a centralized structure. He was the *gendarme nécessaire*, maintaining order as the initial condition for any civilizing transformation. Positivism's determinist evolution was under way![4]

Although the presumed need for "order" became the ideological justification for the tyrannical regime of Gómez, the important thing was that the project of modernization did not come to an end with his death. The politicians who followed him, and the social process they brought about, carried on the ideas of progress and modernization, although all would hold themselves philosophically aloof from the tenets of *gomecismo*.[5]

When the dictator died in 1936, Venezuela was experiencing the impulse of modernizing change. With the opening of political debate under civil-military governments less intolerant than that of Gómez, the national project of modernization ceased to be élitist and extended to the masses. Incipient political groupings, formed in exile under the dictatorship, began to develop the debate, each designing its own project for the nation. The different political forces anxious to lead the country offered a great variety of options: Marxist, reformist, and even *gomecista*. Regardless of their diverse ideologies, all were to coincide in the two elements that would form the base of what has been Venezuela's political project up to the present. Of course, differences in their ideologies, methods, and styles meant that their political platforms were far from identical.

The first element, a legacy of Gómez, was the notion of modernization; the second, owing to the characteristics which the Venezuelan state acquired, was the dominant role of government in directing the development of the nation. Little need be added about the first element, development and modernization. Suffice it to say that different political currents proposed slower or more drastic advances in the political sphere, that is, in the establishment of an open society where widely varying social forces would participate; as regards socio-economic modernization there were no major differences. Two existing conditions guaranteed the second element, the state as director of the modernizing plan. First, the state, once consolidated, became the only organized social space in society and thus the sole sector from which change could be brought about. The other sectors of what we would today call civil society had no organic structures, except for a few élitist groups organized into political parties opposing the government élite. Second, the state's central role was assured by its control of the initial oil income. By this time oil already represented the main source of income for the nation; the infrastructures of production that had been created with the concessions of the 1910s and '20s were now fully set up and in operation. Thus oil was already an alternative for financing development.

It was precisely the idea of modernizing the country under the aegis of the state that made oil the privileged source of income for Venezuela. With the arrival of the transnational companies at the start of the century, the conditions for granting rights concessions changed as the government élites designed new ways of entering into the oil business. Since conditions in the country did not permit a role in production and there was little likelihood of Venezuela's participating as direct producer or consumer, the path chosen was that of handing down concessions. The Venezuelan state, as proprietor of the oil resources, would demand from the direct producer suitable remuneration for the extraction of its resources. The government wanted the state to share in what the oil companies earned from the sale of oil on the world market. Naturally, this participation by the state as proprietor of the oil fields was not present from the start. That would require the development of a rent-consciousness among the governing classes, and was determined by many factors: competition among the companies seeking concessions and, more important, the possibility that the state could count on money from the oil contracts to accelerate the country's modernization.[6]

Herein lay the source of the ultimate justification for the confrontations between the proprietor-state and the foreign companies, the attempts by the state to maximize the income from concessions in order to accelerate the development of productive and social forces of a backward country in the first third of this century. That confrontation clearly defined the interests of the Venezuelan oil sector, beginning in 1943 with the *Ley de Hidrocarburos*, whereby the transnational companies recognized the right of the proprietor to exact payment for its resources. From then on, Venezuela defined its oil profile and policy and the use of these resources for its modernization.

Oil income can thus be seen to serve a double function. On the one hand, it was the source of accumulating capital to provide for private and public investment; on the other, it allowed for the distribution of income for the improvement of life for the general population. This included the transformation of the physical environment, the creation of infrastructures for urbanizing the country, and the betterment of the population's health, education, and nutrition. The result was that in less than five decades, from 1920 to the start of the 1970s, the country was to change radically, but with social costs and levels of open violence far below those usually accompanying such rapid processes of social change.

Oil is not the whole story

It could be said that modernization in Venezuela from 1920 to 1976 had its basis in oil revenues. The magnitude of this process is apparent today in every walk of life, and the experience of modernization appears to have been successful, despite the problems and maladjustments that it provoked – indeed, to have been Venezuela's most important national achievement so far.

In that period Venezuela ceased to be a principally rural country. Today, 82 per cent of its population is urban. Economic growth reached 3.9 per cent per annum, while that of the industrialized economies of the world reached 2.1 per cent. Real wages grew by 3.8 per cent a year, while those in Latin America as a whole grew by only 2.1 per cent and in developed countries by 3.1 per cent. Illiteracy virtually disappeared and levels of school attendance grew; more than 80 per cent of children of school age attended both elementary and high school. At the same time, all health services improved, and endemic illnesses, which had afflicted broad sectors of the population, tended to disappear.[7] "The process cost not a single life." On the contrary, these changes contributed greatly to enhancing the chances of living for all Venezuelans. Their quality of life got better and better and their individual rights came to be within their reach.

Although political modernization lagged behind the rapid socio-economic advances, the transformation to a democratic state from an authoritarian one entailed much less violence than in other countries of Latin America. From 1936, when democracy began, until 1958, when its definitive consolidation took place, many obstacles had to be overcome; but, in comparison with other forms of government, that was no doubt that this one demanded less violence to guarantee its maintenance. On the contrary, the transition from authoritarianism to democracy took place through negotiation between divergent interests, who reached agreement without civil wars or armed confrontations such as had happened in the nineteenth century.

From 1936 to 1945 the opposition was entirely of a civilian nature. Political life was expressed in the encounter between leaders and people and the first attempts to organize workers, peasants, students, and even entrepreneurs. With the exception of some cases of exile carried out under the López Contreras regime (1936–1941) as a deterrent to the regime's political opponents, it was not until 1945 that a section of the military, allied with the emerging political party Acción Democrática, carried out a successful *coup d'état* on 18 October. This event initiated the first fully democratic experiment during the following three years (1945–1948).

However, this pact between young military men and social democratic leaders did not last long, and on 24 November 1948 Rómulo Gallegos, the writer who had won a landslide victory in the first direct presidential elections on an Acción Democrática ticket, was toppled by the same military who had reached a coalition with his party three years previously. The coup marked the beginning of the last dictatorship. It lasted ten years, until a popular revolt brought it down on 23 January 1958.

During his eight years in office, Marcos Pérez Jiménez (1950–1958) led a carefully selective violence against democratic political leaders and tried to dismember every kind of voluntary association. He went too far, however, and his allies of the first years – the Church, the businessmen, and sectors of the armed forces – abandoned him. From that moment on his fate was sealed, and the pacts and negotiations that were to became a feature of the Venezuelan democratic process began.[8]

The consolidation of democracy, although it was not without its problems, guaranteed that socio-economic transformations took place. The fact that the dictatorship had based its legitimacy on the expansion of economic well-being imposed on democracy the obligation to prove that it could do it better, and emphasis was put on political liberties and not only on economic matters. Normalcy was imposed on the political succession – no small achievement! – and on the non-violent solution of conflicts. The issue of oil, in the meantime, lay in the background of these events.

"Happy democracy"

Democracy as a political system is characterized by the creation of a set of procedures and institutions whose ultimate end is to solve conflicts, differences, and dissent through peaceful means. Democracy can thus be construed as the political entity which guarantees the least violence in social relations. Democracy and the democratic process mean that social unrest is out of the question.

In Venezuela, the consolidation of a democratic system from 1958 onward, where political rights for citizens were the norm, where there existed individual liberties for the exercise of those rights, and where the presence of an electoral system guaranteed peaceful accession to power, was achieved thanks to agreement worked out by the main power groups in the country.[9]

With the so-called Pact of Punto Fijo, the main democratic parties – Acción Democrática, the Social Christian COPEI (Comité de Organización Política Electoral Independiente), and the Unión Republicana Demócrata – together with the armed forces, the Catholic Church, the businessmen's organization Fedecamaras, and the rest of those civil associations "connected to the political parties," formed a democratic bloc that was to back the building of the newly-won democratic political system. The pact between workers and entrepreneurs and the arrival at a *modus vivendi* with the Vatican facilitated the absence of strikes and ensured the Church's goodwill toward the new system. Consensus among partners was achieved through negotiation. Any conflicts that arose between them were worked out in this way and the maintenance of democracy became a desideratum for everyone concerned. This inclusiveness was very strong in the first two presidential periods, those of Rómulo Betancourt (1959–1964) and Raúl Leoni (1964–1969). These were coalition regimes, despite the obvious and overwhelming majority of Acción Democrática deputies, and they tried very carefully not to exclude any party, except the "subversive" left, from government. Exclusion was a dirty word!

But the most radicalized leftist groups were excluded from this "pacted democracy." This was the price to be paid by the new system in order to keep the support of the conservative groups, which were still very powerful and would not have participated if the "commies" – the Partido Comunista de Venezuela (PCV) – were included. It was only a matter of time, therefore, before the latter joined the armed struggle. The emergence of the Cuban Revolution accelerated such a possibility. For five years armed struggle was the path chosen by the left and imposed by the intransigence of the Betancourt administration.

By 1962, however, it was clear to everyone that the Fuerzas Armadas Revolucionaras (FAR) had been badly beaten, and the FAR's appeal for electoral abstention was totally ignored at the polls in December 1963. But it was not until 1968 that president-elect Rafael Caldera, the first Social Christian to win the presidency, began his peace-making policies. During his five-year administration, slowly but surely, the left re-entered the political arena through the formation of recognized and legitimate political parties. By 1973 they went to the polls like any other political party.

The military and political defeat of the armed struggle sustained by the left meant the consolidation of democracy. It was obvious that the population did not back armed rebellion, and the pacts agreed upon by the rest of the political spectrum never came into question. The new political system, therefore, was seen to be definitive and to have proved its staying power. As for the left, only one way was left open. Either it accepted the system or it would face certain extinction. The system, on the other hand, had its existence guaranteed thanks to the acceptance of the political agreements which lay at its foundations. It also drew its strength from its constant willingness to compromise and from the fact that any political party could enforce compromise if necessary. No discernible threat lay on the horizon.

The government's commitment to action rested upon two assumptions which became policies for different administrations: (*a*) the idea of sustained economic growth, and (*b*) the guarantee that all social sectors would partake of the benefits of such growth. It was necessary for the oil state to intervene in order to ensure that benefits reached everyone. Such promises were possible in Venezuela because it had become a peculiar kind of welfare state. The fact that oil income was a transfer of money from buyers to Venezuela as a country meant that oil became a national resource capable of satisfying the enormous demands that the people made on the political system. Venezuela could meet such demands without having to exact resources from any group in particular. Social peace, therefore, cost no one but the oil buyers. The Venezuelan democratic state did not have to depend on anyone to finance social demands. Thus it could enjoy considerable freedom in deciding on the use of its resources and could placate those demands, no matter how urgent they were, or how divergent from one group to another. It became possible for no one to lose out in the process.

Thanks to its financial autonomy and the amount of its revenues, therefore, the democratic state could subsidize producers while maintaining low and stable prices to consumers. The public sector, moreover, took charge of many functions – social as well as economic – according to distributive criteria, maintaining a set of stimuli designed to improve economic growth and proceeding to control the economy, while all the time making sure no one would lose. The capacity to do this endeared the democratic state to the people and won it the loyalty of the population. The distributive character of public spending, accompanied by the client system favoured by the political parties in power, imposed a "paternalistic" state, whose public policies were designed with this character in mind.

The fact that the state received the oil revenues directly and then proceeded to distribute them throughout the body politic imposed on it a double mission: to modernize the country and to keep social conflicts at bay. It dedicated all its energies to those ends. Society, in the meantime, was delighted for the state to assume such a role. Nevertheless, it was inevitable that a system which guaranteed a public behaviour that did not create losers, but at worst unequal winners, should reach a point where social demands surpassed the availability both of economic resources, coming mainly from the oil fields, and of political resources, which had hitherto enabled the state either to satisfy or to postpone such demands.

The scheme of democratic modernization itself rested on oil revenues. In the absence of any threat, it did not look for a viable alternative if things should change. It did not seek to create an equilibrium between demands and resources beyond oil-generated wealth. The multiplication of demanding actors led to an overworked state which did not have to hand institutionalized channels for responding to those demands. This led to crisis, and reaccommodations were necessary in order to build a new model of economic and social development.

For the reasons mentioned above this could not be an easy task. In the long term, the "happy democracy" had a limit beyond which it could not go. Even if the oil revenues had kept growing at a normal rate, the exponential growth of social demands due to the increase in social heterogeneity, typical of any modernizing process, would have made the oil revenues useless for the task of attenuating social conflicts. The only way open to the state was to design other means for the control of social demands that were both peaceful and acceptable to all. Reality, however, did not work that way. External debt and constantly falling oil prices accelerated the crisis and compromised "the two feet of the Venezuelan democratic system": unlimited economic growth and the continued enjoyment of it by all Venezuelans.

Dream, awakening, and reality

From the late sixties onward it was clear to everyone that the economic system based on oil was coming to a "dead end." An economy which was open to imports and, with the exception of oil, closed to exports, and which had been so designed by the interaction of many different mechanisms for the distribution of oil revenues, such as the overvalued bolívar, led the system toward disinvestment, low productivity, and capital flight.[10] Such a situation had been envisaged well before the "oil boom" of the seventies. It had been a part of the national rhetoric from the very moment that oil revenues became the core of the economy during the 1940s. The so-called "sowing of oil" had been a classic piece of national rhetoric. At the same time, no group in the country had ever presented a model any different from the one which had been presented after the death of the dictator Gómez and rewritten at the beginning of the democratic era. It was abundantly clear, as the crisis of the eighties showed, that the "oil dream" would remain in place until it became impossible.

Catastrophe was avoided during the seventies, thanks to the Middle East crisis in the early years of the decade. The fourfold rise in the price of oil provoked spectacular growth in Venezuela's export revenues. The political system was thus granted a breathing space, in which it inevitably overemphasized the use of those revenues to placate social demands and postpone conflicts. At the same time, part of the revenues went to finance ambitious development projects in basic industries – iron, aluminium, and hydroelectricity – which were presented as viable alternatives for oil.

During this period the system became obsessed with economics. The oversupply of oil revenues gave rise to the idea that "the economy was the locomotive to pull the political and social wagons." And yet the way the political system had been working over the years left little room for manoeuvre if the revenues should fall. The possibility of resolving conflicts by means of "indiscriminate gratification" pushed the system toward its closure, a stage in which the decision-making process would be elaborated exclusively by the élites and the mechanisms of universal representation decayed. Power became concentrated in fewer hands and the political parties transformed into élites without links to the population – a situation known as *cogollocracia*, government by the party bosses. Elections held only every five years meant promises that went unfulfilled every five years, and the paraphernalia of presidential candidacies consisted of hundreds of "party stalwarts" but no real representation.[11]

Crisis point was reached on the infamous "Black Friday" in 1983, when the international banking establishment refused any more credits and the state suddenly found itself without money. The fact that since 1979 Venezuela had had negative economic growth added further problems; the net result was that, for the second time in the democratic era, the bolívar was devalued, inflation mounted, and public investment halted and then declined. By 1986, three years later, oil prices had descended even further, falling to $10 per barrel from the $34 paid in 1981. Economic crisis became an entirely structural problem, going far beyond the mere ups and downs of oil prices on the international market. It was abundantly clear that the former economic model, and with it the national project of a "happy democracy," was at an end.

The fall in revenues "blew away" everything the last thirty years had kept "safe." The political system began to show its intolerance, its inability to solve conflicts in any other way than by handing out money to anyone who presented a grievance and who had any political backing. Dissent, as a distinctive element in any mature democracy, had no place in the web of pacts and agreements elaborated during the "fat years." Discredit and low prestige became the normal attitude toward every national institution.

In social terms, the panorama was more critical. Beginning in 1981, the real wage decreased notably, reaching levels lower than those of 1968.[12] Poverty increased, to encompass over 70 per cent of the population, and – more importantly – expectations of climbing higher on the social ladder were no longer part of the ordinary aspirations of Venezuelans. In view of this social deterioration, the infrastructure of the state was not capable of compensating or guaranteeing social services beyond putting price controls on basic items. Health, education, and other public services diminished at the same pace as the income of the state, with ever-increasing public expenditure in recent years.

Thus, the crisis had global implications, which went beyond the economic to touch the political and social levels and generated drastic measures that undermined the very bases guaranteed by the democratic system.

Violence is discovered again

The panorama described above can be identified as partially responsible for producing the conditions capable of upsetting the social and political order. The possibility that the crisis would curtail the democratic process became a very real alternative, in view of the drastic changes and the end of the prosperity generated by oil. However, only a simplistic determinism would argue that the degree of prosperity is directly proportional to the degree of democracy within a society. On the contrary, the Venezuelan experience has shown that the greater the oil bonanza, the narrower the space for dissent and the fewer the channels of access to the decision-making process.

An economic crisis, to liquidate the democratic stability of a country, would have to be accompanied by the political conditions sufficient to achieve such a purpose. These conditions do not seem to be present in Venezuela. A fundamental condition for compromising the continuance of a political system is the existence of a clear disloyal opposition to the established order. By "disloyal opposition" we mean those political groupings whose actions are intended to destroy the rules of the political game established by the system. If these actions are not present, popular discontent and conflict resulting from economic conditions will not harm the political order. Even supposing the existence of such opponents, only by channelling the chief power blocs in the direction of their interest – that is, if the disloyal opposition is seen, rightly or not, as the solution to the problems – will the established order be seriously jeopardized. In democracies, disloyal opponents who have been successful in undermining the system have not, to date, come from the masses but rather from the élite. No democracy has ever fallen through a popular revolution. Rather, democracies have fallen through alliances of élites with the armed forces.[13] In all cases, conservative élites look to the military either to re-establish order or to act as mediators for democratic governments unable to maintain order in a state of violence.

In the case of Venezuela, this political condition does not seem to be present at the time of writing (mid-1991). The country does not seem to have disloyal opponents, and the few that exist are insufficient to upset the established order. As a historical hypothesis, if the present socio-economic conditions had been present in the 1960s, the Venezuelan democracy would perhaps not have survived. But that is not the present reality: the Venezuelan political system has destroyed such opposition groups and no alternatives exist today to unite or inspire the sympathy of the population. Likewise there are no élite groups of a kind which would be determinant in the final analysis. The present crisis puts at risk the continuity of the current government, which has provided more peace for the country through indirect violence resulting from the increase in poverty. However, this aspect has not acquired a political dimension, as no social sector of importance identifies the rules of the democratic game as the cause of the problem. This seems to be the guarantee of stability, though one should be aware of the possibility of a *coup d'état*, in which the last to know are always the analysts and the ordinary citizens.

For these reasons, political violence has not reappeared in Venezuela, but social violence has. Beyond the implicit violence caused by the poverty and the limited possibilities of Venezuelans today to upgrade socially, a direct social violence has been unleashed, in a disorganized way and with the sole objective of enhancing personal benefits. This direct violence is characterized by delinquency, self-defence, taking advantage of the defenceless, the invasion of others' property and rights, a system of complicity, lack of justice, and generalized fear among ordinary citizens.

On the other hand, and within the context mentioned above, the increase in crime and violent social relations between citizens has presented problems which seem under control in Venezuela. This is the case with drug trafficking, which has infiltrated both the political and judicial institutions as a method developed for the drug-dealers and in other continental societies for social pseudo-legitimacy.

With the lack of credible political alternatives intended to set in motion a new social project that embraces a collective hope that the present situation can be overcome, the severe change resulting from a depressed economy has stimulated innovations by individuals seeking methods to obtain the objective – seemingly an acquired right – of economic success. Such innovations in method – conceived of by Robert Merton as a cause of deviant conduct – are not only on the margins of formal legality, but also presuppose a disproportionate increase in the use of violence in social relations.

If we study the statistics regarding delinquent acts involving direct physical violence against the victim, taking into account the tendency towards very low estimates due to under-reporting of crimes which is a feature of police statistics, the figures show that in 1989 two out of every hundred people were victims of delinquent violence. If this crime rate is maintained this year – which is unlikely, taking into account the registered increase in violent crime of 71 per cent since the beginning of the crisis – a Venezuelan is likely to become the subject of violent crime 1.5 times during his or her lifetime, with a 1.03 per cent probability of loss of life.[14] Some sociologists, using these figures, suggest that the listing of murders over a weekend in Monday's newspapers constitute veritable "war dispatches". This has brought the attention of the populace, according to each one's economic possibilities, to the development of self-defence mechanisms. Privately, some organized communities are contracting or forming defence groups ready to use necessary force for their own protection. This, however, merely promotes violent relations in a national population which is already violent.

The large-scale expression of unorganized social violence – which is without collective objectives, as opposed to political, religious, or nationalist violence – was evidenced in the social explosion of 27–8 February 1989. Today, given the strong methods of reprisal utilized to restore order, this unorganized violence shows up in the individual, unrestrained criminal instinct. Thus, in analysing the causes provoking this social explosion, we see that the immediate motivation is the individual and personal response; structural features of the social and political order can be identified as causes only at a deeper level, below the surface. Since the alarming increase in daily violence in Venezuela – as a phenomenon embracing common crime, repression, and other, less defined kinds of violence, such as profit-seeking and corruption – originates in the globality of the economic crisis in the country, and in the relative change from bonanza to depression, the reduction of the violence to "normal" levels probably requires the resolution of the macro-social problems which gave rise to it. In this sense, police protection or state repression in some way determine the limit, or the privileged action, of the new process of peace-building in Venezuela.

The time of adjustment, or violence as transition

The increased daily violence in Venezuela has two aspects, springing from the same origin. The first is that violence which endangers people's very lives. The second, less evident than the first, is the violence that occurs when the rights of others are not respected by those in positions of privilege or individual power which enable them to act in spite of institutionality, overriding what is legal and violating the concept of equality of all citizens. The origin of both these aspects of violence can be seen in the deepening or globalization of the Venezuelan crisis, which not only entails the increase of poverty and the steady descent of all social strata into lower classes, but also has extended to a decaying of the level of institutionality of the system and a loss of credibility of its methods of resolving conflicts and disputes. In tracing the rise of daily violence – specifically, violence in the Venezuelan and Latin American context – according to these two levels the two problems do not necessarily have to be seen as separate. On the contrary, delinquency as much as the violation of rights can be analysed as a consequence of the failure of Venezuela's social project and its crisis.

Relationships of causality between poverty and daily violence are by no means a new discovery in the social sciences. Although this constant is evident, it can lead to two extreme positions as solutions for resolution of the problem. One position supposes that it is only by acting on the principle underlying the problem that one can combat this violence. This means that only by doing away with poverty as a social reality can concrete steps be taken to eradicate street violence. Such a perspective implies paralysing society as a whole and its public institutions in particular, in the hope that a reconstruction of society might occur further down the line. The other perspective is repressive and is located within the increase in social control by the police. Striving for this short-term gratification would require the militarization of society and would thus increase the very violence the approach aims to combat, by carrying social control, as a prophylaxis or as repression, to the extreme. Moreover, this kind of action would in no way correct the daily violence that arises from the invasion of others' rights, especially with the aim of gaining some advantage or benefit over others.

There is no doubt that the state should keep its control of violence, whether to confront political threats or to prevent private sectors from exercising their self-defence. If it does not do so, order may be secured, in either case, but at the risk of unforeseen consequences. According to this view, under Venezuela's present conditions, the state should increase its protection of people and their rights, with the aim being to avoid the further privatization of violence or the institutional order's continued failure to defend those rights. Neither the defence of one's rights nor self-defence against delinquency can acceptably be assured by obtaining privileges, in the former case, or by the construction of private "bunkers", in the latter. The new peace process in Venezuela should be one in which, at the micro level, the state guarantees public security and exercises its legitimate control of violence. But it should act at the same time on reforms at the macro level. The state should convert itself into an instrument of compulsion that does not go beyond the principle of the democratic state. Thus, in the long term, the ending of daily violence – or at least its reduction to tolerable levels – requires the recovery of democracy's promises, so that the collectivity may re-experience the possibility of a better future, and the strengthening of its institutionality, so that privilege will not become the way to defend oneself or to attack.

Setting the problem in its macro-social dimension, it can be said that, in the field of economic relations, the solution is not in doubt. There is no space here to describe in detail the principles underlying the hypothesis that the country has a way of getting out of the crisis in its strictly economic dimension; but one can say that the proposed changes in the economic sphere, together with the development and fruitful diversification of the country's main economic activity, oil, offer grounds for belief in the future growth of the economy. Nevertheless, if the country cannot find a way out of its social and political problems, however great its economic growth, it will not automatically become a more democratic country or a more equitable one in terms of its social conditions. Economic development is not the basis of democratization, and there are noteworthy examples of this in the rest of Latin America, such as Brazil and, more recently, Chile. Similarly, the best social policies will not result from economic growth if there are no guarantees that the benefits of growth will be transferred to the different social sectors.

The social and political problems that Venezuela faces, which are the origin of the current increase in disorganized violence, do not appear to have any prospect of solution. On the social side, there is the loss of the state's capacity to act as a benefactor by resolving, compensating for, or diminishing social evils, since it has not been able to overcome the structural impediments that it had been able to hide thanks to the oil revenue. On the political side, there is more and more institutional deterioration: it has now pervaded the political parties, the state agencies, the judicial system, and the political organization of unions, reaching even to the armed forces. Far from being overcome, this deterioration appears to be deepening, in the absence of a new project with the ability to hold the political system together and to have any degree of credibility with the different social forces. The loss of the system's institutionality and of democratic channels for resolving conflicts conveys to the different social forces the message that they must confront each other with only their own naked attributes of power: politicians discredit each other; students demonstrate; businesspeople bribe; workers strike; the police repress; and, in extreme cases, the military takes over.

This situation of non-institutionalization of the social forces is what conspires against the maintenance of non-violent relations in democracy and can bring forth an authoritarian system without even touching or interrupting the constitutional fabric. As we have previously stated, focusing upon social problems and the recuperation of the lost institutionality are clearly bases for building peace in the country.

In terms of the optimistic hypothesis of development we have suggested, one could argue that the increase in daily violence in the two aspects we have discussed above forms part of a process of adjustment which the country is experiencing since the decline in oil revenues. In other words, a certain time is needed for the development of a more viable social project for the country. The construction of a new development paradigm, which supplants that formulated in the middle of the century, has accompanied the unarticulated violence, lacking a structural objective, from which many Venezuelans suffer, but which they will be able to overcome if they are resolved or if the deepest causes of violence are diminished.

However, there is a second, more pessimistic, hypothesis, which in concrete terms would entail taking into account the successes achieved by Venezuelan society in favour of peace. This view is that, in the absence of successful attempts to lessen the social and political crisis of the country, this disorganized violence will acquire the dimensions of social chaos, making it unmanageable within a democratic system and provoking a violent outcome.

At the moment, the outcome according to either hypothesis would seem more or less equally probable. Perhaps this may be the time of transition, albeit a very short time, in which to be able to alter the definitive process in the country. At any rate, it may help to achieve a democratic, and therefore less violent, outcome, the one which seems to be desired by the great majority of Venezuelans, who want Venezuela to continue being the "boring" country of which the German reporter spoke after the painful events of February 1989.

Notes

1. Comisión Económica para América Latina, *Series históricas del crecimiento de América Latina* (Cuadernos Estadísticos de la CEPAL), Santiago de Chile: United Nations, 1978.
2. Banco Mundial, *Informe sobre el desarrollo mundial*, Washington D.C.: World Bank, 1980.
3. Diego Batista Urbaneja, "Pluralismo caudillista", in *Politeia*, Revista de la Facultad de Ciencias Politicas y Jurídicas de la Universidad Central de Venezuela (Caracas: 1975), pp. 53–96.
4. Arturo Sosa A., *El pensamiento político positivista en Venezuela*, Caracas: Centauro, 1985.
5. Arturo Sosa A., "Modernización, programas y sujetos políticos en Venezuela," unpublished document, Caracas, 1984.
6. Asdrúbal Baptista and Bernard Mommer, "Renta petrolera y distribución factorial del ingreso," in Hans-Peter Nissen and Bernard Mommer, *Adios a la bonanza? Crisis de la distribución del ingreso en Venezuela* (Caracas: Ildis-Cendes, Editorial Nueva Sociedad, 1989) pp. 15–40; Luis Pedro España, *Democracia y renta petrolera*, Caracas: UCAB, 1989.
7. Asdrúbal Baptista, "Mas allá del optimismo y del pesimismo: las transformaciones fundamentales del país," in Moisés Naím and Ramón Piñango, *El caso Venezuela, una ilusión de armonía* (Caracas: IESA, 1984), pp. 15–36.
8. Andrés Stambouli, *Crisis política. Venezuela 1945–1958*, Caracas: Ateneo de Caracas, 1980.
9. Daniel Levine, *Conflict and Political Change in Venezuela*, Princeton, NJ: Princeton University Press, 1973.
10. Juan Pablo Pérez Alfonso, *Petróleo y dependencia*, Caracas: Monte Avila Editores, 1971.
11. España, op. cit.
12. Banco Central de Venezuela, *Anuario de cuentas nacionales*, Caracas, various years; Oficina Central de Estadística e Informática, *Encuesta de hogares por muestreo*, Caracas, various years.
13. Juan Linz, *El quiebre de las democracias*, Madrid: Editorial Alianza, 1987.
14. Oficina Central de Estadística e Informática, *Anuario estadístico de Venezuela*, Caracas, various years.

8

State terrorism and death squads in the New World Order

Miles D. Wolpin

If there is one thing that most observers of the "global village" can agree upon in the early 1990s, it is that significant, indeed radical, change is occurring. This affects not only the political balance of power and movements, but also economic systems, ecological stability, and the role of intergovernmental organizations. Few political analysts or "scientists" in the mid-1980s could have predicted the dramatic political and economic transformations that have occurred during the past five years alone. While some previously noted trends continued apace, the unanticipated events are salient reminders that we must be extremely tentative here in prognosticating any future long-term developments.

This necessarily applies to respect for human rights in the political or socio-economic area. While state terrorism properly speaking belongs to the political sphere, it is in some important ways related to the latter. How will be specified shortly. At this point we shall only summarize the thesis that informs this work: that, while the early 1990s will see a modest decline in state terrorism, it will be more pronounced for official violence than for that executed by death squads or vigilantes. This, in turn, is related to *why* an increasing number of states have resorted to such forms of citizen intimidation since the early 1970s. More tentatively, a U-curve is anticipated for death squad salience as the 1990s wear on. More sophisticated indirect links to the state seem likely to appear, as may a rising proportion of state-tolerated or -supported vigilante units organized by ethnic or local interests.

1 Objectives of this analysis

Even if the "New World Order" may be relatively accurate in its assessment of such trends as the expansion of global capitalism and the decline of socialist opposition, we shall suggest certain elements of distortion, omission, and exaggeration that severely qualify its projections of a diminution in global – particularly internal – violence. These aspects will be addressed in summary rather than extended fashion, as the points will either be obvious or are the subject of extensive scholarship. Furthermore, rather than being the primary focus of this discussion, our less benign "realist scenario" is of value only as the essential systemic parameter for assessing the functions and likely prevalence of state terrorism.

In examining some theoretical contributions on the aetiology of state terrorism, we may note that while much study is oriented more to extreme repression than to the specific death squad instrumentality, several analyses do deal with the latter. Our emphasis here will be upon the South and the relationships to the global system dominated by the North. Our discussion will also refer to findings that explicitly focus upon peaceful societies or behaviour. In this way we shall highlight attributes that distinguish systems with relatively low levels of violence.

A synthetic paradigm underscoring structural relationships essential to state terrorism will then be presented, with special attention to the functionality of state-sponsored or state-tolerated death squads. This will be followed by a heuristic elaboration of ten hypotheses, encompassing assumptions concerning the relationship of states to internal élites and external groups in highly stratified class and ethnic systems. Some deal explicitly with vigilantism. The major challenge will be to identify which actors are associated with a state's propensity to engage in terrorism, since that is a precondition for any resort to death squads. Salvadorean peasants, for example, were no better off for being bombed by the air force or massacred in flight by troops than murdered in front of their families or friends by death squadrons.

2 Sources and functions of state terrorism:
Theoretical perspectives

The significance and scholarly salience of state terrorism

The search for theoretical work yields only a modest number of contributions. This cannot be explained by the absence of a common or accepted definition of terrorism (Kegley, 1990:11–16), for, despite this "definitional confusion," there exists a veritable flood of publications focusing upon insurgent and "international" terrorism. Mirroring Kegley was Schmid's (1983:119–52) exhaustive research analysis seven years earlier. He identified approximately a hundred definitions, most of which also pertained to insurgent and international variants. Much of the literature dealt with non-state terrorism, i.e. that which was not targeted by a state upon its own citizens.

Socio-politically, the minuscule proportion of theoretical work dealing with state terrorism may be better explained by the dependence of most researchers upon dominant institutions, including the state, within their own societies (Perdue, 1989:3–9) than by Kegley's (1990:5) proposition that most indigenous acts have an international dimension. This quite simply because the number of victims and extent of physical damage inflicted by domestic terrorism *dwarf* those of the conventionally described international variant.

Thus, Michael Stohl cautions that:

Insurgent terrorism may make the headlines, but the fact is that most of the terrorism in the world goes unnoticed and unreported by the Western media. United States Department of State reports on the incidence of international terrorism worldwide cite approximately 5,000 events and threats of events in the ten years between 1975 and 1985. These events resulted in fewer than 5,000 deaths. In the worst year, 1973, 720 deaths were reported from events, most of which occurred in Europe and the Middle East.

During the period that the Department of State has kept statistics on international terrorism, tens of thousands of people have perished at the hands of government terrorism and death squads, and even more have been the direct victims of torture and intimidation in places such as Guatemala, Uganda, South Africa, East Timor, Chile, and Kampuchea. The actions of Latin American governments in the 1970s turned a verb, to "disappear," into a tragic and intimidating noun, the disappeared, the *desaparecidos*. This terror far outstrips the insurgent terror that gains most Western press notice. (1990:82)

Herman (1982) characterizes the latter as well as "international" acts as "retail" in contrast to the "wholesale" terrorism attributed to states. In his view, the latter may account not for "tens of thousands" but for millions of deaths since the early 1960s.[1] The enormous disparity in research output may also reflect a well-known but seldom-stated relationship: most of the funding for such intellectual work is US in origin. At the same time, Washington is the primary object of such international acts and the hegemonic ally of many of the regimes targeted by insurgents. On the other hand, such governments are often perpetrators of state terrorism which has historically been directed at anti-imperialist and leftist movements. This may help to explain the high level of scholarly tolerance for "definitional confusion," since it facilitates both political and academic use of the term to delegitimize revolutionary or national liberation movements (e.g. the Palestine Liberation Organization).

There is one hypothetical explanation that may be handily disposed of. It runs as follows: while state terrorism may indeed be the "wholesale" variant, it is clearly in decline as a global atrocity – thanks to such organizations as Amnesty International, the employment of sanctions by the USA and the UN, its anachronistic character in an era of technocratic "modernization" and transnational capital, and so on. An assessment of 102 developing countries on the basis of frequent or patterned (as opposed to exceptional) "torture" including disappearances, executions, and penal brutality against government opporients (Wolpin, 1986a:100), revealed that "such practices declined from roughly 2/3 in the 1970–1975 period to about 55% during the 1976–1979 years."[2] By 1980 the figure had fallen to 37 per cent. The basic sources for these classifications were Amnesty International and Ruth Leger Sivard's *World Military and Social Expenditures*. Yet with the resurgence of the hard right in the United States and elsewhere – a process that began in the mid-1970s (Saunders, 1983) and came to fruition in the early 1980s – we note a levelling off in such progress.

The 1981 classification of 113 low- and middle-income states by Sivard identified about 35 per cent which were "highly repressive" in the sense of frequent reports of "torture and brutality" against citizens (1982:1). Nine years later, Sivard (1991:18) revealed that 41 out of the 113 belonged to the "highly repressive category."[3] Half of the 64 military-dominant states were so classified, as were nine of the 49 civilian-rule systems. (Actually the figure should be 10 out of 50, for Sivard has inexplicably excluded Israel, which properly (Finkelstein, 1991) belongs in the brutal category.) While it is clear that military-dominant regimes are more frequently brutally repressive than civilian ones, roughly 20 per cent of the latter belonged to the brutal category in 1990, whereas less than 17 per cent did so nine years earlier. Yet this should not obscure the fact that during the 1980s, approximately "92 per cent of military controlled governments [had] used force and repression against the public" (Schmid, 1991:15).

Furthermore, the trend toward military dominance has continued. Fifty per cent of states were so classified in 1981, while 58 per cent belonged to the category in 1990. The latter were also characterized by far more coups and years of war, 300 per cent higher military manpower burdens and enormously higher casualties (predominantly civilian) from war. Similar patterns were found in the 1970s (Wolpin, 1986a), as was a growing proportion of military-dominant systems since the early 1960s, when approximately 15 per cent could be so denoted. Although between 1990 and 1992 new civilian governments have replaced overtly military ones, in many the armed forces either continue to function as a "state within a state" (e.g. Chile) or, as in the Philippines and Mexico, the civilians are so dependent that there is an effective veto over policy in the vaguely defined "security" area.

Another qualification to ostensible "progress" is demographic. According to Sivard (1982, 1991) the population under "frequently violent" regimes rose from 1.7 to 3.2 billion persons between 1981 and 1990. (Population estimates are for three years preceding.) For those characterized by little or no extreme violence against citizens, the demographic change was from 225.1 to 105.9 million!

Political conflict theorists

Well before terrorism became a fashionable catchword in the late 1970s, a few scholars began to analyse regime terrorism. As described by Schmid (1983:171–8), these focused upon a number of distinctive geo-historical settings and even today provide varying degrees of insight. Eugene Walters (1969), for example, asked "why rulers [in African tribal communities] who already have authority nevertheless choose to rule by violence and fear," and concluded that they did so "to overcome the threat of resistance and secure cooperation."

According to Walters, terror had to be both discriminating and limited rather than general. While ideologically sanctioned, it was necessary to intimidate specific power challengers rather than being impulse-led or gratuitous. In this, Walter's perspective is consonant with modern political conflict theories as well as the "materialist" school of anthropology.

The latter (see Ferguson, 1984) not only emphasizes the magnitude of differences in the peacefulness of various tribes (rebutting the *usefulness* of socio-biological theories of innate "killer instinct" aggressiveness), but also stresses the importance of geographical proximity and ecological scarcity or adequacy, as well as threats by others.

The material interests of decision-makers can take the form of six strategic objectives of war: (1) to increase access to fixed resources; (2) to capture movable valuables; (3) to impose an exploitative relationship on another independent group; (4) to conquer and incorporate another group; (5) to use external conflict as a means of enhancing the decision-makers' position within their own society; and (6) to forestall attacks by others. (Ferguson, 1990:30)

Whether or not violence *actually erupts* will hinge upon other factors such as political customs, organization, and cultural violence.[4]

A rival school places primacy on non-ecological societal attributes. Thus, cultural anthropologists differ in viewing some tribal violence as a result of socialization or learning of cultural values, legitimizing it in certain situations associated with revenge/feuding, religious ritual, sexism, or "sport." Indeed, it seems that many US television viewers of Washington's massive air assault against Iraq experienced it as a type of sporting diversion or event! By contrast, William Perdue, one of the last theorists to be considered here, would classify that massacre as state terrorism.

Less radical are theorists who have associated terrorism with totalitarian rule. Although preoccupied with Stalinism, they saw the political dynamics of Nazism and Communism as those of symbiotic twins.[5] Thus, Dallin and Breslauer (1970), even more than Walters, not only regard terror as instrumental for control, but also view it as "a sign of weakness." Such a need of systemic intimidation is likely to exist when "a communist party which comes to power by revolution ... lacks normative [legitimacy] and material resources to ensure obedience from citizens and to satisfy the followers." There is little or no need for terror, however, when the movement prior to the takeover had substantial popular support and considerable penetration of dominant societal institutions including the state. Another attribute often found in such cases is leadership adeptness in outmanoeuvring, discrediting, and isolating opponents. Titoist Yugoslavia in the late 1940s or Viet Nam in the late 1970s might epitomize this "benign" end of the continuum, whereas Romania in the mid-1980s would be close to the Stalinist orthodox pole.

The two theories previously summarized, then, tend to regard terror as a rational or instrumental policy choice intended to intimidate opponents or threats from below. There is a similar assumption of cost-effectiveness in Abram de Swaan's (1977) analysis of the use of torture as the "linchpin" of terrorist regimes. Essential to its effectiveness are both unpredictability as well as predictability; similarly, rumours in a context of secrecy. The consequence of these dualities is an "ever-present fear of arrest, of ill treatment, of mutilation, of betrayal, of death." Optimally this generates "so much fear in people that of their own account they will abstain from things that otherwise would be hard for the regime to detect or prevent." Even more, "they will not just abstain from what is forbidden, but will avoid whatever has not expressly been allowed." This level of effectiveness is rarely attained, one suspects, though Guatemala, East Timor, and Saudi Arabia may approximate such an "ideal type."

More recently, R. Duvall and Michael Stohl (1983) have created a third-world-focused "expected utility" model that synthesizes elements of the preceding approaches. Their essential hypothesis is that state terror is employed because it appears more effective or *less ineffective* "than alternative means in eliminating or quieting some actual or perceived potential challenge or threat." Elsewhere Lopez and Stohl (1986:74) hypothesize that state violence or terror may also be resorted to as "an extension of an oppression or repression system," and as "a method for the consolidation of power." According to Duvall and Stohl, it is now pervasive only in the third world, where its targets are potential political opponents, especially "the left."[6]

They emphasize that the reason "weak" states commonly engage in terror is not their belief that it is "highly efficacious" but a perception "that other available means of rule are quite inefficacious." As for strong states, these too may engage in terror when they are "reclusive" with a "low vulnerability to international pressure and domestic retribution or when they show features of either a militaristic-state or an ideological-mission syndrome." With respect to this last variable, it seems the explanation transcends simple expediency of cost-effectiveness rationality. Yet, upon reflection, even non-ideologically fanatic élites managing "strong" states presumably have alternative, equally efficacious, means of weakening opposition groups. The fact that the costs of terrorism are reasonable does not cast light upon *why* this course was adopted.

Helpful here are three additional non-utilitarian variables which Stohl identifies (1986:211–21) as likely to constrain or promote state terrorism. The first is to what degree non-violence is valued – a variable both within and among cultures. Second is the social distance and ease with which one can deny the attributes of human identity to the target. Finally, there is routinization within a context of bureaucratic irresponsibility, so that no single individual views himself as personally responsible for the behaviour. Given the growth of bureaucratic institutionalization in the South as well as the global intensification of ethnic and other particularisms that enhance social distance, the prospects for the employment of such coercion in conflicts of the 1990s seem rather strong.

Beyond the political conflict theorists whose key points have been summarized above as they appear in Schmid's impressive compendium (1983:171–8), there is one major theorist of political violence who offers us a number of provocative hypotheses from a background of extensive cross-cultural empirical work. Drawing upon that of Schmid as well as Duvall and Stohl, Ted Robert Gurr (1986:46–8) begins by elaborating an intent-based definition of state terrorism: the use by a state, or by those it makes no serious efforts to control, of life-threatening violence against opponents; an intent not only to immobilize the latter but also through symbolic demonstration effects to influence the behaviour of other potential supporters or opponents; in a manner reflecting "*patterned activity* in which instrumental violence recurs often enough that threats of similar violence, made then or later, have their intended effects on conflict outcomes."

After considering when state terrorism may be justified from the perspective of "rational" state managers, Gurr (1986:51–3) emphasizes a "necessary condition" of "a group, class, or party that is regarded by ruling élites as an active threat to their continued rule," by making claims upon "the prevailing distribution of power and resources." Gurr's specific hypotheses involving "challengers" are as follows: (1) the greater the political threat posed by challengers, the greater the likelihood that a regime will respond with violence; (2) the greater the latent support for revolutionary challengers in a population, the greater the likelihood that a regime will respond with terrorism; (3) challengers who rely on terrorist and guerrilla tactics are likely to be countered by state terror; (4) regimes are more likely to use terrorism against politically marginal groups than against opposition groups that have influence on or supporters among the élite. The second of these is really subsumed by the first, while the last two are not specifically geared to the magnitude of challenge. Thus a popular reformist movement led by a *déclassé* sector of the dominant oligarchy (e.g. Allende's Unidad Popular) may constitute a far greater threat than an isolated guerrilla force (Honduras) or even an insurgency confined to a dominated ethnic (Iraq or Kenya) or racial group (Malaysia or Peru).

Like the preceding ones, several variables involving state and political culture attributes pertain to violence *per se*, while others focus upon the form defined at the outset as terrorism. To follow Gurr's (1986:53–8) sequence, they are: (5) weak regimes are more likely to use violence in response to challengers than strong ones, since "coercion is relatively cheap and within the capacity of any rulers who have a standing army"; (6) élites which have secured and/or maintained their position by violence develop norms and "specially trained units" which contribute to the future employment of violent means against challengers; (7) successful situational uses of state terror in polarized societies are likely to lead to institutionalized terror via specialized units which may even engage in "pre-emptive" terror to maintain political control; (8) the initial decision of a challenged élite to use state terror is usually modelled on others' successful uses of state terror;[7] (9) democratic values, institutions, and traditions inhibit the use of state violence and terror in particular.[8]

The last of these is so obvious as to be almost tautological, while the fifth may be regarded as problematic. We shall now proceed to several of a more structural nature. The first two pertain to group identity and social distance. Thus: (10) the greater the (ethnic/religious/racial) heterogeneity and stratification (inequality) in a society, the greater the likelihood that a regime will use violence as a principal means of social control; and (11) ethnic, religious, or tribal minority élites in highly stratified societies are likely to use terror routinely as an instrument of rule. Yet, even in more ethnically homogeneous societies, high stratification implies minority rule, as has also been observed (see Gurr 1986:58). Others, like Glossop (1987) have also noted the propensity of the rich to employ violence against popular movements of *descamisados*.[9]

The last group of Gurr's (1986:60–1) hypotheses pertains to exogenous factors. Three are highlighted: (12) external threats are likely to induce regimes to use violence against domestic opponents – particularly in ethnically heterogeneous societies; (13) regimes involved in proxy big-power conflicts are likely to use the most extreme forms of violence against challengers, including state terrorism;[10] and (14) peripheral regimes in the world system that are more autarkic and less vulnerable to international sanctions are more prone to rule by violence.

In his concluding section, Gurr (1986:65–6) theorizes that while structural factors that define the relations of élites with their opponents, along with "dispositional variables" such as beliefs or norms, account for regimes' willingness to employ violence, the adoption of terrorism is largely a function of the domestic balance of power with opponents.[11] He adds:

Probably most important of all the immediate determinants of state terrorism is another situational factor, the availability of agencies practised in tactics of terrorist [sic] control. In contrast to these situational variables, we can identify only one structural condition, the exigencies of minority elite rule in a highly stratified society, closely associated with policies of state terror. Dispositional variables, however, seem essential. Historical traditions of state terror, as in Russia and China, and the demonstration effect of successful uses of state terror elsewhere, as among conservative Latin American regimes, probably encourage elites to use terror elsewhere, irrespective of this or other structural factors.

Yet empirically there seems to be a strong association between such traditions of terror initiation in highly stratified systems as well as where the regime is endeavouring to heighten or reverse stratification patterns among ethnic groups and/or classes (e.g. Amin in Uganda, Pol Pot in Cambodia).

Dependency and social structure theorists

Just as some of our political conflict theorists have focused primarily upon regime violence *per se* while others also, or alternatively, have examined hypothesized conditions associated with its terrorist forms, a similar pattern of differentiation is revealed among works considered here. Although such theorists ignore the political, they presume that the *unbalanced character* of existing North/South structure is the primary source of tension-producing violence. Unlike those political conflict theorists who stress social distances associated with class or ethnic stratification *per se*, here the emphasis is upon the asymmetrical *qualitative* aspects of intergroup relations. Hence this orientation might help to explain violence-prone tensions where little social distance existed. Several recent empirical studies (Mitchell and McCormick, 1988; Henderson, 1991; Jongman, 1991) have found that the level of development itself is inversely associated with the more savage forms of repression, particularly when the former is extremely low.

One interesting approach in this genre is Gernot Kohler's (1982) "Global Apartheid." Central to that work is a North/South estimate using 1965 data of differences in the magnitudes of both overt and "structural" violence.[12] The latter is for premature mortality due to the failure of institutions to adopt life-promoting policies. It accounts for the preponderance (14–18 million) of lives lost. While civil violence took 92,000 lives and international violence between 11,500 and 23,000, Kohler's main point is the North/South disparity. The latter, with less than 70 per cent of the world's population, nevertheless experienced 91 per cent of the international violence, 96 per cent of the structural violence, and almost 100 per cent of the civil violence!

Notwithstanding his acknowledgement that "global inequality of income is even more severe than income inequality within national societies," Kohler's basis for using the term "apartheid" is the strong association of the foregoing disparities with race. Yet Kohler rejects the centre–periphery model as being only "partly true," since opposition to the system can be found not only in the South but among élites and mass sectors in the North. Ultimately, however, "reform" of "global apartheid" will require sufficient "unruly" resistance in the South to raise the costs of maintaining the status quo to the point where it will be in the self-interest of its former beneficiaries to accept such reforms.[13] By implication, then, North-supported or North-sponsored state violence and terror in the South would function to suppress such "unruly" resistance movements, but Kohler does not explicitly treat how unruliness should be organized. He similarly ignores the payoffs and integration of comprador and pliant élite sectors in the South that – "racial" differences notwithstanding – have readily assimilated into the North-dominated system, as have the Japanese and the NICs.

Less radically directed – or optimistic, for that matter – are Mason and Krane (1989), who not only focus explicitly upon death squad functionality but also see this as being employed by comprador regimes as a matter of rational choice, because such regimes lack the resources to introduce mass-oriented redistributive reforms to alleviate the distress consequential upon adoption of the agro-export growth model – a model widely associated with a decline in living standards and security for mass sectors. The easiest response becomes selective violence against opposition trade union, peasant organization, and political party leaders – and this is encouraged by military dominance and the bias of external security assistance.

Mason and Krane argue that this sets off a dynamic in which younger regime opponents begin to employ violent tactics to defend their movement for mass betterment. To this reactive violence, the regime responds not only with an escalation, but by first targeting supporters and then, indiscriminately, the lower-sector population base, which had heretofore been equivocal. As a result, widespread indiscriminate violence may in fact lead to greater active support for the opposition. Eventually, however, the coercive resources become exhausted and a stalemate results which leads to disorientation within the regime.[14]

Interestingly, their model is El Salvador, which received very high injections of external "aid" funds that could have financed *major* reforms, while redistributive ones in particular can cost relatively little, as the MNR (Movimiento Nacionalista Revolucionario) discovered four decades ago in Bolivia. Class interests, élite reference groups or aspirations, as well as ideological commitments to existing exploitative structures might, in my view, better explain the absence of reform vigour. Yet Mason and Krane are prescient in noting that indiscriminate violence drove more citizens with nothing to lose into tacitly supporting the revolutionary movement. This is close to a point made by Aguilera (1980) in reference to Guatemala, where terror by the state and its rightist allies against insurgents and their communities tended to undermine the residual legitimacy of the state. Indeed, a study by Mitchell and McCormick (1988) identified a pattern of extreme repressive violence as associated with non-leftist authoritarian regimes of this genre. While Marxist-oriented states most often imprison opponents, rightist authoritarians such as those dominating Guatemala frequently resorted to torture, disappearances, and the like.

While such indiscriminateness has enabled the revolutionary movement to survive, the savagery of the military response and the efficiency of its urban death squads has constrained the size of the insurgency. Yet in some measure the "exhaustion" predicted by Mason and Krane did eventually bring the Guatemalan armed forces *seriously* to the negotiating table by 1991. In the case of Peru, however, the latter has not occurred (see Kirk, 1991:554–5). Unlike Guatemala and El Salvador, Peruvian regime repression has not targeted several moderate left-of-centre parties, while Sendero Luminoso has! Yet the newest, increasingly illiterate, recruits are even less likely than more educated cadres to equate electoral options with democracy. Repression and particularly its most extreme variants have been found by Henderson (1991) and Jongman (1991) to be inversely related to the salience of democratic institutions.

But it is easy to exaggerate the latter for lower population sectors even when elections are routinely organized. For, as Galeano (1989) cautions, democratic forms have no meaning to desperately poor, homeless, illiterate people. Or as Magdoff (1991:9–10) emphasizes, "privilege, social status, and power are interrelated" regardless of whether a system is authoritarian or formally democratic. Thus, in a context of material scarcity and conflicting interests, elections easily become "instruments for the more powerful getting still more advantages at the expense of the weaker and underprivileged sectors." Since most elections are subject to strong structural sources of bias – including openness to external ones (Herman and Brodhead, 1984) – only exceptional elections yield significant popular outcomes. And these – when leaders don't sell out or become intimidated – tend to be vitiated by military intervention reinforced by external destabilization. Thus the state's electoral legitimacy tends to be limited to upscale sectors. Voting fraud and buying, along with the introduction of "modern" political technology, is reinforcing the de facto electoral bias that favours comprador-dominated parties.

Yet, as Koenig and van Es (1976) have noted, one of the ironies is that while those high in social status and participation tend to harbour the greatest support for the legitimacy of electoral institutions, this is not inversely correlated with support for vigilantism, i.e. the use of extralegal force for political goals. Why this occurs is suggested by Sederberg (1978), who maintains that vigilantism is often "a reaction to a widening range of officially tolerated innovation and [even] the existence of state-sponsored innovation." He underscores the fact that "radicals and presumed radicals historically have been the recipients of vigilante vengeance" (1978:297). Thus, when the state cannot constitutionally act against those perceived to be an overt *or symbolic* threat to the established order, vigilante groups may be organized either under private sponsorship or by a sector of the state apparatus. They tend to recruit those whose status is insecure and who are characterized by authoritarian personalities with a strong power drive and need for hierarchy. This may explain why many are current or former members of the state's coercive apparatus. Further, while some vigilante groups are spontaneous rather than organized, most tend to break the law in practice even though many claim to be defending it. The propensity for this, as well as the degree of violence employed, is governed by two factors in addition to the ability of state sectors to control such behaviour. One, of course, is the magnitude of the perceived threat to the social order and the degree of threat to the social status of the vigilante manpower base. The second is the pervasiveness of violence in the culture itself.[15]

Mention should be made of two psychological dimensions in addition to Sederberg's pinpointing the importance of impulsive and violence-prone personalities being attracted to vigilante roles. Like others, Eckhardt (1982) focuses upon inconsistent and punitive child-rearing in a context devoid of compassion as likely to engender personalities who respond aggressively to those who threaten their perceived status and social hierarchy (see also Trevarthen and Logotheti, 1989:177). Second, at a societal level, culturally violent norms are likely – as with individuals – to be reinforced by prior success in attaining goals by such means (Shy, 1971). These aspects may contribute to explaining the high US propensity for violence both internationally and domestically.

More indirectly, economic insecurity and decline appear to place great stress upon family tranquillity, resulting in parental violence and other forms of abuse (Elshtain and Buell, 1991). The latter, in the form of neglect, is consequential upon a society addicted to competitive consumerism, which is aggravated by the rising structural unemployment and underemployment associated with policy shifts towards a *laissez-faire* "free" market system. Soaring violent crime rates have also been attributed to this orientation (Currie, 1991).

Imperialism theorists

Johan Galtung's global structural violence paradigm (1982:606–8) would seem strikingly analogous to Kohler's, which was examined in the preceding section. But rather than emphasizing race, Galtung focuses upon "capitalist imperialism" as the most important ultimate impediment to the satisfaction of basic needs. As a system of structural dominance, it operates in an exploitative manner primarily between the centre and the periphery. But Galtung qualifies this by emphasizing that within such a world order, also, the exploited may in turn use their superior power resources to take advantage of others weaker than themselves. And exploited groups may exist not only in the periphery, but even within core states.

While Western universalism served as a cultural pretension legitimizing this exploitative system, Galtung (1990:291–301) subsequently addressed the nature of cultural violence itself and its triangular linkages with structural as well as overt (including terrorist) violence. Thus these three forms or types of violence are mutually reinforcing. Conversely, successful efforts to attenuate one variant may promote reduction in another. Yet it may not, for he also warns: "one type of violence may be reduced or controlled at the expense of increase or maintenance of another."

We might ask whether the recent wars against drugs and Iraq illustrate that hypothesized relationship. Similarly, defeat of an egalitarian insurgency, as in the Philippines, could result in a greater structural violence. Although he notes that the "violence cycle" may begin with the structural or exploitative form (where the top dogs get more out of the relationship than the underdogs), Galtung argues that "generally, a causal flow from cultural via structural violence to direct violence can be identified."[16]

Cultural violence is defined as the most "permanent" form, consonant with the anthropological view that symbolic construction is a *basic* attribute of any human society. Galtung proceeds to define cultural violence as those "aspects" of the "symbolic sphere ... that can be used to justify or legitimize direct or structural violence." Examples are drawn from science, mathematics, art, language, religion, and ideology. These include nationalism, chauvinistic "chosen people" religious beliefs, as well as other concepts of the "chosen" group – often also rationalized by appeal to an external divinity – including ones based upon social class, race, gender, or creed.[17]

Rejecting views of innate human propensities for violence because they are "contradicted" by the wide variation in overt, cultural, and structural violence in different societies, Galtung adds that violent norms and beliefs may characterize *more or less* of an entire culture.[18] Yet he recognizes that it is possible to encounter one with "a set of aspects so violent, extensive and diverse, spanning all cultural domains, that the step from talking about cases of cultural violence to violent cultures may be warranted." Inferentially we should expect to find greater overt and structural violence in proportion to the pervasiveness of the cultural variant. According to Galtung, "exploitation and repression go hand in hand as violence: but they are not identical." The latter reinforces the former by impeding consciousness formation and mobilization, two conditions for effective struggle against exploitation. Repression, in turn, operates via four mechanisms: (1) penetration; (2) segmentation, or giving the underdog only a partial view; (3) marginalization, or keeping him on the outside; and (4) fragmentation, or keeping the underdogs away from each other. It is in these last two areas that, presumably, combined private and state violence, including death squads and other forms of terrorism, would be functional.

The significance of cultural violence is that it promotes structural and overt violence which denies human beings four basic needs: survival, well-being, identity, and freedom. Though this is a phenomenon generally identified with the major Western powers of the North, Galtung singles out the salient role played by the USA in furthering values associated with "male, Western, white innate superiority," and adds: "reducing US cultural violence becomes particularly important precisely because that country sets the tone for others." Washington's dominance of the Gulf "coalition" underscores that conclusion.[19]

Within the array of works that attribute responsibility to the USA for state terrorism, we find two tendencies. More complex approaches, like Galtung's, tend to emphasize exploitative internal stratification and institutional roles *within the South* that are *reinforced* by the USA in order to promote their stability. Rubenstein (1987:37, 236) also belongs to what we may call this dual-dimensional category. Although Rubenstein doubts that groups led by disaffected and marginalized social intelligentsia can rely upon terrorist tactics to overthrow a regime in the absence of mass support (when such tactics are unnecessary), his most interesting points address regime terrorism. Historically, such violence has primarily targeted left-of-centre parties, trade unions, and so on, even in the North.[20] Death squads, though guided by middle- and upper-middle-class elements (Rubenstein, 1987:127–30, 137), generally recruit lumpen strata who are paid for "part-time" work and appealed to upon the basis of anti-communism and/or ethnic chauvinism. Rubenstein (1987:129) adds that also in Europe and the USA right-wing extremists and neo-fascists have been linked historically to elements within the bourgeoisie and the coercive apparatus.

A more inclusive definitional perspective also posits the major sources of terrorism as the North and particularly the USA. Here terrorism is equated with *any* major act or threat of state violence designed to intimidate and to induce compliance. Thus Perdue (1989) regards such terrorism as but one element within an array of ideological and coercive instruments of domination by the North, with Washington playing the leading role.[21] The purpose is to ensure access to labour and other raw materials as well as market dominance for global transnational corporations. Thus the term "terrorism" gets selectively applied to liberation movements, and it functions ideologically to mobilize support for suppression, including death squads.

The excessive, indiscriminate, and unnecessary use of overwhelming force against Iraq in early 1991 would fall squarely within this framework. Interestingly, it also conforms to George Bush's own definitional criteria of terrorism as set forth by Perdue:

... the *Public Report of the Vice President's Task Force on Combatting Terrorism* proclaimed in 1986 that "terrorism is a phenomenon that is easier to describe than define." Undeterred, the Bush report cites: "the unlawful use or threat of violence against persons or property to further political or social objectives. It is generally intended to intimidate or coerce government, individuals, or groups to modify their behavior or policies." This cabinet-level attempt at definition also specified the methods of terrorism, including "hostage-taking, aircraft piracy or sabotage, assassination, threats, hoaxes, indiscriminate bombings or shootings." And finally, the document portrayed the targets of terrorism as innocent, noting that "most victims of terrorism seldom have a role in either causing or affecting the terrorist's grievances." (1989:2)

Indeed, when Bush unilaterally lifted economic sanctions from South Africa in July 1991, he informed reporters that had sanctions been given a chance to work against Iraq, the "coalition would have fallen apart." Yet, by January 1991, Iraq had already announced its willingness to withdraw in exchange for a UN-sponsored Middle Eastern peace conference!

Consistent with this perspective is that of Walton (1991), who sees the Gulf massacre as merely the ultimate phase of US expansionism. Similarly, Reed (1991:45), in delineating the implications of the vast US overseas base structure, notes that "a significant proportion of military planning is directed towards threats in the Third World and low intensity conflicts."

Focusing instead upon Washington's enormous inventory of weapons, another observer ("LBO Replies," 1991:3) comments:

They don't build murderous gadgets for the hell of it. The U.S. military has something to do with the fact that 24 rich countries that constitute the OECD have an average per capita income of $17,470, and those that don't, the 96 countries that the World Bank classifies as low- and middle-income, average $750. Would scores of desperately poor countries be dutifully following the IMF austerity line and paying $175 billion a year on their debt if there were no B-52s and CIA?

While this may strike one as simplistic, it should not be dismissed out of hand.[22] Certainly the scale and intensity of the military attack on Iraq was intended to intimidate nationalist regimes and movements. Further, the decline in available US economic "aid" resources implies the need for greater reliance upon extant military capabilities and cover action.

A decade ago Herman (1982) followed Agee (1975) in stressing the role of the CIA in suppressing Latin American popular movements and even conniving with death squads and other forms of terrorism. Vanden (1990:59), for example, notes that death squads were "a by-product of the U.S.-inspired counterinsurgency campaigns of the sixties." Observing that Washington has used Argentina and Israel as proxies, he adds that the CIA itself encouraged the Nicaragnen *contras* to employ death squad tactics against the rural Sandinista infrastructure.

More globally, former CIA officer and National Security Council participant John Stockwell (1991:72, 73) refers to

three thousand major covert operations, over 10,000 minor operations [...] the CIA has overthrown functioning constitutional democracies in over 20 countries. It has manipulated elections in dozens of countries. It has created standing armies and directed them to fight. It has organized ethnic minorities and encouraged them to revolt in numerous volatile areas.

In other cases, ethnic majorities and religious fundamentalists have been encouraged to act as vigilantes in liquidating supporters of a growing popular movement. Indonesia constitutes a "model" of such a successful operation, involving both a coup in 1965 and perhaps the most sweeping death-squad massacre to date. Australian intelligence "put the figure at closer to two million – the rivers were clogged with the bodies of the dead." Stockwell (1991:72–3) adds that "in the summer of 1990, the U.S. State Department acknowledged that it had indeed delivered lists of names, of people who were subsequently killed, to the Indonesian government." Did this also occur in Chile at the time of Pinochet's coup? It is reasonable to surmise that globally such provision of "suspect" lists enhances the efficacy of death squads and regime terrorism. Indeed, while Bush was CIA director, Stockwell had been charged with organizing an ethnic insurgency to overthrow the new government of Angola. As in the case of Kurdish or Afghan rebels, Washington predictably never referred to the South-African-aided Angolan Unita guerrillas – or, for that matter, the even more sanguinary Renamo insurgents of Mozambique – as "terrorists."

215

Like Agee and Herman, Stockwell (1991:133) sees US "militarism" and support for state terrorism, as well as covert action, as being instrumental in protecting the "global financial order" as well as particular "financial interests." Other major sources of US militarism, in his view, are: (1) weapons producers who need foreign threats to justify high levels of armaments appropriations; (2) political manipulation by élites in the context of a militaristic history and culture. Stockwell and other former intelligence officers who organized the Association of National Security Alumni have in recent years focused less upon military terrorism, or what Stohl (1986:215) terms "coercive diplomacy," than upon the lack of effective democratic control over the intelligence apparatus and its nefarious global role in countries such as El Salvador (see White, 1991:1) and Chad (see Hunter, 1991:49, who indicates an Israeli linkage).

What preoccupies Richard Falk and the Association of National Security Alumni, of which Stockwell was national president, is not merely the harm done abroad, but that during the past decade US presidents have employed elements of this parastatal network to subvert constitutional limitations within their own "democratic" system. (See Stockwell, 1991:121–8, 174–8; also Reynolds, 1990; Reynolds, 1991; Scott and Marshall, 1991.)

3 Toward a synthetic paradigm

Our purpose here is not to fix responsibility upon a particular country, but to explain the most salient contemporary sources and dominant patterns of victimization. Stohl (1986:216–30), for example, using a broad definition encompassing coercive diplomacy, clandestine operations, and surrogate terrorism, does not ignore past Soviet roles in supporting a relatively small number of regimes and a somewhat larger number of national liberation movements. But it is clear from his analysis that the preponderance of such activity emanated from Washington, if only because of the disparity in resources and client regimes. And while for the most part Stohl differs from previous analysts in limiting US objectives to furthering its "sphere of influence" and thus neglects divergent socio-economic biases, he does at one point concede that "in the Third World the Soviet presence appears to be relatively benign." In terms of mass socio-economic and cultural needs, it does appear that Soviet military aid beneficiaries performed far better than most US clients (Wolpin, 1986a). Similar patterns appeared with respect to state terrorism.

However, our relative neglect of the USSR and the former client regimes is premised upon two other factors. First is the collapse of the USSR since 1987 as an active or even nominal supporter for most of the "progressive" states and movements in the South. And second, US roles in this area (with regard to, e.g., Native Americans, the Aguinaldo nationalist movement in the Philippines at the turn of the century, Nicaragua prior to Sandino) antedated the Bolshevik Revolution. And they continue – albeit in less clandestine form during the Reagan/Bush era – since the eclipse of Moscow's apparent "superpower" status. There can be no doubt that Washington – with some support from Europe and Japan – is playing the major reinforcement role in maintaining and actually intensifying existing patterns of global stratification.

Exploitative stratification

Before addressing the specific use of death squads, consideration should be given to the structural attributes of state terrorist regimes which employ or acquiesce in their functioning. Since most terrorist regimes and death squads not only kill but also mutilate and torture, the more extreme forms of the latter – even if *only* to extract "confessions" or other information – should be encompassed regardless of constructive intent to intimidate. Put differently, while for certain empirical purposes it might be desirable to employ a very inclusive definition, for ours a more limited one (Sederberg, 1989) is warranted.[23]

As for exploitation, we merely refer to the use of greater power resources by one or more groups directly or indirectly dominating state policy to impose an exchange relationship upon others which would not have been accepted in the absence of a power disparity, and/or sanctions for refusal to accept a relationship where the top dogs get more than the underdogs. Often this exchange pertains to the subordinate groups' wealth, raw materials, or labour power. In societies like the Nordic bloc, where intergroup equality is relatively high both socially and politically, there is little such structural, cultural, or overt violence. State terrorism and political violence are virtually non-existent aside, perhaps, from some occasional reports of police toleration of neo-Nazi skinhead vigilantes with a proclivity for mobbing third world immigrants.

Sivard's (1990:51–6) classification of states which in 1990 are characterized by frequent extreme or brutal violence indicates that on life

217

expectancy, socio-economic standing, and per capita GNP they are much poorer than those with little or no such violence. Furthermore, the former group's military burdens upon their economies are significantly higher. Almost a decade earlier, they were also far more impoverished in per capita terms. Finally, a large proportion of those classified as terrorist in 1990 had been similarly denoted nine years earlier, suggesting an endemic pattern. Assuming that élites and upscale societal sectors live similarly – variations notwithstanding – in most countries, it is reasonable to presume that stratification and exploitation are greatest in the poorest lands.[24]

Both structural violence (exploitation intensity) and social distance are likely to be greatest where there is a reinforcing overlap between class and ascriptive (ethnic, racial, religious) group membership. That is where the subordinated group lacks a significant exploitative upper stratum which in some measure benefits from the system and often has ties with the dominant group. The larger the subgroup, the stronger the links to the dominant one and the greater the "trickle-down" benefits, the more muted will be any latent or over-societal stratification. A similar structure of relationships characterizes the inter-state system. The economic crisis and externally imposed "re-adjustment" process since the 1970s has, however, heightened stratification within and among countries by squeezing down "national" bourgeois and public employee sectors of the intermediate strata and further integrating comprador business and politico-military élites into the transnational corporate-dominated global system. Similar tendencies are apparent in the North and particularly its current unipolar centre. (Wolpin, 1991; see also Coffin, 1991b:3, citing Bill Moyers, a former high official in the Kennedy administration.)

The militant diffusion of social Darwinist "free-market" or "dog-eat-dog" ideology has been used to intensify exploitation and heighten stratification globally. This implies, to use Gurr's terminology, a secular rise in relative deprivation when reference points are either one's past situation or that of upscale comprador and other high-consumption groups. Rubenstein (1987) contends that even if particular resistance movements are co-opted or suppressed, these structural inequities will be the source of new insurgencies. What is ignored is that *laissez-faire* capitalism in itself has seldom brought mass prosperity to the citizens of any society.[25] Access to the wealth or labour of others, strong trade union or farmers' movements, and ultimately enlarged state economic and social roles have been correlates of such outcomes in a few "mixed" economies.

Thus the heightened stratification resulting from the transfer of increased wealth from the South to the North globally, and from the bottom to the top in both regions, suggests a secular rise in latent and eventually overt tensions. Fewer states will be "strong" in terms of legitimacy domains, administrative effectiveness, or resources for reform. Even redistributive reform measures will become more rare in the context of heightened societal antagonisms. Upscale fear will rise that "uncorking the bottle" even a little will catalyse escalated underdog demands and result in unruliness and instability in the system. Hence, while state terrorism may function in a more sophisticated manner due to enhanced "security" assistance, it is unlikely to become, like slavery, a relic of the past.

We have focused here upon the structural aspects rather than the situational ones, which tend to be secondary or derivative. On the other hand, it is not suggested here that in the absence of "capitalist imperialism" all the societies in the South would have "developed" or attained high incomes. Nor is there any implication that, if the North (and particularly the United States) abruptly terminated interventionism, dramatic reductions in structural, overt, and cultural violence would occur in the short run – simply that one massive source of reinforcement might disappear. Not only would exploitative stratification remain, but cultural values (ethnic or religious chauvinism, sexism, etc.) and desires to revenge past exploitation or worse would also be operative. Use of the state to maintain privileged status or to enhance upward mobility itself would – given cultural reinforcement – predispose many to violence.[26] Beyond that would be expansionist tendencies, to which larger or militantly chauvinistic theocratic states seem peculiarly attracted, like the regional dominance aspirations of India, Brazil, Israel, or Nigeria. Yet without military and police training, advisory roles, and at least some of the higher-tech weaponry that is subsidized by security as well as economic "aid", the *scale* of violence might in general be attenuated, with the relative weakening of coercive institutions. They in turn not only reinforce extant stratification structures but also account for a preponderance of the overt internal violence. Similarly, prospects for groups seeking to lessen structural and cultural violence would be enhanced.

The significance of death squads

There are instances where weak states cannot control organized private vigilantes who seek to destroy and/or intimidate opponents in order to alter the stratification system and/or simply for revenge. Here we may cite the *Época de la Violencia* of the late 1940s in Colombia, Lebanon between the late 1970s and the recent invasion by Syria, perhaps even Sri Lanka with respect to rival Tamil and Sinhalese racial groups. Where the armed forces lack sufficient resources or perhaps fear disunity, it would be improper to attribute responsibility to the state for such terrorism. Indeed, these epitomize truly "weak" states devoid of a legitimate preponderance of physical coercion.

Yet in most cases the state's coercive apparatus – and often sectors of its civilian arm as well – will sympathetically tolerate or covertly aid one of the vigilante groups. These may be essentially non-violent, such as the CDRs (Committees for the Defence of the Revolution) in Cuba, or quite lethal, as in the case of Inkatha's or the regime's own death squads in South Africa (McDougall and Soderbergh, 1990), or the Anti-Communist Alliance in the Philippines. In highly stratified societies with a growing opposition, this can be a very effective means of weakening the more threatening group by dividing (or "segmenting," to use Galtung's term) the exploited sectors. A quarter of a century ago, the Indonesian military command – with vital assistance from the CIA – consolidated its coup by encouraging Muslims to mass-murder leftists and ethnic Chinese.

When antecedent antipathies exist between two or more groups, this mechanism scores highly on any cost-benefit calculus. Stohl (1984) stresses that the magnitude and *form* of terrorism are generally a function of: (1) vulnerability; (2) manageability; and (3) presumed effectiveness. Often there is also the crucial element of *deniability*. Yet we would hypothesize that state terrorist regimes employ such surrogate death squad vigilantes only under certain conditions – usually when the opposition movement is both growing and constitutes a major threat to the exploitative stratification system. There are two principal reasons for this. First, deniability may be compromised because of the informal and uninstitutionalized links with such quasi-autonomous death squads. The latter is the second reason – lack of total regime control over them. At best this can lead to counter-productive, totally indiscriminate brutality, as the Renamo pattern illustrated in Mozambique. Even worse, it may prove difficult to disarm the group effectively after it has been successful, thus symbolizing a new threat to the regime's power to enforce the existing system of privilege.

The "ideal" death squad, then, is one staffed by professional personnel belonging to the regime's political police, military intelligence, or special forces, who are trained to perform such activities. Here lapses of control are minimized and deniability is maximized.

Death squads have not been limited to Latin America, although they have been most salient in this region. We underscored the role of the special forces because they, along with the CIA (McClintock, 1985), were both US innovations and "exports" to Latin America. Through the AID Office of Public Safety, the CIA trained, aided, and advised political police in Latin America – as well as elsewhere – in "anti-subversive" operations. Similarly, special forces counter-insurgency units, first formalized after the Cuban Revolution, contributed to the creation of similar units. The growing popular liberation movements in Indo-China and elsewhere also played a role. Special forces generally recruit the most sanguinary military regulars while specializing in sabotage, assassination, and terror.

In rural areas their activities against non-combatants are generally deniable. Further, once an actual insurgency has begun, repressive regimes generally need such élite "irregulars." Yet these uprisings are often reactive to urban repression. As noted, trade union membership is low for regimes engaging in frequent brutal violence (Wolpin, 1986a). When urban political and trade union movements are relatively strong and growing, existing police death squads may be too few to suppress the threat. Or, if expanded, the problem of deniability may become acute. Thus the optimum cost-benefit policy is to employ *volunteer* proto-fascists as informal, part-time torturers, mutilators, and the like. Often organized by higher officers in the "security establishment," members in other cases may be recruited by fanatical secular (e.g. World Anti-Communist League) or religious (Causa/ Unification Church) groups. The latter strategy is particularly functional when civilian elements (e.g. Duarte, Aquino, Cerezo) personally oppose the creation of new official units for this purpose but lack more than nominal control over an autonomous military.

When overtly state-linked terrorism assumes an indiscriminate character, and/or also targets "respectable" or "moderate" opposition élites, negative repercussions may occur. To take a US example, only a small minority of social democratic liberals in the Democratic Party responds not only to human rights interest groups but to their recognition that the proto-fascist mind seldom draws fine distinctions between their own liberal international reference groups and more principled egalitarian militants. Even so, in contradistinction to cases – relatively few in number – where the "left" has targeted the rich, sanctions are weak, while other responses are more symbolic than punitive.

Our main point is that such de facto regime vigilante death squads have become a key instrument of terror because of the growing need for deniability, on the one hand, and because of the strength of *largely urban-based* leftist opposition movements, on the other. They are also more organizationally "efficient" than other sectors of relatively weak states. This is due not only to fanaticism or a financial reward system, but also to official and "private," largely US-based, high- and low-tech assistance (McClintock, 1985), as well as training. Other former major imperial powers, like Britain and France, have provided similar "security" assistance in various parts of Africa, the Middle East, and Asia, as has Israel in Latin America and South Africa (see McDougall and Soderbergh, 1990).

Yet opposition movements in most of these countries have been less well organized than in Latin America. Further, because there is more social distance between their élites and "the West," sensitivity to human rights criticism – and, concomitantly, deniability – are less important. Moreover, the opposition often tends to be rural and/or ethnically based, thus rendering the military rather than death squads the most cost-effective or suitable repressive instrumentality. Hence military terrorism serves as a rural functional equivalent for death squad terrorism. Landowners and ethnic allies of the armed forces may, of course, provide supplementary vigilante units.

Death squad hypotheses

The foregoing discussion can be viewed as a tentative exploration of some key relationships and patterns. What is needed are comparative in-depth case studies and systematic empirical research to build upon this heuristic treatment. The following ten hypothesized relationships flow from the assessment elaborated in preceding sections:

1. The highest levels of structural violence and social inequality are associated with one or more of the following: extremely low per capita income and low retention of external earnings within the society; relatively high levels of external control over economic policy; substantial ethnic and/or racial heterogeneity.
2. Structural violence and stratified inequalities will intensify during periods of economic stagnation and particularly with economic decline, fiscal crisis, and public sector austerity.
3. High or rising levels of structural violence, when reinforced by

cultural violence, will be associated with state terrorism where there is a perceived overt or symbolic threat to the stratification system generally and/or the élite level; this is particularly true for military-dominant systems.

4. For situations described in the preceding hypothesis, state terrorism will be most intense where there are high levels of exploitation as well as overlap between socio-economic class and ascriptive ethnic and/or racial group membership; yet overt acts may be rare and a consequence of past success in fragmenting, demobilizing, and/or co-opting opposition movements.

5. Off-duty covert state-sponsored death squads are more likely to be employed when opposition groups are strong as well as urban-based, and where deniability is important for domestic and/or international reasons; thus, in electoral systems when *success* in mobilizing structural bias against "popular" left and/or ethnic opposition movements is problematic, death squads and other forms of intimidation are likely to be employed to compensate for the *absence* of sufficient electoral bias mobilization; the latter is particularly likely for extremely low-income countries.

6. Against rural movement opposition, direct military terror will sometimes be employed by special forces death squad units, overtly or incognito, by impersonating the insurgent movement; they may cooperate with "private" ethnic – or, more often, oligarchic – vigilante units.

7. Covert action networks employed by constitutional states will, over a substantial period of time, develop sufficient autonomy and a propensity to subvert the constitutional process when moderate elements within the state seek to alter external and/or internal repressive policies; this may extend to intimidation or death squad assassination of such officials.

8. Regime external reference groups, dependence, and vulnerability will intensify state terror and enhance death squad efficacy when the external power is itself characterized by high levels of structural and cultural violence – particularly when endogenous opponents or their external supporters oppose the existing transnational corporate-dominated stratification system; converse external linkages, when preponderant, are likely to ameliorate such tendencies over time.

9. Major redistributive and anti-discrimination reform measures that benefit lower strata and/or previously exploited or marginalized sectors – particularly when reinforced by developmental na-

tionalism – will be associated with a low or declining propensity to engage in state terror, with the exception of defence against counter-revolutionary movements, particularly when externally supported.

10. Regardless of any particular configuration of structural or situational variables, a strong historical tradition of intergroup animosity or feuding is likely to function in the short and even medium term as an independent source of cultural and overt violence; the latter will be most probable and intense where one group is attempting to modify the stratification system by altering the power balance with the state.

Any research generated by these ten hypotheses may necessitate revisions and/or result in the elaboration of additional hypotheses. Not only have some circumstantial factors been ignored, but so has one emphasized by other historical investigations (Melko, 1973; Powell, 1982:42–3) – that is, the values, quality, and cohesion of the leadership stratum. To this we might add the socio-political and/or economic alternatives available to the "outs." Thus, even in relatively "strong" states (in terms of resources and administrative effectiveness), an ideology high in cultural violence (e.g. "predatory" as opposed to "social" marketism) may inhibit egalitarian concessions, whether via redistribution and/or state-financed social programmes. Similarly, we need measures of exploitation intensity in stratification systems and thresholds that predispose state managers towards terrorism against opponents. And yet another equally important level, the former's relationship to the assimilation of culturally violent norms in childhood socialization, ought to be an object of sustained research.

4 Prospects for a more peaceful world order

It is easy to confuse the current dominance of transnational corporate capitalism and its leading militarist enforcer with the "success" of the system in providing for the basic needs and equitable development of the third world. Worse, a social Darwinist ideology that ignores market power disparities and celebrates possessive individualism indirectly reinforces other rationales for private or group self-seeking at the expense of others. Moreover, its acceptance of the most common denominator of mass media advertising ratings precludes serious efforts to transform extant culturally violent values, tastes, and propensities.

The present defeat, co-optation, or reverses of movements inspired by cooperative and sustainable ideologies by no means implies their extinction. What it does suggest is a decline in opposition to Galtung's capitalist imperialism during the early 1990s, and this may be associated with an attenuation of state terrorism and even the use of death squads. Indeed, this change has become apparent over the past five years. So has the rise in both variants of structural violence, associated with growing public sector austerity and a general increase in unemployment as well as a decline in real wages – these reflecting excessive indebtedness and global economic restructuring. And the last involves a decline of economic pluralism, due to transnational corporate takeovers of national financial and manufacturing entities.

Thus the present era is characterized by demoralization of egalitarian alternative development movements, national self-determination aspirations, and an intensification of mass relative deprivation. This is exacerbated by growing economic insecurity contrasted with the opulent lifestyles that are conveyed by external media infusions and exposure to comprador elements within societies. As relative deprivation escalates, we may expect a rise in ethnic and other ascriptive conflicts.

But so long as such conflicts do not target or threaten the basic state-enforced stratification system, its terrorism and death squad capability potential will remain latent. Similarly, such conflicts will be only minor irritants to transnational capital. Intense ethnic conflict, however, may disrupt orderly markets. Indeed, given the paucity of ethno-linguistically homogeneous societies, Hobsbawm (1991) predicts that the upsurge of virulent nationalism in Eastern Europe is likely to yield violent resistance by minorities to the suppression of customary equal rights.

When trans-ethnic movements for greater class equality and alternative development strategies reappear, most of the "new democracies" and relatively non-violent systems will relapse into violent repression, as they have done in the past. In none have former state terrorist unit participants been severely incapacitated as a stratum. It is particularly instructive that state terrorism occurred ubiquitously between the early 1960s and late 1970s – the very era of death squad prominence – when economic "aid" and actual growth characterized much of the South. This was a veritable heyday of optimism, despite the seldom-noted massive comprador and politico-military élite recycling of hard currency to the North – an amount today which probably equals half or more of the public debt owed by the

South. Those élites who attempted to provide increased mass pur-
chasing power and to stimulate domestically oriented mass production to broaden the basis of regime legitimacy were deposed –
usually by destabilization (Stockwell, 1991), which in turn resulted in
economic crisis and military intervention.

Global economic stagnation in the 1990s will heighten the repressive prospects for new and resurgent popular movements. When electoral manipulation fails to marginalize such elements, repression will
operate increasingly through overt forms such as death squads rather
than as "official" regime violence. This is because of the heightened
need for "deniability" that has come with new global human rights
norms. Decades, perhaps half a century, will be required before the
latter are sufficiently intensified to inhibit such practices. And this
presumes not only an upsurge in economic growth for the South but
also a much widened diffusion of its benefits, consequential upon the
adoption of domestically oriented development strategies that emphasize sustainability, lateral linkages, local initiative, appropriate
technology, self-reliance, and ethnic as well as class equity.

Notes

1. Guest (1983), for example, refers to a study by Kenyan lawyer Amos Wako, who concluded
   that "at least two million people have been summarily executed around the world in the last
   15 years for their opposition to governments." Wako's report was prepared for the February 1983 session of the UN Human Rights Commission.
2. *Frequent* extreme violence *may* not be necessary for relatively effective states to terrorize,
   particularly in the circumstances addressed in the following note. On the other hand, great
   frequency may reflect ineffectiveness, i.e. a failure to terrorize, when confronted by a highly
   organized, competently led and growing insurgent movement (Kirk, 1991) such as Sendero
   Luminoso in Peru.
3. The proportion of highly repressive regimes in 1990 *may* be even higher, because prior
   "frequent" use of brutal violence may have decimated opposition leadership and terrorized movement supporters. This would be particularly true where there was no leadership
   hiatus or when – even if there had been – terrorist officials or units remained immune from
   significant state sanctions and even continued to be employed occasionally "as a reminder"
   by the state's coercive apparatus.
4. Much of this comparative cross-cultural work indirectly pertains to our concern by focusing
   upon societal violence and warfare. Thus a recent anthropological conference (McCauley,
   1990:2–16) concluded again that the innate aggressiveness or "killer instinct" hypothesis,
   whether assumed to be a function of genetic adaptation or innate, was not useful in explaining major differences in the extent of violence characterizing varying cultures or such short-
   run changes as have occurred in particular cultures. A second theme was that material/eco-
   logical scarcity in band and tribal societies was of problematic utility in predicting war, since
   reactions to material adversity were heavily influenced by particular cultural norms – especially as cultures became more hierarchically organized and acquainted with using technology to enhance productivity.

5. This ignores qualitative differences. Fascism, and particularly its Nazi variant, were militaristic – positively glorifying the use of force against demonized ideological protagonists (especially communists) and "inferior" or "alien" racial, religious, and ethnic groups. Thus we have a partial parallel with contemporary death squad ideology and some aspects of "national security doctrine" ideology in Latin America and elsewhere.

6. In the "first world," only limited state terrorism occurs and is generally targeted against socially isolated groups that are distrusted by the general population. Gurr (1986:49–50), for example, notes that "in the United States, the Federal Bureau of Investigation and police campaign against the Black Panthers in 1969–1970 was terrorist in intent and effect." Yet, according to one expert (Ratner, 1991:142), torture is widely practised by urban police departments today within the USA, involving thousands of victims, many in minority areas. On Chicago, see Muwakkil (1991). As for the now non-existent "second world," Duvall and Stohl (1983) saw only "quite limited terror," even though in the past it had been pervasive against non-revolutionary classes, members of the revolutionary party, and most recently the dissident intelligentsia.

7. As his most recent example of such "diffusion," Gurr (1986:57) refers to "the spreading use among conservative Latin American regimes of enforcement terror by special military units or by vigilante groups operating with the tacit approval of authorities ... by the end of the 1970s, such policies had been used to counter actual and threatened revolutionary (and sometimes reformist) opposition in Uruguay, Paraguay, Argentina, Chile, and El Salvador. Indicative of the level of enforcement terror relative to revolutionary terror is the estimate that in Argentina between 1976 and 1979 guerrillas killed around 700 people contrasted with some 20,000 killed by the military." This recalls Herman's (1982) distinction between insurgent "retail" and "wholesale" state terror.

8. Thus he acknowledges that Argentina, Brazil, Chile, and Uruguay illustrate this since it was only after the collapse or overthrow of democratic regimes that the military resorted to "wholesale" terror. Yet "democratic" electoral systems have often employed or tolerated violence against labour and ethnic or racial groups, domestically even to the extent of death squads. And this ignores their use of violence and terror against other countries.

9. "The use of violence by those in control can also occur within nations when the poor are making too many gains by nonviolent means ... This incident [military ouster of the Allende government] is not unique, but in most situations the poor do not get so far before being repressed. The elite are able to exercise control by using government power to arrest, imprison, or otherwise silence anyone who might in the future threaten them." (Glossop, 1987:155–6)

10. "In El Salvador the U.S. government does not overtly support death squad terrorism but has been prepared to tolerate it, just as it tolerates the presence in Florida of right-wing Salvadorian exiles who are a principle source of direction and funding for such terrorism."

11. With respect to beliefs as "decisional criteria that will trigger a government's movement from increased centralization of economic, political, military functions to torture, disappearances, and assassination as standard political practice," Lopez (1986) pinpoints the national security doctrine of such major Latin American states as Brazil, Argentina, Peru, and Chile during the 1960s and 1970s. In much of this, opponents are defined as mortal threats to the economic development of the society via state (military) managed capitalism, and thus to its very viability in the modern world. Although ignored by Lopez, US military influence in this area is examined at length in Wolpin (1973).

12. "Structural violence" should be distinguished from armed violence. While armed violence is violence exerted by persons against persons with the use of arms, structural violence is violence exerted by situations, by institutions, by social, political, and economic structures. Thus, when a person dies because he/she has no access to food, the effect is violent as far as that person is concerned, yet there is no individual actor who could be identified as the source of this violence. It is the system of food production and distribution that is to blame. The violence is thus exerted by an anonymous "structure." The measurement of

227

the number of persons killed through structural violence uses statistics of life expectancy. By comparing the life expectancy of affluent regions with that of poor regions, one can estimate how many persons died in a poor region on account of poverty and poverty-related conditions (e.g. lack of doctors, clean water, food, etc.) which can be interpreted as "structural violence."

13. Paulo Freire (1982:47–8) emphasized earlier, in his famous *Pedagogy of the Oppressed*, the crucial importance of a new consciousness and self-responsibility in the struggle from below to transform structures rather than punishing their beneficiaries. This is distinguished from token reforms or "aid," which remain integral to and legitimize the institutional sources of structural exploitation.

14. Yet Rubenstein (1987:70–2) highlights how the "savagery" of the military regimes in Uruguay and especially Argentina, "supported by secret army organizations," was sufficiently extreme to isolate the Tupamaros and Montoneros effectively from their mass constituencies. With respect to the latter, Izaguirre (1990) calls this a social "rupture strategy," while Buchanan (1987) emphasizes how overt and more subtle forms of state terror were systematically used by the military regime and its civilian allies to disrupt the economic and political strength of those believed responsible for the chaotic social conditions they inherited. Those targeted were not only the organized working classes, but also sectors of the domestic bourgeoisie.

15. The USA today has probably the most violent culture of all "developed" states. (See Gitlin, 1991:245; also NPR, 1991, which note that the average US child has watched about 25,000 murders on television by the age of eighteen!)

16. Illustrative is Garcia's (1983) contention that violence, particularly in Latin America, is largely a product of an educational system transmitting norms associated with Western philosophy that define "manhood" as achievable "only through domination" which often implies violence. Analogously, Newman and Lynch (1987) posit that such "protracted violence" as feuding and terroristic behaviours is linked to an "ideology of vengeance" which is reinforced by values of honour and manliness.

17. According to McCauley (1990:19–25) most of these attributes have been found in peaceful as well as highly coercive societies. To incite hostility and conflict, a perception of inequity (unfairness or illegitimacy) must be wedded to "absolutist" moral norms which are viewed as justifying violence. On the other hand, behaviourist learning theory can explain other instances of violence for those socialized into punitive or vengeful subcultures in which "peace" is *not* a highly valued norm. Thus death squad participation may be less a function of internalized "moral absolutism" than Sederberg's (1978) status threat, material rewards (i.e. money), "sport," or some combination.

18. McCauley refers to psychological and anthropological findings that are consistent with Galtung's rejection of innate instinctual as well as frustration-aggression assumptions unmodified by learning theory. Impulsive violence may, of course, operate at a personal level, but organized internal or external violence is largely instrumental. Many soldiers, especially conscripts, would prefer to *avoid* combat. Thus much organized violent participation must be coerced or reinforced by status or other rewards as well as by ideological absolution.

19. As does the popularity of war toys and video games. See "Toys" (1991) for further details, such as the fact that war-toy sales in the USA have increased 600 per cent since 1982.

20. Within the USA, targets of state terror have included Blacks and Native Americans (Saxton, 1991) as well as trade unionists and unemployed protestors (Folsom, 1991). Puerto Rican *independencistas* and rapprochement-oriented Cuban exiles have also been victimized.

21. Thus Noam Chomsky estimates the total number of people killed in US-sponsored activities in South-East Asia at four million (cited in Stockwell, 1991:149).

22. Not only did Schoultz (1981) find a strong US foreign aid bias for Latin American regimes that were notorious violators of human rights during the 1970–76 period, but, more globally, Wolpin (1986) identified the following correlates of extreme repressive brutality: (1) high levels of US military training; (2) high levels of US arms transfers; (3) large actual

US military presence; (4) military dominance. Conversely, such regimes boasted the lowest percentages of organized labour.

23. Yet we are *more restrictive* than the new US-ratified convention that prohibits mild as well as *extreme* torture. The latter is defined as "severe physical or mental pain inflicted by a public official for such purposes as obtaining a confession, punishment or for any reason based on discrimination."

24. Thus the immediate or proximate catalyst of violence can be found in the relative position and exploitation of groups rather than in the extreme poverty of particular countries. See, for instance, Ferguson (1990:49).

25. Even in the now defunct state socialist systems, the mass sectors received a far more impressive improvement in their living standards than in comparatively underdeveloped *laissez-faire* ones.

26. This is premised not only upon the ubiquitous ethnic conflict, much of which is at best indirectly related to global capitalist imperialism, but on Melko's (1973) findings of internal conflict prior to the modern era. Some residual violence would still continue owing to cultural values, historical animosities, fear, and perhaps differential socialization of the young.

References

Agee, Philip. 1975. *Inside the Company: CIA Diary*. New York: Bantam Books.

Aguilera P., Gabriel. 1980. "El estado, la lucha de clases y la violencia." *Revista Mexicana de Sociología* 42:2 (April–June), pp. 525–58.

Ahmad, Feroz. 1991. "Arab Nationalism, Radicalism, and the Specter of Neocolonialism." *Monthly Review*, February, pp. 30–7.

Altemeyer, Bob. 1988. "Marching in Step: A Psychological Explanation of State Terror." *The Sciences* 28:2 (March–April), pp. 30–8.

Amin, Samir. 1991. "The Real Stakes in the Gulf War." *Monthly Review*, July–August, pp. 14–24.

Amnesty International. 1983. *Political Killings by Governments*. London: Amnesty International.

Amnesty International. 1984. *Torture in the Eighties*. London: Amnesty International.

Ananthu, T.S. 1990. "New Trends Around the World: The Growing Sustainability Movement." *Gandhi Marg* 12:3 (October–December), pp. 343–51.

"As the Pope Sees It: Communism, Capitalism Are Both Losers." 1991. *In These Times*, 22 May, p. 14.

Avruch, Kevina, and Peter W. Black. 1991. "The Conflict Question and Conflict Resolution." *Peace and Change* 16:1 (January), pp. 22–45.

Bacchus, Wilfred A. 1990. *Mission in Mufti: Brazil's Military Regimes 1964–1985*. New York: Greenwood.

Barhoum, Khalil. 1991. "Perception and Reality." *Peace Review*, Summer, pp. 23–6.

Barkin, David. 1990. *Distorted Development: Mexico in the World Economy*. Boulder, CO: Westview.

Baron, Larry, and Murray A. Straus. 1988. "Cultural and Economic Sources of Homicide in the United States." *The Sociological Quarterly* 29:3 (September) pp. 371–90.

Bello, Walden, and Stephanie Rosenfeld. 1990. *Dragons in Distress*. Washington, DC: Institute for Policy Studies (Food First).

Bennis, Phyllis. 1991. "The U.N. in the New World Order: Bush's Tool and Victim." *Covert Action Information Bulletin* 37, Summer, pp. 4–8.

Black, Ian, and Benny Morris. 1991. *Israel's Secret Wars: A History of Israel's Intelligence Services*. New York: Grove Weidenfeld.

Blaker, James R. 1990. *United States Overseas Basing: An Anatomy of the Dilemma*. New York: Praeger.

Blechman, Barry, and Stephen Kaplan. 1978. *Force Without War*. Washington, DC: Brookings Institution.

Blum, William H. 1987. *The CIA: A Forgotten History – US Global Interventions Since World War II*. London: Zed Books.

Buchanan, Paul. 1987. "The Varied Faces of Domination: State Terror, Economic Policy, and Social Rupture during the Argentina 'Proceso', 1976–81." *American Journal of Political Science* 31:2 (May), 336–82.

Callahan, David. 1991. "A Dangerous Victory." *Nuclear Times*, Summer, pp. 13–18.

Campbell, Bruce. 1991. "Free Trade: Beggar Thy Neighbor." *NACLA Report on the Americas* 24:6 (May), pp. 22–9.

Challenge to the South: The Report of the South Commission. 1990. New York: Oxford University Press.

Chaudhri, Mohammed Ahsen. 1991. "The Gulf War and Islam." *Peace Review*, Summer, pp. 23–6.

Clark, Ramsey. 1991. Editorial, *The Nation*, 11 March, pp. 293–4.

Cockburn, Alexander. 1991a. "Teamsters Elections Sound Hopeful Note for a U.S. Labor Movement in Decline." *In These Times*, 22 May, p. 17.

———. 1991b. "Beat the Devil." *The Nation*, 8 July, pp. 42–3.

———. 1991c. "Beat the Devil." *The Nation*, 9 September, pp. 254–5.

Coffin, Tristram. 1991a. "FYI, Items of Interest from Spectator Files." *The Washington Spectator*, 1 June, p. 4.

———. 1991b. "A Lesson for Politicians." *The Washington Spectator*, 1 July, pp. 1–3.

Cohen, Ronald. 1984. "Warfare and State Formation: Wars Make States and States Make Wars." In Ferguson, 1984a, pp. 329–58.

Cohen, Tracy. 1991. "Covering the Peace Movement." *Nuclear Times*, Summer, pp. 24–6.

Commoner, Barry. 1990. *Making Peace With the Planet*. New York: Pantheon.

Corn, David. 1991. "What Harkin May Herald." *The Nation*, 29 July–5 August, pp. 156, 158–60.

Cortright, David. 1991. "Assessing Peace Movement Effectiveness in the 1980s." *Peace and Change* 16:1 (January), pp. 46–63.

"Covert Operations." 1991a. *Unclassified*, June–July, pp. 11–12.

"Crimes Against Humanity." 1991b. *Unclassified*, April–May, p. 10.

Currie, Elliott. 1991. "Crime in the Market Society." *Dissent*, Spring, pp. 254–9.

Dallin, Alexander, and G.W. Breslauer. 1970. *Political Terror in Communist Systems*. Stanford, CA: Stanford University Press.

Deere, Carmen Diana. 1991. "Cuba's Struggle for Self-Sufficiency." *Monthly Review*, July–August, pp. 55–73.

De Swaan, Abram. 1977. "Terror as a Government Service." In M. Hoefnagels (ed.), *Repression and Repressive Violence*. Amsterdam: Swets and Zeitlinger.

Divale, William Tulio, and Marvin Harris. 1976. "Population, Warfare, and the Male Supremacist Complex," *American Anthropologist* 78:3 (September), pp. 521–38.

Dumas, Lloyd. 1986. *The Overburdened Economy*. Berkeley: University of California Press.

Duvall, Raymond D., and Michael Stohl. 1983. "Governance by Terror." In Michael Stohl (ed.), *The Politics of Terrorism*. 2nd edn. Marcel Dekker.

Eckhardt, William. 1982. "Atrocities, Civilizations, and Savages: Ways to Avoid a Nuclear Holocaust." *Bulletin of Peace Proposals* 13:4, pp. 343–50.

Elshtain, Jean Bethke, and John Buell. 1991. "Families in Trouble." *Dissent*, Spring, pp. 262–6.

Falk, Richard, Samuel S. Kin, and Saul H. Mendlovitz (eds.). 1982. *Toward a Just World Order*, vol. 1. Boulder, CO: Westview.

Ferguson, R. Brian. 1984. "Studying War." In Ferguson, 1984a, pp. 1–81.

———. 1984a. *Warfare, Culture, and Environment*. Orlando, FL: Academic Press.

———. 1990. "Explaining War." In Haas, 1990, pp. 26–55.

Finkelstein, Norman G. 1991. "Israel and Iraq: A Double Standard in the Application." *Monthly Review* July–August, pp. 25–54.

Fogarty, Brian E. 1991. "The Function of Military Waste." *Peace and Change* 16:2 (April), pp. 162–75.

Folsom, Franklin. 1991. *Impatient Armies of the Poor: The Story of Collective Action of the Unemployed, 1808–1942*. Denver: University Press of Colorado.

Freire, Paulo. 1982. "Pedagogy of the Oppressed." In Falk, et al., 1982, pp. 47–54.

Friedland, Mary. 1991. Review of *Environmental Hazards of War: Releasing Dangerous Forces in an Industrialized World*," ed. Arthur Westing (London: Sage, 1990). *Peace Review* 3:1, Summer, pp. 45–6.

Galeano, Eduardo. 1989. "Democracy in Latin America: Best is That Which Best Creates." *Social Justice* 16:1 (Spring), pp. 119–26.

Galtung, Johan. 1982. "Self-Reliance: An Overdue Strategy for Transition." In Falk et al., 1982, pp. 602–22.

———. 1990. "Cultural Violence." *Journal of Peace Research* 27:3 (August), pp. 291–305.

Garcia, Celina. 1983. "Latin American Traditions and Perspectives," *International Review of Education* 29:3, pp. 369–83.

George, Susan. 1989. *A Fate Worse Than Debt: The World Financial Crisis and the Poor*. New York: Grove Press.

Gerson, Joseph. 1991. "The War and the New World Order." *Peace Review*, Summer, pp. 31–5.

Gitlin, Tod. 1991. "On Thrills and Kills: Sadomasochism in the Movies." *Dissent*, Spring, pp. 245–8.

Glossop, Ronald J. 1987. *Confronting War: An Examination of Humanity's Most Pressing Problem*. Jefferson, NC: McFarland.

Gregor, Thomas. 1990. "Uneasy Peace: Intertribal Relations in Brazil's Upper Xingu." In Haas, 1990, pp. 105–24.

Guest, Iain. 1983. "Report to UN Panel Cites 2 Million Executions." *International Herald Tribune*, 17 February, p. 3.

Gurr, Ted Robert. 1986. "The Political Origins of State Violence and Terror: A Theoretical Analysis." In Stohl and Lopez, 1986, pp. 45–71.

Haas, Jonathan (ed.). 1990. *The Anthropology of War*. Cambridge and New York: Cambridge University Press.

Harff, Barbara, 1986. "Genocide as State Terrorism." In Stohl and Lopez, 1986, pp. 165–87.

Heelas, Paul. 1989. "Identifying Peaceful Societies." In Howell and Willis, 1989, pp. 225–43.

Henderson, Conway W. 1991. "Conditions Affecting the Use of Political Repression." *Journal of Conflict Resolution* 35:1, pp. 120–42.

Henwood, Doug. 1991. "Recovery? Not by a Long Shot." *The Nation*, 9 September, pp. 262–4.

Herman, Edward. 1982. *The Real Terror Network*. Boston: South End Press.

Herman, Edward, and Frank Brodhead. 1984. *Demonstration Elections: U.S. Staged Elections in the Dominican Republic, Vietnam and El Salvador*. Boston: South End Press.

Hobsbawm, Eric. 1991. "¡The Perils of the New Nationalism." *The Nation*, 4 November, pp. 555–6.

Hockenos, Paul. 1991. "IMF Austerity Measures: Bitter Medicine to Swallow." *These Times*, 1–7 May, p. 11.

Howell, Signe, and Roy Willis (eds). 1989. *Societies at Peace: Anthropological Perspectives*. New York and London: Routledge.

Hunter, Jane. 1991. "Dismantling the War on Libya." *Covert Action Information Bulletin* 37, Summer, pp. 47–51.

Izaguirre, Ines. 1990. "Ruptura de relaciones sociales: una estrategia conceptual para el análisis del terrorismo de estado en Argentina." Paper presented at International Studies Association meeting.

Jacobson, Julius. 1991. "Pax Americana: The New World Order." *New Politics* III (3), pp. 5–24.

Jonas, Susanne. 1990. "'New Thinking' or More of the Same? Bush Administration Policy on Central America." *New Political Science* 18/19 (Fall/Winter), pp. 165–80.

Jongman, Berto. 1991. "Why Some States Kill and Torture While Others Do Not." *PIOOM Newsletter and Progress Report*, Summer, pp. 8–11.

Kang, Mili. 1991. "North Korea, The Next Target?" *Covert Action Information Bulletin* 37, Summer, pp. 14–19.

Kegley, Charles W., Jr. (ed.). 1990. *International Terrorism: Characteristics, Causes, Controls*. New York: St Martin's Press.

Kennedy, Paul. 1987. *The Rise and Fall of the Great Powers*. New York: Random House.

Kirk, Robin. 1991. "Shining Path Is Gaining in Peru." *The Nation*, 29 April, pp. 552–5.

Knapp, Peter, and Alan J. Spector. 1991. *Crisis and Change*. Chicago: Nelson-Hall.

Koenig, Daniel J., and J.C. van Es. 1976. "Social Status and Extremist Political Attidues." *Sociological Quarterly* 17:1 (Winter), pp. 16–26.

Kohler, Gernot. 1982. "Global Apartheid," in Falk et al., 1982, pp. 315–25.

Kolko, Joyce. 1988. *Restructuring the World Economy*. New York: Pantheon.

Kothari, Rajni. 1989. *State Against Democracy: In Search of Humane Governance*. New York: New Horizons Press.

LaRoque, Gene. 1991. "Rear Admiral Gene La Roque Speaks Out on Peace, Democracy, Militarism." *New Patriot*, July–August, pp. 6–7.

Lauria, Joe. 1991. "Panel To Probe U.S. Led War Crimes in Iraq." *Guardian* (NY), 10 April, p. 5.

"LBO Replies: War and Waste." 1991. *Left Business Observer*, p. 3.

Light, Julie. 1991. "Nicaragua: Speaking Bitterness." *NACLA Report on the Americas* 24:6 (May), pp. 4–7.

Lindgren, Stefan. 1991. "Of Human and Social Rights and the Freedom From Want." *These Times*, 22 May, p. 16.

Little, Craig B., and Christopher P. Sheffield. 1983. "Frontiers and Criminal Justice: English Private Prosecution Societies and American Vigilantism in the Eighteenth and Nineteenth Centuries." *American Sociological Review* 48:6 (December), pp. 796–808.

Lopez, George. 1986. "National Security Ideology as an Impetus to State Violence and State Terror." In Stohl and Lopez, 1986, pp. 74–95.

Lowrey, Amy, and David Corn. 1991. "Mexican Trade Bill: Fast Track to Unemployment." *The Nation*, 3 June, pp. 735–8.

Luban, David. 1987. "The Legacies of Nuremberg." *Social Research* 54:4 (Winter), 779–829.

MacEwan, Arthur. 1991. "Why the Emperor Can't Afford New Clothes: International Change and Fiscal Disorder in the United States." *Monthly Review*, July–August, pp. 74–94.

Magdoff, Harry. 1991. "Are There Lessons to be Learned?" *Monthly Review*, February, pp. 1–19.

Marshall, Jonathan, Dale Scott and Jane Hunter. 1987. *The Iran Contra Connection: Secret Teams and Covert Operations in the Reagan Era.* Boston: South End Press.

Mason, T. David, and Dale A. Krane. 1989. "The Political Economy of Death Squads: Toward a Theory of the Impact of State-Sanctioned Terror." *International Studies Quarterly* 33:2 (June), pp. 175–98.

Mayer, Tom. 1991. "Imperialism and The Gulf War." *Monthly Review*, April, pp. 1–11.

McCauley, Clark. 1990. "Conference Overview." In Haas, 1990, pp. 1–25.

McClintock, Michael. 1985. *The American Connection.* Vol. 1: *State Terror and Popular Resistance in El Salvador*; vol. 2: *State Terror and Popular Resistance in Guatemala.* London: Zed Books (2nd edn).

McDougall, Gay J., and Carl E.S. Soderbergh. 1990. *South Africa's Death Squads.* Lawyers Committee for Civil Rights Under Law, Washington DC.

McGehee, Ralph W. 1983. *Deadly Deceits: My 25 Years in the CIA.* New York: Sheridan Square Press.

McSherry, J. Patrice. 1990. "The Roots of U.S. Policy toward Latin America." *New Political Science* 18/19 (Fall/Winter), pp. 195–207.

Melko, Matthew. 1973. *52 Peaceful Societies.* Oakville, Ontario: CPRI Press.

Melman, Seymour. 1988. *The Demilitarized Society. Disarmament and Conversion.* Montreal: Harvest Books.

Meyer, David S. 1991. "Peace Movements and National Security Policy: A Research Agenda." *Peace and Change* 16:2 (April), pp. 131–61.

Miliband, Ralph. 1991. "Socialism in Question." *Monthly Review*, March, pp. 16–26.

Mitchell, Christopher, Michael Stohl, David Carleton, and George A. Lopez. 1986. "State Terrorism: Issue of Concept and Measurement," in Stohl and Lopez, 1986, pp. 3–25.

Mitchell, Neil, and James M. McCormick. 1988. "Economic and Political Explanations of Human Rights Violations." *World Politics* 40:4, pp. 476–98.

Muwakkil, Salim. 1991. "New Trends in Brutality from Chicago's Finest." *In These Times.*

Navarro, Vicente. 1985. "The Road Ahead." *Monthly Review*, July–August, pp. 30–58.

Newman, Graeme, and Michael J. Lynch. 1987. "From Feuding to Terrorism: The Ideology of Vengeance." *Contemporary Crises* 11:3, pp. 223–42.

233

NPR, 1991. Interview with Newton Minow, in "Morning Report." Washington DC: National Public Radio, 1 July.

"October Update." *Unclassified*, June–July 1991, pp. 12–16.

Parenti, Michael. 1989. *The Sword and the Dollar*. New York: St Martin's Press.

Patterson, Orlando. 1977. *Ethnic Chauvinism: The Reactionary Impulse*. New York: Stein and Day.

Perdue, William D. 1989. *Terrorism and the State*. Westport, CT: Greenwood Press (Praeger).

Petras, James, 1990. "Transformation and the Future of Socialism in Latin America." *New Political Science* 18/19 (Fall/Winter), pp. 181–93.

Powell, Bingham G. 1982. *Contemporary Democracies: Participation, Stability and Violence*. Cambridge, MA: Harvard University Press.

"Pox Americana: Review of the Month." *Monthly Review*, July–August, 1991, pp. 1–13.

Ratner, Michael. 1991. "Home Truths About Torture." *The Nation*, 29 July–5 August, p. 142.

Ray, Ellen, and William H. Schaap. 1991. "Behind the Veil: Disinformation and Covert Operations." *Covert Action Information Bulletin* 37, Summer, pp. 9–14.

Reardon, Betty. 1991. Review of *Societies at Peace: Anthropological Perspectives*, ed. Signe Howell and Roy Willis. *Peace and Change* 16:1 (January), pp. 116–18.

Reed, Laura. 1991. "An Obscured Dimension of the Arms Race: A Review of *The Sun Never Sets*, edited by Bruce Birchard and Joseph Gerson (South End Press)." *Nuclear Times*, Summer, pp. 45–6.

Reich, Robert B. 1991. "Who Champions the Working Class?" *New Patriot*, July–August, p. 11.

Reynolds, Diana. 1990. "FEMA and the NSC: The Rise of the National Security State." *Covert Action Information Bulletin* 33 (Winter), pp. 54–8.

———. 1991. "Domestic Consequences of the Gulf War." *Covert Action Information Bulletin* 37, Summer, pp. 36–41.

Robarchek, Clayton. 1990. "Motivations and Material Causes: On the Explanation of Conflict and War." In Haas, 1990, pp. 26–55.

Rubenstein, Richard E. 1987. *Alchemists of Revolution: Terrorism in the Modern World*. New York: Basic Books.

Saunders, Jerry W. 1983. *Peddlers in Crisis: The Committee on the Present Danger*. Boston, MA: South End Press.

———. 1991. "The Gulf War and Bush's Folly." *Peace Review*, Summer, pp. 27–30.

Saxton, Alexander. 1991. *The Rise and Fall of the White Republic: Class Politics and Mass Culture in Nineteenth-Century America*. London: Verso.

Schmid, Alex P. 1983. *Political Terrorism: A Research Guide to Concepts, Theories, Data Bases and Literature*. Amsterdam North-Holland.

———. 1991. "Repression and the Military." *PIOOM* 3:1 (Summer), p. 15.

Schoultz, Lars. 1981. "U.S. Foreign Policy and Human Rights Violations in Latin America: A Comparative Analysis of Foreign Aid Distribution." *Comparative Politics* 13 (January), pp. 149–70.

Scott, Peter Dale, and Jonathan Marshall. 1991. *Cocaine Politics: Drugs, Armies, and the CIA in Central America*. Berkeley, CA: University of California Press.

Sederberg, Peter C. 1978. "The Phenomenology of Vigilantism in Contemporary America: An Interpretation." *Terrorism* 1:3–4, pp. 287–305.

————. 1989. *Terrorist Myths: Illusion, Rhetoric, and Reality*. Englewood Cliffs, NJ: Prentice Hall.

————. 1990. "Responses to Dissident Terrorism: From Myth to Maturity." In Kegley, 1990, pp. 262–80.

Serrano F., Alfonso. 1991. "Poverty and Intervention: The U.S. Legacy in Central America." *Nuclear Times*, Summer, pp. 36–8.

Shah, Sonia. 1991. "Allahu Akbar! The Political Impact of Islam." *Nuclear Times*, Summer, pp. 21–33.

Shields, James, and Leonard Weinberg. 1976. "Reactive Violence and the American Frontier: A Contemporary Evaluation." *Western Political Quarterly* 29:1 (March), pp. 86–101.

Shy, John. 1971. "The American Military Experience: History and Learning." *Journal of Interdisciplinary History* 1:2, pp. 205–28.

Simon, Joel. 1991. "Mexico's Free Traders: Salinas Repeals the Revolution." *The Nation*, 24 June, pp. 842–4.

Singer, Daniel. 1991. "Socialism's Setting Sun." *The Nation*, 3 June, pp. 732–4.

Sivard, Ruth Leger. 1982. *World Military and Social Expenditures: 1982*. Leesburg, VA: World Priorities.

————. 1990. *World Military and Social Expenditures: 1990*. Washington, DC: World Priorities.

————. 1991. *World Military and Social Expenditures: 1991*. Washington, DC: World Priorities.

Social Breakdown in the United States. Ed. Fred Siegel. *Dissent*, Spring 1991, pp. 163–304.

Stockwell, John. 1991. *The Praetorian Guard: The U.S. Role in the New World Order*. Boston: South End Press.

Stohl, Michael. 1982. "International Dimensions of State Terrorism." In Michael Stohl and George Lopez (eds), *The State as Terrorist*. Westport, CT: Greenwood.

————. 1986. "The Superpowers and International Terrorism." In Stohl and Lopez, 1986, pp. 207–34.

————. 1990. "Demystifying the Mystery of International Terrorism." In Kegley, 1990, pp. 81–96.

Stohl, Michael, and George A. Lopez (eds.). 1986. *Government Violence and Repression: An Agenda for Research*. Westport, CT: Greenwood Press.

Sweezy, Paul M. 1991. "What's New in the New World Order?" *Monthly Review*, June, pp. 1–4.

Tirman, John. 1991. "The Fickle Public." *Nuclear Times*, Summer, pp. 4–5.

"Toys." 1991. *These Times*, 26 June, p. 6.

Trainor, F.E. 1989; "Reconstructing Radical Development Theory." *Alternatives* 14:4 (October), pp. 481–515.

Trevarthen, Colwyn, and Katerina Logotheti. 1989. "Child in Society, and Society in Children. The Nature of Basic Trust." In Howell and Willis, 1989, pp. 165–86.

Vanden, Harry E. 1990. "Terrorism, Law, and State Policy in Central America: The Eighties." *New Political Science* 18/19 (Fall/Winter), pp. 55–73.

Walters, Eugene V. 1969. *Terror and Resistance*. New York: Oxford University Press.

Walton, Richard J. 1991. "What Are We Fighting For?" [Review of *The Vietnam Wars 1945–1990*, by Marilyn B. Young] *The Nation*, 27 May, pp. 709–11.

Where Are We Going: Review of the Month." *Monthly Review*, March 1991, pp. 1–15.

Miles D. Wolpin

White, Robert. 1991. "Ambassador White Speaks Out." *Unclassified*, June–July, pp. 1–2.

Windmiller, Marshall. 1991. "Dialogue: Justice, Law and a Few Other Strong Words for the Left." *These Times*, 10–23 July, p. 16.

Wolpin, Miles D. 1973. *Military Aid and Counterrevolution in the Third World*. Lexington, MA: D.C. Heath.

———. 1986a. "State Terrorism and Repression in the Third World." In Stohl and Lopez, 1986, pp. 97–164.

———. 1986b. *Militarization, Repression and Social Welfare in the Third World*. London: Croom Helm.

———. 1991. *America Insecure: Arms Transfers, Global Interventionism, and the Erosion of National Security*. Jefferson, NC: McFarland.

———. 1992. "Third World Military Roles and Environmental Security," *New Political Science*, Fall, no. 23, pp. 108–14.

World Bank. 1991a. *Financial Systems and Development*. Excerpted from *World Bank Development Report 1989*. Washington, DC: World Bank.

———. 1991b. *Urban Policy and Economic Development: An Agenda for the 1990s*. Washington, DC: World Bank.

———. 1991c. *Social Spending in Latin America*. Compiled by Margaret E. Grosh. Washington, DC: World Bank.

Zunes, Stephen. 1991. "Arab Nationalism and the Gulf War." *Peace Review*, Summer, pp. 8–12.

9

Violence and culture in the United States

Robert Brent Toplin

For about a quarter of a century – from the mid-1930s to the early 1960s – Americans enjoyed perhaps the most tranquil period in their history with respect to violence in everyday life. Then, during the 1960s, Americans were shocked to see new outbreaks of violence. Violent crime soared during the decade; groups of protesting blacks, college students, anti-war activists broke the quiet of cities and college campuses, and the assassinations of President John F. Kennedy, Martin Luther King, Jr., and other prominent public figures shook public confidence. Excitement over these developments in Washington led to the creation of national commissions to study the causes of violence and to recommend possible remedies. Out of these efforts came three lengthy reports. The 1966–67 President's Commission on Law Enforcement and Administration of Justice examined the criminal justice system and prospects for preventing crime; The National Advisory Commission on Civil Disorders of 1968 (often called the Kerner Commission) assessed the urban race riots and recommended improvements for blacks in the city ghettos. Finally, the National Commission on the Causes and Prevention of Violence offered the broadest view of violence in its 1969 report by investigating the sources of diverse kinds of violent behaviour.

America's escalating role in the Viet Nam conflict during the 1960s also pushed fundamental questions about violence and culture into public debates. US intervention in Viet Nam divided the nation as no previous twentieth-century war had done. Many American critics of the fighting in South-East Asia argued that the killing in Viet Nam was unnecessary and immoral; they claimed the nation was carrying anti-communist ideology to extremes. Cold War thinking had grown so intense that Americans were ready to sanction brutal military actions against any people in the world who attempted to experiment with socialism or communism, they argued. Such attacks excited a wide-ranging examination of the sources of American aggressiveness in foreign policy. Scholars looked back into American history in the 1960s and 1970s with increased interest in finding the roots of the United States' lively twentieth-century record of military action in world affairs. Anguish over the suffering of both American soldiers and Asians in the Viet Nam war helped to bring this interest in the connections between violence and culture to the fore.

When these developments first occurred in the 1960s, it was difficult to gain perspective. The violent events had appeared so quickly on the landscape that it was hard to determine whether the trouble represented only a temporary problem or long-term troubles concerning a culture of violence in the United States. Now, a quarter of a century after the tumult of the sixties, we can more effectively place these examples of violence in the larger context of American history. While this discussion is not limited to violence in the sixties, it suggests that it is useful to begin with a view of the outbursts in that decade in order to give structure to the discussion. The 1960s serve as a pivotal point from which to view both the historical trends and the lessons for the 1990s.

In the broadest sense, four kinds of violence attracted the interest of the public as well as scholars in the 1960s, and still today these four categories represent the most important divisions in major discussions about violence in the United States. The first category may be described as collective and political violence. It includes group protests, demonstrations, strikes, riots, and related activities. The second broad category concerns criminal violence. This subject involves acts by individuals or small groups and includes assaults, robbery, murder, rape, and related problems. The third grouping, which includes assassinations, mass "gratuitous" violence, and serial killings, may be identified as psychopathic violence. This topic has received considerably less attention in scholarship than the first two. Finally, the discussion examines the problem of violence in late twentieth-century American foreign policy.

Collective and political violence

Numerous outbursts of collective and political violence in the United States attracted attention in the 1960s, and these disturbing developments left many Americans asking if their country was as homogeneous in outlook as they had thought. Popular scholarship in the 1950s and early 1960s described the United States as a nation built on consensus. According to this viewpoint, individuals and groups in the country differed about small details, but they agreed on a number of essential matters. They respected private property, maintained faith in the democratic process, and viewed their country as a land of economic opportunity. This "liberal tradition" made the United States different from many other societies around the world, where, it was said, feudal-style conditions gave land, education, opportunity, and political power to only a few.[1] Upheaval in the sixties, however, shattered much of this confidence in "consensus" and made conflict, not agreement, look like the standard of life in America.

The early collective outbursts in the 1960s involved African-Americans and students, and both of these groups figured prominently in the violence that spread through the decade. With respect to African-Americans, a relatively small-scale riot in the black ghetto of Harlem (a section of New York City) in 1964 was followed by much more destructive outbursts in Watts (a neighbourhood of Los Angeles) in 1965, Cleveland in 1966, Newark and Detroit in 1967, and numerous cities across the United States in 1968. Most of this protest activity occurred in northern cities; ghetto riots in the South occurred on a much smaller scale. By the late sixties, African-American "radicals" such as Stokely Carmichael were angering moderate and conservative whites with cries of "Black Power," and the American people had become deeply troubled by the growing trend toward racial confrontation.[2] Most of the violent college student protests (led generally but not exclusively by whites) began modestly, with the activities of the Free Speech Movement at the University of California at Berkeley in 1964, and then became more widespread in later years as student groups took up a number of causes, including the integration of blacks on the campuses. The greatest catalyst for student protest came from resistance to the Viet Nam War. Student demonstrations against the war and the military draft were usually non-violent with respect to personal injury, but occasionally individual students or recent graduates who considered themselves "radicals" damaged property. Only a few collected weapons or made

239

bombs. The students' sense of frustration and anger grew on the campuses until it exploded in the spring of 1970 in protest against President Richard Nixon's decision to send American and South Vietnamese troops into Cambodia. Strikes broke out on almost 450 campuses, a few protesters firebombed military education buildings on the campuses, and at Kent State University students and national guardsmen clashed for a few days before the guardsmen fired their rifles in a broadside that killed four students.[3] Kent State represented both the high point of the student confrontations and the beginning of the end of the wave of violent confrontations. The incident profoundly shocked the nation and made both defenders and critics of the war in Viet Nam realize how polarized American society had become. After Kent State, policy-makers in Washington emphasized that they were de-escalating the US military commitment in South-East Asia. University campuses then turned calmer.

In view of the seriousness of the students' cause (which, above all, was to stop the killing in South-East Asia), it is remarkable that their protests remained, for the most part, quite peaceful. Most of the student activity against the Viet Nam war involved meetings, rallies, marches, and demonstrations. Assaults on property or people were rare, and just a few Americans lost their lives in the active period of collective protest between 1965 and 1970.

Many factors explain the wave of protest in the sixties, but few stand out, particularly in the scholarly literature. With respect to African-American protest, a number of scholars have emphasized the concept of rising expectations. Opportunities for blacks were not becoming worse in the sixties, they argue; in fact, the economic condition of African-Americans improved somewhat in comparison to conditions in previous decades. But American society could not deliver its full promise. President Lyndon Johnson may have aggravated the situation unknowingly by promoting the creation of "The Great Society." Such language inspired hope, but as blacks became aware that their expectations could not be realized, their dissatisfaction grew.[4] With regard to student protests, the Viet Nam War badly undermined the "consensus" ideal. Anger over the war broke down the sense of legitimacy – the population's traditional respect for the government, the political leadership, the flag, and other symbols of a national community. When the irritant of American participation in a long and unpopular war began to disappear in the early 1970s, interest in collective protest and violence waned quickly.

There is also an international dimension to the wave of protest.

Student upheaval somewhat similar to that in American patterns broke out in a number of cities around the world, especially in 1968 (for instance, in Paris, Prague, Mexico City, and Rio de Janeiro). Any study of the conditions in the United States during this period should consider the international context as well.

The conditions which caused student unrest in the late 1960s were primarily short-term. Collective protests of college students diminished dramatically in the second half of 1970 and in 1971. Since that time, there has been very little collective or political violence involving university students. In this context the upheavals of the sixties have appeared anachronistic, the product of specific conditions during a unique period in recent American history.

Collective protest by African-Americans also diminished significantly, but the potential for flare-ups continued. In the 1970s, '80s and '90s many blacks in the United States remained outside the economic mainstream. Millions were identified as part of an underemployed and unemployed "underclass" concentrated in America's large cities. Many from the underclass continued to demonstrate resentment about the poor opportunities for obtaining jobs, housing, and education. Occasionally their anger excited national attention, as in the case of the riots in Miami's Liberty City in 1980. That violent protest occurred after an all-white jury acquitted four former Miami police officers in a case involving the fatal beating of a black insurance executive. The worst of the new racial riots took place in 1992 in Los Angeles, when African-Americans protested the acquittal of four police officers on all but one state charge associated with the beating of Rodney King. The assault had been recorded on videotape, and television news programmes had broadcast the shocking footage frequently. Fifty-eight persons died in the rioting, 11,900 were arrested, and more than a billion dollars in property damage occurred in the five days of upheaval in Los Angeles. Around the same time, smaller-scale flare-ups occurred in Las Vegas, San Francisco, Atlanta, Miami, and Seattle. The next year, citizens in Los Angeles remained tense as they awaited the outcome of another jury decision in the Rodney King case, this time involving federal charges that the police officers violated King's civil rights. When a jury convicted two of the officers, many African-Americans in Los Angeles cheered the verdict, and the city remained calm.

While the violence in Los Angeles excited considerable discussion about racial tensions in the United States, it did not demonstrate that widespread rioting resulting from enmity between blacks and whites was as likely to explode in the 1990s as it had in the 1960s. Most of the tumult of 1992 was concentrated in southern California. Furthermore, the "racial" character of the confrontations was much more complex than in the case of the 1960s riots. Many Hispanics joined African-Americans in the looting and burning in 1992, and Korean immigrants figured prominently among the people whose businesses were attacked. The increasingly multi-ethnic character of the country's urban population made it appear that the large-scale, nationwide black–white clashes of the 1960s were not likely to be repeated. The political environment also made an impact. Discontent over the Viet Nam war and the expectations for social progress spurred by the recent civil rights gains and President Johnson's Great Society programmes had contributed to the enthusiasm for collective protest in the late 1960s. Such factors were absent in later years.

There have been other major episodes of collective violence in US history, of course. Some of them involved fear of radicalism (as in the riots against abolitionists, the leaders of the movement against slavery, in northern cities in the 1830s). Much of the collective violence concerned ethnic tensions, as in the case of the anti-Chinese riot in Los Angeles in 1871. During the period of America's industrial spurt, there were also outbreaks of violence related to the workers' struggle to organize unions. The Railroad Strike of 1877, the Homestead Massacre of 1892, and the Ludlow Strike in the Colorado mining fields in 1913–1914 are among the most dramatic examples of these conflicts. An anthology edited by Richard Hofstadter and Michael Wallace (1971) provides an excellent overview of these violent incidents in American history.

When examining the broad record of American history, these examples of collective violence appear more episodic than endemic. They resulted from the particular circumstances of a period in American history, not from long-standing tensions that would make collective violence a natural feature in the American political landscape. For example, anti-abolitionist violence in the northern states died out quickly by the 1840s, and by the 1850s many of the same leaders who had been targets of angry protest became heroes in their communities. As people in the northern states began to favour anti-slavery politics, the abolitionists' image improved substantially. Ethnic violence also was usually associated with particular social pressures – in this case the thrust of immigration. When newcomers arrived in large numbers rather suddenly in some communities, sometimes Americans from the dominant ethnic groups displayed their resentment through ugly group protest (as in the Philadelphia riots against Irish immigrants in 1844). Later, when the tensions associated with immigration passed, the violence subsided. Similarly, violence in labour–management relations developed out of particular tensions of the times. Most of the worst examples of injury and killing occurred during the 1877–1920 period. That was the era of America's rapid rise as an industrial nation and the struggle to protect the industrial workers through union representation. After unions won the right of representation and collective bargaining in most of the United States' largest manufacturing sectors during the 1930s and 1940s, labour violence dropped dramatically. In short, the outbursts of collective violence were related to temporary tensions, and, for the most part, by the late twentieth century they no longer represented a serious problem.

Of all the historical examples of collective violence in the United States, aggression between whites and African-Americans has been the most persistent. The relationship remained troublesome through much of American history, because racial slavery and segregation were fundamental institutions in the culture of the American South. During the years before the Civil War, whites remained fearful of slave insurrections and employed a variety of violent means to intimidate blacks and keep them deferential. Southern secessionists broke from the Union in large part because they feared abolitionism (the destruction of slavery) and a future in which blacks could enjoy freedom and equality in Southern society. In other words, the foundations of the Civil War in America can be traced to the tensions in white–black relations. After the end of slavery, whites in the South turned to other devices to maintain their dominance. Terrorist organizations such as the Ku Klux Klan played an important role in establishing the new order. Indeed, various forms of intimidation continued to trouble blacks in the American South until the 1960s. The civil rights movement of that decade could not achieve all its goals, but it did bring many of the most glaring racial abuses to an end. African-Americans gained much greater protection from the law, and the racial murders and beatings that had so long been a feature of Southern life diminished dramatically. Especially in the 1960s, individuals guilty of racial attacks came under closer scrutiny from the American justice system.

While the problem of white–black collective violence was much reduced in the American scene by the 1990s, its pattern in US history offers some lessons for people in other nations who seek an understanding of the factors that lead to group conflict. Through much of American history, culture in the American South seemed divided between two "racial" groups. Whites outnumbered blacks in several southern states, and in a few places, such as South Carolina and Mississippi, the numbers were roughly even. In this respect the pattern of two "peoples" and "cultures" in the American South resembled the pattern in many other nations in the world that are divided today by ethnic tensions. In situations where only a few major groups compete for power and one dominates another, the potential for violent conflict is often great. It is noteworthy that the United States has succeeded in removing a great deal of this tension in the late twentieth century by taking measures to ensure equality under the law and seeking ways to integrate its major minority population into the mainstream of economic, political, and social activities. In government, for example, African-Americans were holding the mayors' offices in most of the largest cities in the United States by the early 1990s. The struggle for racial equality in the United States is not complete, of course, but it has made enough substantial progress to relegate most collective white–black violence to the history books.

For the most part, American society has lacked the long-term divisions that have made political and collective violence seem endemic in many countries in the world.[5] The United States has allowed religious freedom and participation to so many groups that it has not experienced intense divisions such as the enmity between Protestants and Catholics in Northern Ireland. Also, the United States has become a homeland to so many diverse immigrant groups that it is not troubled by widespread ethnic and nationalistic violence such as the tension found in former Yugoslavia involving Croatians, Serbs, and others. Furthermore, despite the appearance of many immigrants with their own languages (especially Spanish-speaking newcomers in recent years), the United States remains essentially a one-language nation. Various ethnic groups try to maintain their mother tongues, but the American system of public education ensures that virtually all children of immigrants develop a basic command of English. This common denominator enables most people in the United States to communicate with other Americans, and it operates as a powerful contributor toward "consensus." Nations around the world that have been divided by language often face much greater difficulty in maintaining a sense of unity, and sometimes they are troubled by collective and political violence.

Criminal violence

Just as outbreaks of political and collective violence increased greatly in the 1960s, so did the incidence of criminal violence. Statistics for aggravated assaults, armed robbery, and murder soared during the 1960s. The US Federal Bureau of Investigation's *Uniform Crime Reports* indicated that all aspects of violent crime rose by 156 per cent in the period (the real crime *rate* may have been greater, since many frustrated or fearful people did not report violent crimes to the authorities).[6] The incidence of rape also climbed dramatically, stretching from 17,400 reported cases in 1962 to 46,400 in 1972. Increasingly, acts of violence involved strangers and robbery involved injuries. The growing brutality accompanying petty crimes – the change from non-violent stealing to what Americans came to refer to as "mugging" – raised the American's people's apprehensions and brought demands for "law and order" in the late 1960s and early 1970s.

Unlike political and collective violence, criminal violence did not subside after the 1960s. The problem remained serious and even grew in intensity in various periods. Between 1985 and 1989, for example, violent crime rose by 19 per cent. Even rural areas and small farming towns, which usually escaped such problems, began to suffer.[7] By 1990, drug trafficking and violent crimes were plaguing many once-peaceful communities. The western state of Montana, for instance, saw a 23.4 per cent increase in violent crimes reported to the police in 1990.[8] Not surprisingly, the public's sense of fear and frustration rose as the crime wave continued. A study in the 1980s revealed that about 75 per cent of the American people believed the country was making no real progress against crime and violence.

African-Americans have been particularly affected by the crime wave of the last quarter-century. According to an epidemiologist who wrote a report for the federal government, in some areas in the United States "it is now more likely for a black male between his fifteenth and twenty-fifth birthday to die from homicide that it was a for a United States soldier to be killed on a tour of duty in Vietnam." Young black males in Harlem are less likely to survive to age 40 than young males in Bangladesh. Gun-related homicides are the prevalent factor in these deaths.[9]

Numerous explanations have been posited for the continuing problem of violent crime. Many theorists have tried to trace the problem to poverty, but the correlations between violent crimes and economic

245

conditions often appear contradictory. Violent crime in the United States soared during the prosperous mid-1960s; it remained relatively stable during the painful recession of the early 1980s. Some social scientists placed much of the blame on fertility rates. The baby boom of earlier years produced an abundance of males in the dangerous 15–24 age group, they argued. Once the population explosion subsided, violent crime would subside. Are these theorists right? Age data clearly have some bearing on the question, but these statistics have not delivered an adequate explanation to satisfy most students of violence. Rates of violent crime have not dipped sufficiently in response to changing numbers of young males in the population. Age data represent a partial, not a full, explanation.[10] Other factors also seem to identify facets of the problem but not the total picture. Some scholarship points, for instance, to the media, particularly Hollywood movies. Since the 1960s, Hollywood films have featured much more graphic criminal violence: the trend began with movies such as *Psycho* (1960) and *Bonnie and Clyde* (1967). Some believe that the criminally violent are influenced by graphically violent entertainment and participate in "copycat" behaviour in the commission of crimes.[11] Others speak of the tremendous growth of cocaine use, including the use of crack. Dependence on drugs leads to crime – often violent crime – to maintain a habit.

Questions about the impact of the media became especially intense in 1993, when Congress held hearings to consider ways to reduce the violent content of prime-time television programming in the United States. Legislators were disturbed about the degree of carnage seen on television, and they were aware of the more than 3,000 research studies that identified connections between violence on television and the aggressive or violent behaviour of the viewers. To prevent government intervention in the matter, executives from the major networks agreed to police themselves through a new system of parental advisories. They would give viewers on-screen warnings about excessively violent programmes and provide similar warnings to magazines and newspapers that contained listings of TV programmes. While some Congressmen and TV executives hailed the compromise as a sign of progress, many social scientists criticized the arrangement. Critics noted that many of the smaller stations on cable television often featured greater violent content in their programming than major networks.

Debates about the influence of television programmes and motion pictures concern more citizens than just those of the United States, of course. Millions of people watch American-made TV programmes and movies in Europe, Africa, Asia, Latin America, and the Middle East. If the violent material in US-produced entertainment can stimulate violent behaviour on the part of some viewers, it probably makes an impact on levels of violent crime in diverse societies around the globe.

Scholars also point to a number of cultural factors in explaining the rise of violent crime in the United States. For example, some note the breakdown of a sense of community among urban groups. According to this argument, in earlier years the family, church, and neighbourhood served to keep individual behaviour in line with community standards. Then came vast industrial and commercial change, mobility, and the growth of a rather transient population. A sense of uprootedness developed. Individuals who lacked ties to a community were more likely to become involved in crime. Another factor relates to the growth of single-parent, female-headed households in the United States during the last thirty years. Research indicates that youths who spend their adolescent years without a father-figure present rank disproportionately high in the statistics for violent crime. Still another explanation concerns the status consciousness of young males in poor neighbourhoods. Each day these youngsters see on television and in the city streets the advantages money can buy. They seek upward mobility and social status in the eyes of their peers. From their perspective, drug trafficking and other crimes represent a "rational choice." Lacking skills and with no access to good jobs, they believe crime – often violent crime – provides the best option for quickly turning their dreams into reality.[12]

No discussion of the rise in violent crime in recent US history should overlook the importance of guns. Ownership of firearms, especially handguns, soared during the 1960s. By 1980 about half of all American households reported some gun ownership.[13] Many of the weapons poor Americans owned were purchased without registration. Cheap handguns called "Saturday Night Specials" became abundantly available in America's cities. Handguns were increasingly prominent in violent crimes. In 1960, before the period of "firearms democracy," only 19 per cent of homicides could be traced to handguns; by 1990, the figure was 69 per cent.[14] The United States became the gun murder capital of the industrialized world. For instance, in 1988, gun murders in the United States amounted to 8,915 while seven were recorded in Great Britain, thirteen in Australia, and eight in Canada.[15]

247

While many social scientists point to changes that have occurred since the 1960s in order to explain the surge in criminal violence, others cite historical trends. For example, some trace the problem of violent crime to America's frontier heritage, pointing out that nineteenth-century wars with Indians and fights over gold, cattle, and land made violence socially acceptable in the frontier environment. Furthermore, they note that frontier communities were characterized by the presence of many uprooted people and the absence of adequate law enforcement. These conditions contributed to the culture of violence in the "Wild West." Proponents of this interpretation argue that the legacy of outlaws such as Jesse James and rough frontier towns such as Dodge City can be observed in twentieth-century American life.

While America's nineteenth-century history may offer some insights into the sources of modern-day violence, this explanation has many shortcomings. One of the most important criticisms of the interpretation relates to the mythical quality of popular images of the Wild West. Nineteenth-century figures such as William Cody (Buffalo Bill) and dime novelists made fortunes creating the myth for a growing population of urban Americans (as well as urban Europeans) who eagerly sought out stories about Western adventure. Hollywood film-makers added to the myth-making in the twentieth century. They focused on the lives of a few dramatic figures and the conditions of lawlessness in a few notorious towns. Their pictures of gunslingers marching to shootouts in frightened communities and outlaws holding up banks and stagecoaches were unrepresentative. Criminal violence in the Western communities of post-Civil War America was not as prevalent as it is in the 1990s in places such as East Los Angeles or inner-city Detroit. Furthermore, it is important to note that even the most notorious cities in the "Wild West," such as the Kansas cowtowns of Abilene and Dodge City, experienced high levels of criminal violence only during a few years of their early development. Myth-makers focused tightly on these brief periods of instability and suggested the violent environment represented the norm in Western life.[16]

In searching for clues to the causes of modern-day criminal violence in the United States, data from the twentieth century may be more relevant. Studies indicate that criminal violence had become troublesome in the streets of American cities and in the countryside as well as in various periods from the end of the Civil War to the early 1930s. Beginning around 1934, the rates of violent crime began to drop, and the decades of the 1940s and the 1950s brought some of the most comfortable years with respect to freedom from dangerous crime in the streets of American cities.[17] The incidence of violent crime then began to rise quickly around 1964, and it has remained at high levels since that time. Against this background, it is easy to understand why many Americans were greatly shocked in the sixties. They remembered "the good old days" – meaning recent decades – the time when life in urban streets seemed untroubled by muggings and murders. In view of these data it seems worth while to focus attention on the new developments in American life during the 1960s and 1970s, in order to detect some of the principal causes of the rise in violent behaviour.

Whatever the causes of the problems, it is clear that American society has not found a solution. Public policy leaders have advocated a variety of remedies, but they have not been able to deliver dramatically effective results. When crime rose in the 1960s, some observers, particularly "conservative" politicians, argued that the "cost" of crime was too low for criminals. They maintained that too many criminals succeeded in evading incarceration. In recent decades substantial efforts have been made to expand the prison populations, and today approximately 1.1 million Americans are behind bars. The inmate population is now 426 per 100,000 people, the highest ratio in the world. Many more criminals would be in prison if American society could afford to put them away. Because of the substantial expense involved in keeping a criminal in prison, many convicted criminals are placed on probation rather than incarcerated. As a consequence, the caseloads for probation officers have grown tremendously. In many cities probation officers handle 75 or 100 convicted criminals, and in San Diego, a city that was unprepared for the deluge, officers are responsible for as many as 1,000 cases. Incarceration may deliver a form of justice to the guilty, and it may deter some individuals from committing further crimes, but it has not reduced the incidence of violent crime as dramatically as many conservative thinkers hoped. In the last quarter-century in the United States, punishment has expanded and so has violent crime.[18]

Psychopathic violence

As mentioned earlier, there is a third type of violence that has troubled American society – a type that relates, in part, to both collective and political violence and to criminal violence. Assassination attempts against prominent figures, "gratuitous" massacres against an anonymous public, and serial killings have, on a number of occasions, shocked the public in the last quarter-century.

Assassination attempts were not new to American history (Presidents Lincoln, Garfield, and McKinley died by assassin's bullets), but the frequency of the attacks after the 1963 assassination of President Kennedy was unique in terms of its intensity. Figures such as Robert Kennedy and Martin Luther King, Jr. were killed, and other prominent people such as Governor George Wallace and Presidents Nixon, Ford, and Reagan were targeted by would-be killers. In most of these cases the assailant was deeply troubled psychologically and lacking in self-esteem. The assailants thought they could achieve redemption by committing vicious and well-publicized crimes. The ready availability of guns in the United States facilitated their attempts to play out their fantasies.[19] Thus, while the assassins' actions sometimes made a significant political impact in the country, as individuals these violent men were not themselves significant players in the political affairs of the nation.

Examples of gratuitous mass violence – i.e., undiscriminating murder against several people – has also typically involved this pattern of psychological deviance. The perpetrators have enjoyed easy access to firearms, and that opportunity has enabled them to become very destructive. The 1984 case of James Oliver Huberty, an out-of-work security guard who sprayed a McDonald's restaurant with gunfire and killed 21 people, including many children, is just one example of these cases of gratuitous violence. The cases involving serial killers involve similar patterns. The violent individuals victimize a variety of strangers over an extended period of time, acting out their psychopathic impulses.

There is a pattern to most of the cases of assassination attempts, mass gratuitous violence, and serial killings in the United States. The cases usually involve a person who is caught up in profound psychological difficulties. The individual's motivations almost never have broad political implications, and the episodes do not involve the participation of large groups of people operating in concert. The assailants usually act independently, without support from co-conspirators. Furthermore, the gun-wielding murderers often lack a clear sense of political ideology, or, if they do espouse one, it is frequently of an extreme and distorted variety. In sum, these outbreaks of violence are usually private affairs that reveal a deeply disturbed state of mind.

Violence in foreign policy

Scholars have begun to ask questions about the connections between domestic and international violence. Investigating whether aggressive practices in foreign policy are related, in part, to attitudes about violence that are prominent in the American cultural milieu, they have asked, for example, if popular support for military operations and action in war relates to concepts the American people have learned in their homes, communities, and schools. Richard Maxwell Brown, a prominent scholar who has written a great deal about violence and vigilantism, presents an intriguing example of this type of research through his examination of President Lyndon B. Johnson's approach to the Viet Nam war. Brown traces Johnson's attitudes to the lessons he learned as a youth about the "ethic" of central Texas. Brown observes that Johnson's parents and schoolteachers told him about the Alamo and the way Texans of the nineteenth century had the courage to continue fighting against the Mexicans even though they were greatly outnumbered. President Johnson applied this "I'll-die-before-I'll-run" attitude to the situation in South-East Asia, says Brown; like a good Texan, he would not retreat even though the evidence strongly suggested he had stepped into an unwinnable situation.[20]

The United States' frustrating involvement in Viet Nam stirred many scholars to ask provocative questions about the nation's long record of participation in warfare. Critics of the engagement in Viet Nam looked back at American history and observed the frequency of military activity. They noted the abundant battles with Indian "nations" from the period of early colonial settlement to the late nineteenth century, and they pointed to the way each generation of Americans, from the time of the Revolution onward, confronted new experiences in war. Critics emphasized that the United States fought Britain in 1775 and 1812, fought Mexico in 1846, engaged in civil war in 1861, entered a war with Spain in 1898, went to war against Germany in 1917, fought Germany and Japan in 1941, fought North Korea in 1950, and battled in Viet Nam. Additionally, many small military engagements punctuated American history, such as the fighting in the Philippines in the early 1900s and an invasion of Grenada in 1983. The agony over Viet Nam stirred scholars to ask: was violence deep-rooted in American culture? Did this cultural strain of violence manifest itself frequently in the United States' belligerent actions toward other nations? How could one understand the sources of this aggressiveness? Was it motivated by hunger for territory, a drive of capitalists to find new markets, an exaggerated sense of pride and honour, or other factors?[21]

While the questions raised by these critics provoked useful probes into American history, it appears that broad, sweeping assumptions about connections between culture and foreign- policy often obscured understanding. Scholarship discovered diverse causes behind US commitments to military action and found that simple explanations based on economics, ideology, or other single factors failed to provide sophisticated explanations.

Much of the United States's military posturing since 1945 relates not to single historical influences but to the peculiar circumstances the nation found itself in at the conclusion of the Second World War. The United States emerged from the global conflict as the dominant military power in the world. Other nations that had been strong militarily, such as Germany, Japan, France, and Britain, were terribly weakened by the experience of the world war. Standing almost alone as a military giant in the "Free World," the United States began to act as a protector of world order. Americans saw themselves after the Second World War as the "policemen" of the globe, obliged to take action wherever the forces of trouble and disorder made their appearance. This new US outlook represented an extraordinary change in perspective concerning the country's role in world affairs. Isolationist sentiment had remained strong with the American people up to the time of Pearl Harbor, and it re-emerged when the US Congress took up the debate about international obligations in the post-war years. Internationalists won the arguments for the most part, especially after the outbreak of the Korean war. Before the engagements in Korea, the American military had been reduced to a relatively small size; the start of fighting on the Asian peninsula helped promote a tremendous build-up in the country's military capabilities. By the 1960s, the United States had substantial tactical and strategic forces and expanded capability for counter-insurgency warfare. The country's leaders also demonstrated an interest in covert forms of warfare, including operations promoted by the Central Intelligence Agency (CIA).[22]

A fear of communist expansion motivated much of this military intervention in the years after the Second World War. The fear was fundamentally important in US involvement in smaller-scale actions such as overt intervention in the Dominican Republic (1965) and covert intervention in Guatemala (1954), Cuba (1961), and Nicaragua (in the 1980s). Yet the decline of the communist threat in the late 1980s and early 1990s did not bring a quick retreat from the role of world policeman. For example, when the American military invaded Panama in 1989 to remove General Manuel Noriega from power, the action had little to do with a fear of communism. More important, the United States took the lead in pursuing the Persian Gulf confrontation to the point of war in 1991. That conflict, too, had little relevance to the old patterns of military action motivated by anti-communism. US leadership in the fight against Iraq revealed the persistence of the "policeman" image in American foreign policy, a perspective that was likely to outlast the Cold War against communism. As long as Americans viewed the world as an unstable place needing leadership from a powerful nation that could help guarantee world order, they were likely to continue sanctioning violent intervention in other foreign nations. The demise of the Soviet Union did not result in an immediate reduction in US military involvement in world affairs. Indeed, it could have opened the way for more involvement, as Americans seek to fill the vacuums created by retreating Soviet influence in various regions of the globe.

Conclusions

It appears that the problem of collective and political violence in the 1960s developed out of the peculiar circumstances of the times; it did not reflect a long-term trend towards group or mass violence. Americans remain essentially non-violent with respect to their handling of political issues. Though there are always some exceptions in the long sweep of history, it is fair to say in general that people in the United States do not usually harm each other physically or kill each other over elections, political ideas, or political leaders. Politics in the United States usually does not involve physical violence pitting citizens against the government or the government against citizens. The democratic process is sometimes abused with respect to ethics, as in the cases of Watergate and the Iran–Contra scandal, but it is not usually dishonoured in terms of physical violence.

Quite a different pattern holds with respect to criminal violence. The troubling trends that became evident in the mid-1960s continue to disturb the American people. No dramatically effective solutions have been found for treating the crisis, and public frustration over the continuing threat of criminal violence remains strong. Politicians and scholars who try to interpret the causes of the difficulty disagree strongly about the origins of the wave of criminal violence; consequently public policy does not move dramatically toward particular remedies. The same applies to psychopathic violence. Whatever the causes, it is evident that most of the criminal and psychopathic acts are committed with firearms and that a diminution in the number of guns privately owned would help in reducing these violent incidents. Political leaders are very cautious, however, in dealing with measures to control firearms. The tradition of gun ownership in America is almost as old and as treasured as the tradition of owning private property. Many Americans eagerly oppose any laws that deny what they consider their "constitutional" right to own firearms. In view of these conditions, the spectres of criminal and psychopathic violence that grew substantially in the 1960s are not likely to go away soon. Americans may have to wait a long time before seeing again a situation approximating the relatively peaceful urban environment of the 1950s.

The culture of violence is also reflected in US foreign policy, and scholars interested in tracing connections between domestic violence and violence as it is practised in military activities may discover rich material for analysis. With respect to the escalation of US military involvement in world affairs since the end of the Second World War, the concept of world leadership has made a substantial impact on American diplomacy. Many Americans, including architects of diplomacy in Washington, believe the United States is the only nation in the late twentieth century that has the economic and military clout to preserve international order. Acting from this perspective, they sanction large military budgets and a foreign policy that frequently turns interventionist. A number of people have begun to question how long we can afford to maintain this burden of leadership, however. Paul Kennedy's 1987 book, *The Rise and Fall of the Great Powers*, represented one of the most popular critiques of this ambitious international role. Kennedy argued that many powerful nations in history had weakened their economies through aggressive foreign policies and participation in war, which overtaxed their resources. Kennedy suggested that the United States could decline in a similar fashion if it did not bring its foreign policy into line with economic realities.[23]

Notes

1. Louis Hartz (1955) develops this outlook.
2. Viewpoints expressed in the period of the urban riots appear in a number of edited volumes, including Meier and Rudwick, 1970; Marx, 1971; Geschwender, 1971.

3. See, for example, Brooks, 1979.
4. Davies, 1979.
5. An excellent review of some of these examples of collective violence can be found in Hofstadter and Wallace, 1970.
6. *Crime in the United States: Uniform Crime Reports – 1970* (US Government Printing Office: Washington, DC, 1971), pp. 2–21.
7. *Newsweek*, cxvii, no. 12, 25 March 1991, pp. 35–6.
8. *Wilmington Star News*, Wilmington, North Carolina, 19 June 1991, p. 2A.
9. *New York Times*, 7 December 1990, p. 1.
10. Wilson, 1983:19–25; Weiner and Wolfgang, 1985:27–8.
11. Toplin, 1975:182–208.
12. Comer, 1985:63–71.
13. Zimring, 1985:138.
14. *New York Times*, 19 April 1991, p. A10.
15. Reported by Handgun Control, Inc. (Washington, DC) in 1990.
16. See, for example, Dykstra, 1968; Frantz and Choate, 1955; Cawelti, 1984. For an excellent overview of the problem of violence in American history and culture, including violence on the frontier, see Brown, 1975.
17. Silberman, 1978:29–31.
18. *New York Times*, 19 June 1990, pp. 1, A10.
19. See, for example, Kirkham, Levy, and Crotty, 1970.
20. Brown, 1975:287–9.
21. For critical perspectives of US foreign policy that stress economic factors, see Kolko, 1969; Williams, 1972.
22. Diplomatic historians disagree in identifying the important beginnings of the United States' commitment to protecting a world order. For example, Lloyd C. Gardner (1984:xii–xiv, 3–28) traces the interest in a "covenant with power" to Woodrow Wilson's leadership. A good comprehensive overview of the growing US role in world affairs since World War II can be found in Ambrose, 1980.
23. Kennedy, 1987.

References

Ambrose, S. 1980. *Rise to Globalism: American Foreign Policy, 1938–1980*. New York: Penguin.

Brooks, R. 1979. "Domestic Violence and American Wars: An Historical Interpretation." In Graham and Gurr, 1979, pp. 307–27.

Brown, R.M. 1975. *Strain of Violence: Historical Studies of American Violence and Vigilantism*. New York: Oxford University Press.

Cawelti, J. 1984. *The Six-Gun Mystique*. Bowling Green, Ohio: Bowling Green University Press.

Comer, J.P. 1985. "Black Violence and Public Policy." In Curtis, 1985.

Curtis, L. (ed). 1985. *American Violence and Public Policy: An Update of the National Commission on the Causes and Prevention of Violence*. New Haven and London: Yale University Press.

Davies, J.C. "The J-Curve of Rising and Declining Satisfactions as a Cause of Revolution and Rebellion." In Graham and Gurr, 1979, pp. 415–36.

Dykstra, R. 1968. *The Cattle Towns*. New York: Alfred Knopf.

Frantz, J.B., and J.E. Choate, Jr. 1955. *The American Cowboy: The Myth and the Reality*. Norman: University of Oklahoma Press.

Gardner, L. 1984. *A Covenant With Power: America and the World Order From Wilson to Reagan*. New York and Toronto: Oxford University Press.

Geschwender, J. 1971. *The Black Revolt: The Civil Rights Movement, Ghetto Uprisings, and Separatism*. Englewood Cliffs, NJ: Prentice-Hall.

Graham, H., and T.R. Gurr. 1979. *Violence in American: Historical and Comparative Perspectives*. Beverly Hills and London: Sage.

Hartz, L. 1955. *The Liberal Tradition in America: An Interpretation of American Political Thought since the Revolution*. New York: Harcourt Brace.

Hofstadter, R., and M. Wallace (eds). 1971. *American Violence: A Documentary History*. New York: Alfred Knopf.

Kennedy, P. 1987. *The Rise and Fall of the Great Powers: Economic Change and Military Conflict from 1500 to 2000*. New York: Random House.

Kirkham, J.F., S.G. Levy, and W.J. Crotty. 1970. *Assassination and Political Violence: A Report to the National Commission on the Causes and Prevention of Violence*. New York: US Government Printing Office.

Kolko, G. 1969. *The Roots of American Foreign Policy*. Boston: Little, Brown.

Marx, G.T. 1971. *Racial Conflict: Tension and Change in American Society*. Boston: Little, Brown.

Meier, A., and E. Rudwick (eds). 1970. *Black Protest in the Sixties*. Chicago: Quadrangle Books.

Silberman, Charles E. 1978. *Criminal Violence, Criminal Justice*. New York: Random House.

Toplin, R. 1975. *Unchallenged Violence: An American Ordeal*. Westport, CT: Greenwood Press.

Wilson, J.Q. 1983. *Thinking About Crime*. Rev. ed. New York: Basic Books.

Williams, W.A. 1972. *The Tragedy of American Diplomacy*. New York: Dell.

Weiner, N., and M. Wolfgang. 1985. "Violent Crime in America 1969–1982." In Curtis, 1985.

Zimring, F.E. 1985. "Violence and Firearms Policy." In Curtis, 1985.

10

Children in the city of violence: The case of Brazil

Irene Rizzini

Children are a serious matter

The child is the beginning without end.[1] The end of the child is the beginning of the end. When a society allows its children to be killed it is because it has begun its own suicide as a society. When it does not love the child it is because it has failed to recognize its humanity.

If I do not see a child in the child it is because someone has violated him, and what I see is what remains from all that was taken away. But this child that I see on the street without a father, without a mother, bed and food, this child who lives in the solitude of nights with no one near, is a cry, is a terror. In the face of this child, the world ought to stop in order to begin a new encounter, because the child is the beginning without end and his end is the end of all of us.[2]

In his novel *The Outsider*, Albert Camus (1989:99) attributes the cause of a brutal assassination to the sun: "The judge replied ... that before hearing my lawyer, he would be happy to have me specify the motives which had inspired my act. Mixing up my words a bit and realizing that I sounded ridiculous, I said quickly that it was because of the sun."

Another writer, Bertolt Brecht, in his famous conversation with Mr Keuner, confronted the force of violence with courage of the violated. Without alternatives, the violated live with the hope that one day they will see the violators disappear so that they can then be

257

affirmed as a person: "'What did you say?' asked Violence. 'I was speaking out in favour of Violence,' replied Mr Keuner ... Later, his pupils asked him about his 'backbone'. Mr Keuner replied: 'I have no backbone that I'd like to see broken. I must live longer than Violence.'" (Brecht, 1989:11; English translation from Portuguese-language edition)

Between these two extremes, social researchers who find violence permeating all social classes as a global phenomenon of the third world and, particularly, Latin America, are challenged to arrive at objective positions on a panorama which has to be proven and diagnosed so that it will not be incorporated inexorably into our fate as Latin Americans.

We reject simplistic formulations, such as those which suggest that violence generates violence, or that disadvantaged classes are solely responsible for spreading violence. A deep vein of violence is entangled in the history of our continent and resides in our collective unconscious. Our forerunners, the indigenous peoples, were decimated by the colonizers. Slaves coming from Africa and born on this continent pass on to us, together with their heroism and resistance, memories of the violence committed against them by the colonizers. We are united by threads of violence that were woven into our rulers' strategies for conquest, domination, and the maintenance of power. The heroes of our histories did not leave us worthy examples for the formation of nations constructed for the good of all our citizens. Meanwhile, we find ourselves suffering economic backwardness, grave social imbalance, and a profound disrespect for human life and dignity. Economic backwardness is another form of violence.

The enormously unequal distribution of income in Latin America and, in particular, Brazil, favours the perpetuation of violence.[3] Also, international political relations hinder us from developing more just social solutions, as they take from our already impoverished economies a substantial part of our productive efforts. The foreign debt of third world countries drains part of national hard currency stocks; the absence of direct foreign investment in our countries diminishes economic growth; and lack of technological competitiveness leads us to real dependence on the developed countries.

In Brazil, social and economic impoverishment in recent decades have created new multitudes of marginalized people, especially in the big cities. The 1980s are now regarded as a lost decade, in which social inequality intensified. Violence is increasingly present in the lives of Brazilian citizens, with muggings, attacks, kidnappings, torture, drug trafficking vying with attempts to legalize the death penalty. But most serious is the practice of extermination, which, in the name of defending society, has not spared even children. There are reactions by the government; there are denunciations by individual citizens; there are protests by organized social groups; there is international assistance – but the protests seem fragile and ineffective in the face of unbridled violence.

The problems which affect youth have, for good reasons, been the target of growing outrage. It is estimated that nearly 30 million children and adolescents live in conditions which are subhuman and completely inadequate for their full development. The violence which characterizes the lives and deaths of these children is the subject of this paper. This article argues that despite the great show of concern that has been made about the growing number of children and young people who have been mercilessly assassinated throughout the country, violence against children has persisted in both subtle and direct ways. This violence is indicated by data on infant mortality, illiteracy, income, and other social indicators. We will pay special attention to the violence against the so-called "street kids," a phenomenon today recognized internationally. And, finally, we will consider the extreme form of violence – the extermination of children.

Consensual violence: The situation of childhood in Brazil

"Humanity ought to give children its very best." (*Declaration of the United Nations on the Rights of the Child*, 1959)

It is estimated that today in Brazil there are approximately 60 million children and adolescents aged 0 to 17 years, representing 41 per cent of the entire population.[4] This number has been falling as the fertility rate for Brazilian women has suffered a significant reduction since the second half of the 1960s. The average number of children born to women in Brazil has fallen from 5.76 in 1970 to 3.53 in 1984, though the rate remains high among women with less education (6.63) and among poorer women (6.94).

Levels of family income, as well as family composition, constitute revealing data on childhood in the country. In 1989, more than 50 per cent of children and teenagers lived in domestic units characterized as "in a situation of relative poverty" or "in a situation of absolute poverty," corresponding respectively to families whose monthly per capita income ranged from half to a quarter of the minimum salary (US$40–20). Contrary to common belief, most children and adolescents found "abandoned" on the streets of the big cities belong to families: 74 per cent belong to families composed of a couple with children, 12.2 per cent to families headed by single mothers.

The first challenge a Brazilian child faces is survival. The infant mortality rate, at 63 infant deaths per 1,000 live births, is six times the rate in the United States, whose rate is one of the worst in the first world. Between 1985 and 1990, approximately 20 million children were born in Brazil; of these more than 1,300,000 died in their first year. It is shameful to find that the greater part of these deaths were caused by easily avoidable illnesses, such as malnutrition and acute respiratory infections due to inadequate conditions in nutrition, hygiene, sewage, housing, and medical care. Among adolescents, the 1980s saw a growth in the number of deaths from external causes (accidents, suicides, homicides, poisonings). These cases are responsible for 51 per cent of the deaths among 10- to 14-year-olds and for 66 per cent of mortality among adolescents aged 15 to 17. Non-accidental violent deaths (homicides and suicides) constituted in 1987 the primary cause of death in the 15- to 17-year-old age group in several of Brazil's principal cities (IBGE/UNICEF, 1989:29).

When they reach school age, children confront a series of difficulties that are also associated with poverty: learning problems, irregular school attendance, the need to work in order to contribute to family income. These difficulties are illustrated by elevated indices of illiteracy, drop-out, and repeating grades. It is calculated that at 14 years of age, less than 10 per cent of children are found in the grade appropriate to their age and that at 17 years of age only 44 per cent are still attending school. The issue of education is directly related to that of work. In the face of growing financial difficulties, children and teenagers in low-income families suffer an enormous pressure to leave school for activities which will give them some financial return. These young workers sometimes provide 20–30 per cent of their families' income. They join the workforce to guarantee the survival of the family.

It is bad enough that children should risk their education for work, but that is not the worst news. The work of children and adolescents born into poor families has the common marks of exploitation, be it performed on the streets, in the fields, or in the formal labour sector. These children perform activities which require few qualifications and which are characterized by long working days, lack of workers' protection, and low remuneration. The premature initiation of these children into work obviously closes many doors to the future for them, but it is also an immediate threat to their well-being.

Public violence

Boys and girls: In the streets?

During the 1980s, the streets of Brazilian cities became the stage for a drama hitherto little commented upon – the presence *en masse* of children and young people, the so-called "street kids." A number of these children – exactly how many is not known – become disconnected from their families and come to live on the streets, exposed to every type of abuse and violence and frequently involved in illegal activities such as drug trafficking, mugging, and prostitution, as studies conducted throughout the various regions of the country have shown (Gonçalves, 1979; Ferreira, 1980; Rizzini, 1986; Oliveira, 1989).

As the phenomenon of street kids[5] acquired visibility throughout the country, many social researchers became interested in the theme and attempted to differentiate among children observed on the streets. In particular, the researchers differentiated the majority of street children, who maintained contacts with their families – "kids in the street" – from the minority, who severed ties with their families, the true "street kids." Despite the fact that most of the "kids in the street" are there to contribute to the family's income, Brazilian society has very ambivalent feelings towards them. The children make people feel uncomfortable because of their appearance of abandonment and poverty, because they approach drivers with their merchandise, and because they steal. Some citizens attempt to help them, some ignore them, and some are revolted by their presence and are of the opinion that they ought to be rounded up and severely punished. Unfortunately, there are also those who believe that eliminating these children would help to resolve the problem of criminality and violence.

Even today, when better information is available on the characteristics of these children, the polemic is intense. What are we to do with them? How do we avoid their migrating to the streets, effectively turning into "street kids"? How do we protect them from the violence to which they are exposed every moment they spend on the streets? The answers are complex, but many people are attempting to find solutions. One thing is certain – one cannot accept the street as a place for children to live. They do not belong on the streets. Directives to this effect appear in the Brazilian Constitution (1988, article 227) and in the legislation referring to the rights of the child and adolescent (Statute on Children and Adolescents, 1990, article 4), which stipulate that children and adolescents should have the right to "life, health, food, education, leisure, professional training, culture, dignity, respect, liberty, and the right to live with family and community" – that is, the conditions necessary for full development.

What is known about kids in the streets?

Most of the children and youngsters encountered in the streets are male.[6] Only 10 per cent of them are girls. The research suggests that families attempt to keep the girls at home, either as helpers with household chores or to avoid their falling into prostitution rings. However, the figure for the number of girls on the street is unreliable because most of the studies do not record the gender of the street children who are interviewed.

The studies show that children are initiated into street-related activities between the ages of seven and 12 years, with the average age of initiation being nine. These young people tend to remain in the streets until 15 or 16 years of age. In Rio de Janeiro, of 300 children interviewed, only 17 per cent were older than 14 (Rizzini, 1986), and in Fortaleza (Ceará state), young people between the ages of 14 and 18 comprised only 12.3 per cent of the sample (Governo do Estado do Ceará, 1988). Research has not focused on the occupations of the adolescents as they approach adulthood. All signs indicate that a good proportion of them abandon street activities in search of a more regular job. Few studies make reference to the ethnic origin of the children, though they do suggest that the children are, in the majority, Black or of mixed race. The children in general come from shanty-town slums and the peripheral areas of large cities, where low-income populations are concentrated.

The family and the street

Contrary to the common belief, the studies show that most of the children seen on the streets have families and live with both parents (table 1). Little is known about the history of those children on the streets who have lost contact with their parents, and in particular the motives which brought them to the streets. Testimony from the chil-

Table 1 **Family status of street children**

Place	Year	Living with both parents (%)	Living with one parent (%)	Other (%)
Belém	1979	44	39	2
R. Janeiro	1986	41	35	6
São Paulo	1988	58	30	
Fortaleza	1988	52	36	4
Recife[7]	1989	36	33	16
Recife	1989	52	21	5
Goiania	1990	47	40	4

Sources: FLACSO et al., 1991, Gonçalves, 1979; Governo do Estado do Ceará/Secretaria de Ação Social, 1988; Pires, 1988; Rizzini, 1986.

Table taken from Rizzini and Rizzini, 1991. It is worth noting, for the purposes of clarification, that "family" as defined here does not necessarily involve blood ties, either in the case of mother-headed or father-headed households.

dren themselves suggests that there are other pressures beyond the need to earn money. The children speak of serious familial conflicts, frequently involving episodes of abuse and violence.

The accusation is often made that families whose children remain on the streets are negligent. This view is a simplification of the real situation. Until the beginning of the 1980s, the families of poor children were invariably portrayed as unstructured, owing to the absence of the fathers and to unofficial marriage unions. Recent studies have attempted to reconceptualize the notion of family structure, relating it to the particularities of different social classes. For example, a recent study (FLACSO et al., 1991) focuses on the family dynamic of children in the streets and concludes that the mere physical presence of the parents is not sufficient to guarantee family integrity. Factors such as economic pressure, together with disunity and hostility between family members, compromise the integrity of the family even when there are parents in the home.

While we have learned a great deal about street children in the last ten years, there is still much to learn both about the children who retain ties to their parents and those who do not.

What do children do on the streets?

Children are involved in a series of activities on the streets, but the most common is that of "roaming vendor" – accounting for 64 per cent in Belem (Gonçalves, 1979), 40 per cent in Recife (Oliveira, 1989), 26 per cent in Rio de Janeiro (Rizzini, 1986), and 21 per cent in groups studied in other states of the country (Myers, 1988). In the streets, boys and girls sell almost anything – candies, chewing gum, fruit, cookies, and so on. They also shine shoes, guard and wash cars, carry groceries in street markets and supermarkets. In sum, the children are a true army of little workers in the informal labour market. The conditions which characterize the work of children on the streets are similar to those of other under-age workers – long work days, low-skill tasks, poor wages, and danger. In the streets, children are completely unprotected. Their life on the streets is replete with bitter experiences of violence, abuse, and exploitation (see box 1).

One of the key characteristics of street children that affects their futures is their lack of access to education. A significant percentage of the children do two or three jobs to earn money, remaining in the streets up to 48 hours weekly. A large number of street children once attended school, though they attended irregularly. The demands of street life, however, lead a significant number of them to abandon school. Those who do continue studying are generally not performing at their age level.

Box 1: **Violence in the daily lives of children on the streets**

I am 10 years old, I sleep in the shopping centre every day and every day at midnight the military police go there to bother us and bring us inside. They beat us up, make us eat roaches, they make us eat shit, they throw hot water at us, they hit us over the head, and then they do a whole lot of stuff. (Male)

I'm 12 years old. Here in the square the police beat us up for no reason at all. They beat us up yesterday 'cause I was there playing, me and my buddy, and they went there to beat on us ... I hang out there playing, asking people for something to eat. (Male)

Why is my life involved with this stealing business? My mother can't work, and so I steal. Work? Bosses rob us because they want to pay us a pittance. If you're gonna make so little, I'd rather steal. The problem is that the cops rob from us. (Female, 16 years old)

I'm 15 ... they grab us and take us to the DPO [military police street corps]. There they want us to suck their dicks ... they call us whores ... they take our clothes off and finger us. They want to take advantage of us, they want us to give them money. (Female)

Source: CEAP, 1989.

Despite their poor educational performance, a significant number of street children have plans to continue their education. As a strategy for overcoming the situation in which they find themselves, the children place strong value on study, work, and personal initiative. In one of the first surveys conducted in Brazil (Rizzini, 1986), I interviewed 300 children and young people on the streets of Rio de Janeiro and concluded that, in fact, education and work are their principal aspirations. The testimonies which appeared with the greatest frequency were the following:

I've got to arrange a job. If not, I'm never gonna get out of this life. I'm young, I don't want to die early. I'm thinking about going back to school to study. I'd like to be a jewellery engraver. (15 years old)

I don't have any other future, so I sell candy. I'd like to work at a real job, like being a doorman, a guard in a bank, or carrying boxes of olive oil. (13 years old)

I want to be a doctor in a hospital, or maybe a driver. I think those are nice jobs. I really intend to do it. When you really want something, you can get it. (17 years old)

It is worth stressing here that, obviously, not all the children limit themselves to earning money through work. There are other forms of earning, some of which are much easier and more lucrative than working day to day as vendors or shoe-shiners. Many children, for example, beg. However, the same children do admit reluctantly that they sporadically engage in illegal activities – stealing, drug trafficking, and prostitution – in order "to make a little extra."

Uncontained violence: The assassination of children

Brazil has received with some discomfort the accusation that thousands of children and adolescents are assassinated every year in different states in the country. We have been the target of harsh criticisms from the international community, principally from organizations dedicated to the defence of human rights. In 1988, Defence for Children International, in the face of accusations presented in the European press, sponsored a Brazilian organization (the Centre for the Mobilization of Marginalized Populations) to conduct a survey investigating the assassination of children in Rio de Janeiro. The research was published in the form of a dossier in 1989 (CEAP, 1989). In June 1990, a report compiled by representatives of Amnesty International after a series of visits to Brazil was disseminated (Amnesty

International, 1990b). The report presented a detailed description of cases of violence and the violation of rights perpetrated against children and adolescents in Brazil. The international dissemination of information on the incidence of violence against children had enormous repercussions in Brazil, with headlines such as "Brazil Already Knows How To Resolve the Problem of Its Children – Kill Them" (a quote attributed to Amnesty International by the Brazilian press in 1990). These and other documents served as a base for the formation of complaint boards and investigatory commissions whose task is to pressure the government to take urgent action in combating violence.

It is believed that many of the authors of these crimes are professionals, frequently connected with police, who are contracted to eliminate these children. They are the so-called "extermination groups" or "death squads." The motivation for the murder of children is linked to the belief that such illegal and brutal actions are justified by the need to keep our cities "safe." Part of the evidence for the extermination campaign are the official statistics on infant and youth mortality, according to which violence is responsible for more than half of the deaths that occur among adolescents. Violent, non-accidental deaths, such as homicides and suicides, constitute the primary cause of death among young people in the principal Brazilian cities (IBGE/UNICEF, 1989).

A study conducted by the Department of Federal Police of the Ministry of Justice in 1991 also presented data on the occurrence of violent deaths among children and adolescents in the 5–17 age group, for the period 1988–1990 in 17 states and the Federal District (see table 2).[8] The evidence for a policy of extermination is obviously incomplete, but researchers started to analyse the issue only in 1990.

Table 2 **Violent deaths of children and adolescents aged 5–17, by region and year of occurrence (number of cases)**[9]

Region	1988	1989	1990	Total
South	21	18	22	61
South-East	765	1,262	1,437	3,464
North-East	266	266	320	852
North	24	22	31	77
Centre-West	62	57	38	157
Total	1,138	1,625	1,848	4,611

Source: Relatório do Departamento da Policia Federal DOPS/APPA, 1991 [Report of the Department of the Federal Police]. In Pinto et al., 1991.

There are many reasons for the differences in the data. Attempts to record cases of violent death are still isolated and reports are not always reliable. Many people fear reprisals if they report suspected assassinations. They believe that police protection is inadequate and that the assassins have remained unpunished in the majority of cases (Pinto et al., 1991). In addition, it is suspected that many of the deaths are not registered as such but rather as cases of disappearance.

The available data enable us to make some analysis of these crimes.

Incidence of killings

The phenomenon has largely been associated with the country's large metropolitan areas, for example São Paulo, Rio de Janeiro, Pernambuco, and Bahia (see table 3). However, cases have recently been recorded with some frequency in the interior of states and in smaller cities, such as Vitoria and Manaus (see map, p. 268).

Table 3 **Violent deaths of children and adolescents aged 5–17 in the states with the highest incidence (number of cases)**

State	1988	1989	1990	Total
São Paulo	449	783	918	2,150
R. Janeiro	294	445	492	1,231
Pernambuco	113	85	127	325
Bahia	65	83	89	237
Total	921	1,396	1,626	3,943

Source: Relatório do Departamento de Policia Federal, DOPS/APPA, 1991. In Pinto et al., 1991.

Characteristics of the assassinations

From data collected by the National Street Kids' Movement (Movimento Nacional de Meninos e Meninas de Rua, MNMMR), several characteristics emerge from cases in different Brazilian states (MNMMR et al., 1991). The crimes are committed by means of massacres and executions by firearms against young males (aged 15 to 17). In the great majority of cases, there are no indications that the victims were involved with the police and drug trafficking networks. Researchers emphasize that in spite of the concentration of crimes in the 15–17 age group, small children have also been assassinated: of 457 cases of killings of children and adolescents (0–18) reported

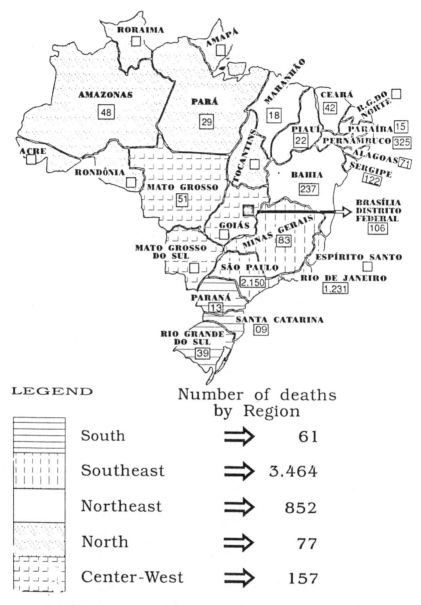

LEGEND

Number of deaths by Region

South ⟹ 61

Southeast ⟹ 3.464

Northeast ⟹ 852

North ⟹ 77

Center-West ⟹ 157

Violent deaths of children and adolescents aged 5–17, by state and region of Brazil, 1988–1990 (number of cases) (Source: Relatório do Departamento da Polícia Federal, DOPS/APPA, in Pinto et al., 1991)

Box 2: **The assassination of children and adolescents in Brazil: victims and aggressors**

Victims
The majority of victims are male between 15 and 17 years of age and of Black or mixed-race ethnic origin. The come from the poor social classes and have little or no formal schooling. The victims are sometimes involved in illicit activities and are codified by the press and police with nomenclatures that deny their personhood as children and teenagers: they are called *pivetes* and delinquents. Nevertheless, according to investigations made, the majority of the victims do not have criminal records.

Aggressors
The majority of aggressors are male and not known to their victims. Using extreme forms of violence, they carry out the acts either for financial gain or for vengeance. While it is not possible to prove the identity of aggressors, it is suspected that the majority are connected with the military police. In accordance with research published by MNMMR, IBASE and NEV-USP (1991), the actions of three groups are highlighted: drug traffickers and organized crime, groups which provide "security" services (officially or not), and groups which "take justice into their own hands." As a rule, official complaints are not filed, the perpetrators of the crimes are not imprisoned, and the certainty of immunity to prosecution is indicated as an incentive for the continuation of these aggressions.

Sources: Pinto et al., 1991; MNMMR et al., 1991.

---

from the largest cities in three states in 1989, 10 victims were under one year of age, 32 were less than 10 years of age, and 66 were 11 to 14 years old (see box 2).

These crimes are also characterized by extreme brutality, such as acts of torture and dismemberment. They have also taken the form of mercy killings following torture, and multiple, point-blank shootings. Children and youngsters are killed on the streets and their bodies frequently left there to intimidate the population and to serve as an example for others. Cases of professional and premeditated crime are typical. The literature has documented a growing number of cases in which the victim is sought out at his or her residence (see box 3).

"A childhood of much suffering"

Just when it was thought that nothing more terrible could happen to Brazilian children, a case of extreme violence shocked the nation.[10]

Box 3: **Typical cases of assassinations of children and adolescents in Brazil**

G.P.S. (17) was imprisoned on 17 July 1987 during a police "blitz." G. was brought to the police station, as records there indicate. Ten days later, the body of the teenager was found "hoisted" on a flag pole at the historic Monte dos Guararapes (Pernambuco state). Records at the police station do not indicate that the victim was ever released from the hands of the authorities.

S.C. (17) and D.R. (18) were kidnapped on 4 December 1988 by five men in civilian clothes, four of whom were later identified as members of the military police. The two bodies were found a day later in a trash deposit showing signs of having been tortured. S. had been raped and had had one of her eyes plucked out before being shot in the head at close range. The body of D. was riddled with bullets. According to the testimony of friends, D. had made public denunciations against the police for extortion in drug-related cases in the city of Novo Friburgo (Rio de Janeiro state), where the tragedy occurred.

F.O.S., a boy of 5 years, was killed by stab wounds, two to the chest and one to the back, by bandits who invaded his house. His father and brother were also killed and his mother, seven months pregnant at the time, was violated and stabbed. She survived only by pretending to be dead. The incident occured in the city of Nova Iguaçu (Rio de Janeiro state), in July 1989.

Four youngsters, C.M. (10), A.C.P. (11), G.F. (12), and L.R. (13), former inmates at FEBEM (the State Foundation for the Welfare of Minors) were captured and shot on 15 November 1990 in the periphery of Aracaju (Sergipe state) by police officer M.H. and drug trafficker M.S.A. who command an extermination group. Youth Court Judge J.R.S. made a statement that a group of *justiceiros* (posse bandits) were killing children who had passed through FEBEM in Sergipe. In only one year, more than 100 teenagers were killed in the state. To date, the police have not identified any of the responsible parties.

On 24 February 1990, five armed men and a woman invaded the shack of a washerwoman in the periphery of Greater Vitória (Espírito Santo state), beat up one of her younger daughters, and kidnapped her 16-year-old son, M.S.S. Four days later, the body of the teenager was found in another area of the periphery riddled with bullets.

Sources: Amnesty International, 1990a; CEAP, 1989; GAJOP/Centro Luis Freire, 1991; MNMMR, 1991b.

On 14 November 1991, when various Congressional Committees of Inquiry[11] investigating the assassination of children and adolescents were in process in several states, a slaughter came to the public eye in which five youngsters were executed and a girl of 15 years of age (A.S.L.) survived to tell the story. It is a story of enormous suffering, which makes us reflect on the various forms of violence perpetrated against children. A.S.L., like so many other Brazilian children, was born into poverty. When she was seven years old, her family moved from Salvador in Bahia state to a *favela* (shanty town) in Rio de Janeiro. One year later, she witnessed the death by stabbing of her mother at the hands of her father, who was drunk at the time. In the same period she was raped in the *favela* where she lived. At ten years of age, she was thrown out of her home by her father "because I looked a lot like my mother." Confused, she was taken by her sister to live with a neighbour, who forced her to work as a prostitute in exchange for food. Some time later, she escaped and went to live in a railway station. There she learned how to use drugs, and, for fear of sleeping on the streets, accepted invitations by men to sleep in motels. At 12 years of age, she moved to the Baixada Fluminense, one of the most violent areas in Rio de Janeiro, where she engaged in petty stealing. At night, she and her companions from the street went to the *favela* where they were later assassinated and, in exchange for sexual favours, received alcoholic beverages, drugs, some food, and small change.

On the night of 14 November, the young woman went to a shack, which was invaded by assassins. She and her friends were beaten. Later, tied up, they were taken to a river bank, where she heard the following explanation: "You're going to die so that you stop stealing." At hearing this, the children began to hug each other and cry. The execution followed and, in order to be assured that their "work" was well done, the assassins kicked the children. Those who reacted were "mercy killed." A.S.L. escaped death by holding her breath and pretending to be dead. The assassins were later identified and imprisoned. Their leader, L.C., 20 years old and the father of a seven-month old daughter, alleged that he had never killed anyone but that "on that night, I had to do justice."[11]

Children in the city of violence: What is to be done?

Born and raised within a political context which has always assured privileges to a minority, Brazilians have absorbed a culture imposed and maintained by force, whose rules are: do not look, do not listen, do not know, do not participate. The country is perplexed in the face of accusations of extreme violence committed against its children and adolescents. But Brazilian society has woken up all of a sudden and reacted with shock to its violence, now exposed.

Through research centres dedicated to children and family issues, the academic world has contributed, since the later 1970s, to the study of social indicators which have revealed a much clearer picture of childhood in Brazil. Ordinary citizens, outraged and united around the cause of children, began to organize themselves. The first centres for the defence of children's rights appeared, and these in turn gave birth in 1985 to a national movement for the rights of children and adolescents, the National Street Kids' Movement. This effort expanded throughout the country and made possible a network which has been critical to the victories obtained in favour of children. In the 1980s, the country witnessed a radical shift in its legislation on children. This process culminated in the passage of an advanced statute (the Statute on Children and Adolescents, 1990), which is the result of long struggles and confrontations on the part of civil society to secure rights.

There have also been changes in state and local government. States and municipalities have revised their constitutions and modernized their practices to recognize the condition of children. There have been unparalleled attempts to reformulate social welfare programmes for poor children. There is a new interest in reforming the educational system to improve the life chances of children. The traditional assistance provided by the Church, principally the Catholic Church, has also passed through a profound revision to recognize the enormous changes in children's lives. Secular orphanages, which had been opened to shelter orphans or abandoned children, also ended up taking children whose parents did not have the resources to care for them. In the last few decades, service providers have devised creative ways to maintain the connections between these children and their parents. The press, despite the sensationalist way it has dealt with some children's issues, has played an important role in describing the condition of children and the grave social problems they suffer. We might have entered the third millennium without realizing the extent of the problem, had it not been for the contribution of the national and international media.

But these changes have been insufficient to prevent violence against children. The judicial system has not responded vigorously to all incidents of violence. It must provide state and federal protection to potential victims of violence. It must pursue all suspected cases to their conclusion. It must make sure all crimes are punished.

We must not, however, lose sight of the fact that no measure will be effective if it is not aimed at structurally modifying the living conditions of a population which confronts continual impoverishment. This will only be possible through a profound change in economic and social policy to confront an inequitable wage policy which keeps millions of families at subsistence level and unable to raise their own children properly. The lives and deaths of so many children on the streets are the visible result of current policies. Thus, we must stress the importance of preventive action characterized by the "profound and radical social change which eliminates the injustices which marginalize and victimize people" (Araujo, 1991).

In conclusion, Brazilian society has reacted with indignation and has achieved considerable improvements in the constitutional and juridical structures that affect children in recent years. There is a national consciousness *vis-à-vis* the situation of childhood. Today there are eyes to see, but there is still much work ahead to be done. It remains for us to understand the meaning of violence and not to fall into the temptation Camus described in attributing its cause to the sun.

Notes

1. In writing this article I counted on the friendly and efficient collaboration of Eneida Larcerda Pamplona (CESPI/USU). I would like to thank Malcolm Bush of Voices for Illinois Children, my former professor at the University of Chicago, for his guidance and helpful comments.
2. Herbert de Souza (1991). In Murray, 1991.
3. It is estimated that in Brazil 10 per cent of the population controls more than 50 per cent of national income. Throughout the 1980s, the distribution of income in Brazil worsened. According to official data, the poorest 50 per cent, who in 1981 held 13.4 per cent of national income, held 10.4 per cent in 1989 (IBGE, 1991).
4. The figures presented here were taken from IBGE/UNICEF, 1989, 1990, 1991; World Bank, 1990.
5. The term "street kids" encompasses both boys and girls and, unless otherwise noted, is used accordingly throughout the text.
6. This profile of street children is based on research produced between 1979 and 1990.
7. The disparity in the results of the two studies done in Recife may be attributed to sampling differences. The first study listed in the table focuses on an open sample of children encountered randomly on the streets of Recife, while the second works with two specific groups of young people working on the streets; also, one is tied to social assistance organizations and the other is autonomous.
8. The causes of these violent deaths include: knifing, shooting, asphyxiation, beating, poisoning, burning, rape, strangulation, and other, non-specified accidents.
9. The data shown in the table present a brief panorama of what is occurring in the country. However, not all states were included in the research, thus making an exact comparison between different regions of the country impossible (see map). Even taking into consideration the limitations of the research which produced these figures, they are revealing. The greatest concentration of cases in the South-Eastern region is due to the high incidence of assassinations in Rio de Janeiro and São Paulo. The almost 100 per cent increase in violent deaths in that region is startling and suggestive.

10. Title of an article in the *Jornal do Brasil*, 20 November 1991.
11. A few days later, the results of the National Congressional Committee of Inquiry hearings were disseminated. After seven months of work, the Committee revealed the existence of more than 7,000 cases of the assassination of children in the last four years and published the names of some of the accused and their actions.

References

Acronyms

CBIA   Centro Brasileiro para a Infância e Adolescência (Brazilian Foundation for Children and Adolescents)
CEAP   Centro de Articulação de Populações Marginalizadas (Centre for Articulation of Marginalized Populations)
CESME   Coordenação de Estudos sobre o Menor (Research Centre on Minors)
FLACSO   Facultad Latinoamericana de Ciencias Sociales (Latin American Faculty of Social Sciences)
GAJOP   Gabinete de Assessoria Jurídica às Organizações Populares (Centre for Judicial Assistance to Popular Organizations)
IBASE   Instituto Brasileiro de Análises Sócio-Econômicas (Brazilian Institute for Socio-Economic Analysis)
IBGE   Instituto Brasileiro de Geografia e Estatistica (Brazilian Institute of Geography and Statistics)
MNMMR   Movimento Nacional de Meninos e Meninas de Rua (National Street Kids' Movement)
NEV   Núcleo de Estudos sobre Violência (Centre for Research on Violence)
USP   Universidade de São Paulo (University of São Paulo)
USU   Universidade de Santa Úrsula (University of Santa Uŕsula)

Amnesty International. 1990a. *Brasil: Tortura e execuções extra-iuridiciais nas cidades brasileiras*. Portuguese translation of *Brazil: Torture and Extrajudicial Execution in Urban Brazil*. London: Amnesty International.
————. 1990b. *Brasil: Crianças vítimas de assassinatos e crueldade*. Portuguese translation of "Brazil: Child Victims of Killing and Cruelty," *Focus*, September 1990. London: Amnesty International.
Araujo João Marcello, Jr. 1991. *Receita contra o crime* [Recipe against crime]. Rio de Janeiro: Jornal do Brasil.
Brecht, Bertolt. 1989. *Histórias do Sr. Keuner* [Stories of Mr Keuner]. São Paulo: Brasiliense. First published in German as *Geschichte vom Herrn Keuner*, c. 1930.
Camus, Albert. 1989. *The Outsider*. Trans. Joseph Laredo. Harmondsworth: Penguin. First published in French as *L'Étranger*, 1942.
CEAP. 1989. *O extermínio de crianças e adolescentes no Brasil* [The killing of children and adolescents in Brazil]. Rio de Janeiro.
FLACSO, UNICEF, and CBIA. 1991. *O trabalho e a rua* [Work and the street]. São Paulo: Cortez Ed.
Ferreira, Rosa Maria F. 1980. *Meninos de Rua. Valores e expectativas de menores marginalizados em São Paulo* [Street kids: The values and expectations of marginalized youngsters in São Paulo]. São Paulo: Comissão de Justiça e Paz.

GAJOP/Centro Luis Freire. 1991. *Grupos de extermínio: a banalização da vida e da morte em Pernambuco* [Extermination groups: the devaluing of life and death in Pernambuco]. Olinda, PE.

Gonçalves, Zuila de Andrade. 1979. *Meninos de rua e a marginalidade urbana em Belém* [Street kids and urban marginalization in Belém]. Belém: Salesianos do Pará.

Governo do Estado do Ceará/Secretaria de Ação Social. 1988. *Perfil do menino e menina de rua de Fortaleza* [Profile of street boys and girls in Fortaleza]. Fortaleza: Jan. 20 fls. Relatório de Pesquisa.

IBGE. 1990. *Sintese de indicadores da pesquisa básica da PNAD de 1981 a 1989* [Synthesis of indicators of basic research from the National Household Survey, 1981–1989]. Rio de Janeiro.

IBGE/UNICEF. 1989. *Crianças e adolescentes: indicadores sociais* [Children and adolescents: social indicators]. Vol. 1. Rio de Janeiro.

———. 1990. *Crianças e adolescentes: indicadores sociais.* Vol. 2. Rio de Janeiro.

———. 1991. *Crianças e adolescentes: indicadores sociais.* Vol. 3. Rio de Janeiro.

MNMMR. 1991a. "Combate a violencia contra crianças e adolescentes: uma proposta de ação" [Combating violence against children and adolescents: a proposal for action]. Brasilia: unpublished report.

———. 1991b. "Dossie sobre o extermínio de crianças e adolescentes no Brasil" [Dossier on the extermination of children and adolescents in Brazil]. Brasilia: mimeo.

MNMMR, IBASE, and NEV-USP. 1991. *Vidas em risco: assassinatos de crianças e adolescentes no Brasil* [Lives at risk: assassinations of children and adolescents in Brazil]. Rio de Janeiro.

Murray, Roseana 1991. *Criança é coisa seria.* [Children are a serious matter]. Rio de Janeiro: AMAIS Editora e Livraria/Memorias Futuras.

Myers, William. 1988. "Characteristics of Some Urban Working Children; A Comparison of Four Surveys from South America." Stanford, CA: Stanford University Law School, mimeo.

Oliveira, Cleide de Fatima Galiza. 1989. *Se essa rua fosse minha – um estudo sobre a trajetória e vivencia dos meninos de rua do Recife* [If this street were mine – a study of the development and life experiences of street kids in Recife]. Recife: UNICEF.

Pinto, Lucia, et al. 1991. *Extermínio de crianças e adolescentes: trajetória, caracterização, análise de investigações (1989–1991)* [Killing of children and adolescents: evolution, characteristic, analysis of investigations]. Rio de Janeiro: CBIA.

Pires, Julio Manuel. 1988. "Trabalho infantil: a necessidade e a persistencia" [Child labour: necessity and persistence]. Master's thesis, University of São Paulo.

Rizzini, Irene. 1986. *A geração da rua: um estudo sobre as crianças marginalizadas no Rio de Janeiro* [The street generation: a study of marginalized children in Rio de Janeiro]. Serie: Estudos e Pesquisa, 1. Rio de Janeiro: USU/CESME.

Rizzini, Irene, and Rizzini, Irma. 1991. *Menores institucionalizados e meninos de rua: os temas de sauisa da decada de 80* [Institutionalized minors and street kids: research themes of the 1980s] In FLACSO et al., 1991.

Rizzini, Irene, and Wiik, Flavio Braune. 1990. *O que o Rio tem feito por suas crianças?* [What has Rio done for its children?]. Rio de Janeiro: CESME–USU/IBASE.

World Bank. 1990. *Informe sobre el desarollo mundial. Indicadores del desarollo mundial* [World development report. Indicators of world development]. Washington, DC: World Bank.

11

Human rights and dictatorship: The case of Chile

Tony Mifsud, S.J.

Since 1973 human rights has been a key word in Chile. In the early years of the military dictatorship, some people suffered direct violent action personally or saw it inflicted on their relatives; others felt impotent in their denunciation of such actions; and still others simply did not believe that such actions were actually taking place, owing to their blind trust in the democratic and legal tradition of the country or their political antagonism to the Allende regime. In 1990, seventeen years later and in the context of a democratic government, the violation of basic human rights under the military dictatorship is a fact that no one doubts. Shown on the national television network, tragic and pathetic scenes of the discovery of clandestine graves and the finding of the skeletons of the victims of massacre have left no possible doubt. Whether such violent action was politically necessary or justified is the only question open for discussion today.

On 13 June 1990, the army issued an official, public declaration stating that the coup of 11 September 1973 was equivalent to "a military operation, that is, an act of war." The military appraisal of the situation is that in 1973 the nation was marching inevitably towards national, political, social, and moral destruction; that the country was on the brink of civil war; that national security was seriously endangered. In this context, the declaration insists, what later seems to have been a "disproportionate" military reaction is fully justified by the fact that at that historical moment the military intervention responded to a situation of war.

On the very same day, the National Conference of Catholic Bishops published a pastoral letter on the need for public knowledge of the truth in a situation where graves and skeletons were being discovered. They stated, furthermore, that in the present circumstances it is imperative "not to justify the unjustifiable on the grounds that in those times the country was at war."

Church and *military*: two national institutions which have shaped the history of Chile. Yet, during the military dictatorship, the public image which they projected was of a totally antagonistic relationship. The violation of human rights was attributable to the military, while the Church was considered as the defender of the victims.

1 A black page in Chilean history

Going back to the years of the dictatorship is still painful to the Chilean soul, because a traditional pride in democratic government was shattered by this long and dreadful ordeal. However, any study on the defence of human rights can only be understood in so far as one has a clear picture of the context in which those rights were constantly violated, though their violation was publicly justified.

In Chile the doctrine of national security[1] defended by the military dictatorship resulted in a total insecurity of the population at large, since basic and elemental civil rights were denied. National Congress was dissolved, political parties were prohibited, university civil authorities were replaced by military officials, the press suffered strict censorship, social organizations and labour unions were destroyed, and many people were simply sent into exile without any judicial process. Above all, any dissent – private or public – was considered to be a sign of betrayal of the nation and was therefore harshly punished. The presence of the secret police created an atmosphere of suspicion and basic mistrust of any unknown person. Thus, in public places or in any social group one was afraid to voice an opinion or comment on national affairs lest he or she be accused of intervening in politics or condemned as a communist for criticizing the military authorities.

A peculiarity of the military dictatorship in Chile was the appearance of legality which the Junta constantly tried to preserve. Respect for the law and the social necessity of the presence of laws to support political measures are features deeply rooted in Chilean culture. This does not necessarily mean that in Chile citizens are more law-abiding; it does mean, however, that the promulgation of a law assures social acceptance. So much so that, on the very first day of the military dictatorship, the Junta proclaimed solemn declarations and also published laws. The Junta reserved for itself the executive, legislative, and constituent powers and made ample use of them. At the same time, the State of Exception was decreed, which gave special powers to the executive. Thus, in the first months courts martial (*Consejos de Guerra*) were set up and people were officially condemned by these military courts reserved for times of war.

Curiously, and sadly enough, in the records of the proceedings of the courts martial strange and tragic contradictions are discovered. For example, some people were condemned to imprisonment for having gone to work on 11 September 1973, while others were condemned for not having gone to work on the same day. This illustrates how politicial repression sought the appearance of legality, even at the cost of basic contradiction and insult to common sense.

Laws were also created to cover up political abuses. Thus, it was discovered that sometimes a person had been first arrested and only then, after his arrest had actually taken place, was the judicial decree issued with a date previous to the arrest. At other times, laws were simply invented to justify atrocities. When skeletons were found in the north of the country, at Pisagua, it was said that the executions had been carried out according to the law against escape (*ley de fuga*), which is non-existent in the civil legal code. This legal circus did not prevent other violent actions which could not be justified legally, such as the "disappearances"; however, military authorities systematically denied that the disappeared (*detenidos-desaparecidos*) had ever been arrested!

Laws exist to protect the citizen. Therefore, when laws are converted or perverted into simple smokescreens for violations against basic civil rights, the vulnerability of any citizen who does not agree with the authorities is complete. This explains the fear which pervaded the population of Chile and turned any small gesture of protest into a symbol of heroic action, for the personal danger involved was considerable and one had to overcome personal and public irrational fear to bring oneself to perform such an action.

In 1978 an Amnesty Law (*Ley de Amnistía*) was promulgated by the military authorities. The immediate effect was the pardoning of all crimes committed during the period from September 1973 to March 1978. However, this law was only applied to the military themselves and, furthermore, prevented any judicial investigation of any crimes committed during that period.

These facts lead us to the conclusion that the judicial system did not act with due independence from the military authorities and that the unilateral intervention in favour of the military heightened the sense of insecurity and fear in the citizen.

2 Violations in numerical terms

In July 1974, the Organization of American States (OAS) published a report in which it stated that "the most moderate calculations speak of about 1,500 deaths, 80 of which belong to the military forces" in the first months of the military regime. In the same report we read that in the first days an estimated 220 persons were shot. At present, the Vicaría de la Solidaridad, the Church-run office for the defence of human rights and support to the families of victims, has officially and judicially claimed that there exist 1,000 cases of disappeared persons who are presumed to be dead. Of these, 877 cases have been officially reported and 123 have been accepted for investigation.

In February 1976, the Director of the National Prison Service (*Servicio Nacional de Detenidos*), Colonel Pedro Espinoza, officially acknowledged that in the Junta's first two years 42,486 persons had been arrested. It is generally accepted that in the first years the majority of political prisoners were psychologically and physically tortured. However, the number of denunciations before the law courts were very limited, for two reasons: mistrust of the law courts, especially since most cases would finish up in the military courts, and fear of reprisals against victims or their families. It was only in June 1978 that the Vicaría de la Solidaridad received testimonies with respect to torture and started presenting these cases to the law courts. In spite of the difficulties mentioned above, the Vicaría presented a total of 2,737 cases legally.

Fear, anguish, suffering, and death can never be translated into numbers. For the family of the victim, one single loss by death is irreplaceable. The psychological consequences of torture are endless and permanent. The experience of fear wounds one's self-respect because it is not easy to distinguish between prudence and cowardice. The figures quoted above are extremely conservative, and can only begin to suggest the magnitude of the tragedy and to show that the consequences of a violent dictatorship are not limited to its direct victims but also include the country as a whole. It is the soul of Chile which has been wounded; a page of its history has been stained with the presence of Cain. Under no previous government has human life been so little appreciated, so lightly judged, and so massively destroyed.

3 The voice of the silenced

On 6 October 1973, just three weeks after the coup, the Comité Pro Paz (Peace Committee – its full title was *Comité de Cooperación para la Paz en Chile*) was formed under the protection of the Catholic Church and the World Council of Churches. Various individuals had approached the different churches asking for help, information, and protection. The purpose of this ecumenical institution was to defend the human rights of Chilean citizens in an organized manner. Thus the Comité not only denounced the atrocities committed, but also organized different programmes related to legal, health, and labour problems.

By December 1975, a year and a half after the coup, an estimated 40,000 persons had approached the Comité; more than 70,000 persons had received basic medical assistance; and more than 35,000 children had attended the daily "soup kitchens" or *comedores infantiles*, which for most of them provided the only meal of the day. The Group of Relatives of the Disappeared (*Familiares de Detenidos-Desaparecidos*) was organized with the help and encouragement of the Comité. Consisting mainly of women, it was renowned because the members carried photographs of their relatives (husbands, sons, and daughters) in many public demonstrations in order to break the circle of silence which surrounded the cases of the disappeared.

However, in December 1975 General Pinochet ordered the immediate dissolution of the Comité. Cardinal Raúl Silva Henríquez had no choice. However, the Cardinal created a "Vicariate of Solidarity" (*Vicaría de la Solidaridad*), depending directly from the Catholic Church, which started working in January 1976. The Vicaría has its buildings right next to the cathedral of Santiago. In spite of the fact that it was an all-Catholic operation, the World Council of Churches was its main financial support for many years.

The Vicaría has received international recognition for its Legal Department, which, over the years, has given legal protection to thousands of victims. Besides continuing the work of the Comité, the Vicaría also published a journal every two weeks, entitled *Soli-*

daridad. At a time when censorship and control of the press was very tight, the journal of the Vicaría and the Jesuit monthly *Mensaje* were the only sources of information on what was really happening in the country. *Solidaridad* reached a circulation of 20,000 copies.

Under the military dictatorship, the Vicaría de la Solidaridad shone out as the symbol of defence of human rights. Obviously enough, however, the Vicaría had to pay the price for its daring. In 1974, three members of the Comité (Alvaro Varela, Francisco Ruiz, and Yésica Ullóa) were arrested. In 1975, the Lutheran bishop and co-president of the Comité, Helmut Frenz, was expelled from the country and two Jesuit priests, Fernando Salas and Patricio Cariola, were arrested. In 1976, a lawyer (José Zalaquett) was arrested and expelled from the country, another (Hernán Montealegre) was imprisoned in the Cuatro Alamos concentration camp for six months, and two more (Jaime Castillo Velasco and Eugenio Velasco Letelier) were expelled from Chile. In 1984, Ignacio Gutiérrez, the Vicar responsible, was not permitted to enter the country. In 1985, the chief of documentation of the Vicaría, José Manuel Parada, was found with his throat cut, together with two other members of the Central Committee of the Communist Party. In 1986, there was an attempt to kidnap the lawyer Luis Toro, while another lawyer, Gustavo Villalobos, and a doctor, Ramiro Olivares, were arrested and spent a year in jail. During 1987, Enrique Pallet, the executive secretary of the Vicaría received constant threats against his life.

The Church's answer to these attacks was to nominate Bishop Sergio Valech as responsible for the Vicaría in 1987. This did not deter the military authorities from continuing their attacks on the Vicaría, but the presence of a bishop in the Vicaría meant that it had the strong and official backing of the Catholic Church. As a result, the military authorities were eventually forced to lessen their pressure, since it was interpreted as a direct attack on the Catholic Church.

4 One objective, different strategies

In a situation where human rights are systematically and "legally" violated, the primary and immediate objective is that of proclaiming and demanding the respect due to any person for the sole and trascendent reason of being a human person with predetermined rights. Thus, the first strategy developed in Chile was direct action to help the victims of the repression. In the first years this meant seeking out the places where people were being detained so that they would not finish up on the list of the disappeared; helping other people to enter foreign embassies in order to save them from execution; offering legal support to students, who were expelled from the universities in great numbers, and to workers who lost their jobs; and creating health services to look after the persecuted. The defence of individual rights was accompanied by an effort to re-establish a generalized situation in which human rights were respected.

Gradually, the public denunciation of the atrocities that were being committed came to contrast deeply with the public image which the military government had skilfully created. The existence of concentration camps, the systematic use of torture, the frequent political executions without judicial process, and other tragic happenings were constantly denied by the military authorities. However, the official statements of the National Conference of Bishops and the reports of the Vicaría insistently accused the authorities of such transgressions. Through the censorship imposed on the media and intervention in newspapers, radios, and television, an official history was being publicized which did not coincide with the yearly condemnation received by the United Nations. Some believed the military, others trusted the Church, still others simply could not or did not want to believe that such perverse atrocities were being committed in a country with such a unique record of political democracy by Latin American standards. But, with the passing of the years and the consolidation of the human rights movements, the facts started to come out into the open.

The military dictatorship justified its proceedings by resorting to a messianic logic. Military intervention in 1973 had saved the country from economic, social, and religious chaos; it was an open and decisive war against national and international communism; and it was not possible to be weak in front of such a powerful enemy, who was deceitful in all respects. This crusade was understood in military terms and the strategy of war was applied. This war atmosphere was sustained daily in all the media and any objection was interpreted as betrayal or, at best, simple naïvety. Thus the physical elimination of people who opposed the regime was justified as a victory over the enemy. When someone was killed, it was quickly explained that the dead man or woman was a communist. And the killing of a communist was not only permitted but also justified as a praiseworthy and patriotic action!

In contrast to this military logic, the Catholic Church, through the declarations of the bishops and the Vicaría, insisted on and preached the equal dignity of all human beings. The role of the Good Samaritan was understood to form an essential part of believing in God. To help the persecuted and to restore peace based on justice became leitmotifs of the Church's preaching, teaching, and practice. The official military language erased the dividing line between right and wrong, for in a war all means are justified by the end in view. The Church maintained a basic human ethical viewpoint: politics is not war, murder can never be justified, everyone has a right to a just trial before being condemned, a political adversary is not an enemy, democracy is superior to dictatorship.

As the years under military government passed, other social agents joined the Church in the defence of human rights. In the years immediately following the military coup, the Church was the only social organization capable of presenting a collective voice which, though evidently repressed, could not be silenced. All other social organizations were prohibited, repressed, and silenced. Yet, gradually, other social agents entered the political scene and joined in the defence of human rights.

Instead of presenting a list of organizations which stood out for the defence of human rights, it is more interesting to discover the common characteristics which helped to form a united front in the defence of the dignity of all citizens.

Organization versus dispersion

The Roman Empire practised the "divide-and-rule" military strategy. The military dictatorship not only prohibited all social organizations but also reinforced collective fear through severe punishment towards any gathering or meeting which did not have the official support of the military authorities. Thus, violations of human rights were reduced to a personal problem of the victim for not abiding by the rules dictated by the authorities.

In this context, the defence of human rights was based on the organization of the victims in order to emphasize the social and political meaning of the violations. As a result it became evident that if a person was arrested, tortured, or disappeared it was for reasons which were not necessarily personal; that is, the mere fact that one was a member of a given party was a sufficient reason to endanger one's life.

Pluralism versus uniformity

The doctrine of national security offers a messianic understanding of politics. It was officially understood that given the danger of spreading communism, the military had the responsibility of waging a total war against Marxism at all its possible levels of expression. The security of the nation and of the whole of Western culture depended on this adamant stand against communism. This doctrine was defended in terms of a crusade and its cause implied a religious adherence. Any expression of weakness was considered a defeat in front of the enemy and any kind or hint of dissent was interpreted as a betrayal of the nation.

In this context, the organized effort to defend human rights assumed a converging pluralism. Differences in political ideology and religious belief were overcome and unity of action was centred around the principle of defence of basic human rights and their various expressions (respect for human life, innocence until proof of guilt, condemnation of torture as a systematic political instrument, and so on).

Political ethics versus military strategy

The military understanding of politics reduces the social scene to a battlefield. The adversary is an enemy and any kind of giving in to his demands is simply considered to be a sign of weakness. The only way to win a war is by defeating and crushing the enemy. The disappearance or humiliation of the enemy is identified with victory. The traditional understanding of politics as a democratic space where the interests of different groups are represented by political parties is simply considered as a degenerate activity of manipulation of the masses. As a result, the violation of human rights was not a question of "abuses," but rather a "systematic procedure."

In this context, the sense of democracy was gradually restored among the vast majority of the population and among people of different political tendencies. Social conflicts are not solved by imposition or repression but by the art of persuasion and dialogue. The dangerous vocation of the enlightened "élite" was gradually replaced by the necessary intervention of the representatives of the people. Due respect for basic human and civil rights was considered as a primary political condition for a democratic future.

Solidarity versus terror

One of the evident effects of collective terror is that people develop an individualistic style of life in order to avoid trouble. The "unknown person" in a group is looked upon as a possible spy and therefore as a possible source of danger and a potential enemy to one's life. Besides, a totally capitalist economic system reducing to the bare minimum any state intervention reinforces an individualistic mentality and perverts the scale of values, since economic welfare becomes more important than human rights issues.

In this context, the organized and pluralistic groups lived the experience of solidarity amongst their members. The victim or his or her family was helped and taken care of. In spite of the natural tendency to build a considerable distance between the victim and oneself, the spirit of solidarity was assumed for reasons of nationality (all belonging to the same country), religion (all brothers and sisters in the common Father), and simple humanity (all belonging to the human race). Besides, the irrationality of a widespread repression emphasized the impression that no one was really safe and that any day anyone could be the next victim.

Peace versus violence

Dictatorship is daily lived as violence because of the sense of insecurity, the experience of civic impotence, and the indignation of a sorrow that cannot be made public. These repressed feelings give the impression that the only possible outlet to overcome a violent system is a violent answer.

In this context, the predominant political and religious reaction was an increasing conversion to an active and non-violent defence of violated human rights. Violent groups are a minority in Chile. The Frente Patriótico, the Movimiento de Izquierda Revolucionario, and Lautaro are small in number and lack popular support. Thus, the option of resorting to legal procedures and the organization of public peaceful protests (1983–1985) bore fruit in 1988, when the military dictatorship was defeated on its own ground and by its own rules in the plebiscite.

Truth versus official versions

During the military government the history of the country possessed two textbooks: the official version of what was happening and the clandestine reports which radically contradicted those versions. Military authorities systematically denied the existence of torture, concentration camps, and the scandal of the disappeared. Furthermore, it was declared that these accusations were an invention of the Marxists and the result of Soviet imperialistic ambitions. The final period of Allende's rule had been traumatic and a return to the social conflicts present during the socialist government was exploited as the only alternative to the military government. Social and political chaos was seen to be implied by any opposition to the military dictatorship.

In this context, it was essential to proclaim the true version of what was really happening. Moreover, the chaos theory of the military authorities was questioned and criticized by the historical perspective which holds that the present cannot be justified on the sole grounds of an escape from the past and the belief in the collective possibility of constructing a future which has learned from the errors of the past.

In the first months of democracy this political truth was socially recognized and the possibility of an alternative political system to the military dictatorship without falling into chaos became a reality beyond doubt.

5 Human rights and democracy

The human rights issue was one of the principal themes in the political programme during the campaign of the present democratic authorities. In his inaugural speech, the President of the Republic solemnly stated his adherence to his promise on human rights. Eventually, he formed a special presidential commission to investigate the violations of human rights which had resulted in the assassination of persons, propose measures of reparation to the victims, and suggest concrete strategies to prevent abuses in the future.

The truth must be known and politically recognized by the highest authority in the nation. This had been understood to be the first step towards the accomplishment of justice. However, in a divided country there is a social agreement that, if the nation is to be reconciled, justice must not be confused with vengeance, but at the same time reconciliation must not be confused with impunity in the case of violations of human rights. Strict justice cannot be accomplished, for what kind of justice can bring back to life the dead and the missing persons? What can repair the physical and psychological damage suffered by the tortured? Besides, it is impossible in practice to bring to court the thousands of cases which imply some degree of abuse against human rights. Furthermore, a prolonged situation of innumerable court cases will only bleed the country to death and entrap the future in the darkness of the past. On the other hand, while the ever-present threat of a new military intervention with massive abuses of human rights has to be taken politically into account, this surely cannot mean the consecration of impunity. Human rights must not be reduced to a merely political or institutional problem.

It is not the time to judge and condemn institutions, since the responsibility falls on the persons who lead these institutions. An institution may be betrayed and misguided, but it may also be reorientated, for everything depends on human decisions. The presidential proclamation of the truth of what really happened is the first national step in closing a chapter of Chilean history. Yet another chapter must be started. The defence of human rights is a progressive social process that will imply the gradual healing of deep wounds and an honest desire to construct a common future for all citizens. The debate on human rights has to be established in human terms. Crime must be called by its proper name. Political convenience cannot mean that what has been considered by humanity as "evil" suddenly turns out to be "good."

In this regard, the elementary ethical dividing line between what is right and what is wrong should be restored and socially recognized. The proclamation of the historical truth of what actually happened and the need to bring to justice those responsible for abuses are first requirements. It is important to achieve them, in order to prevent a social process of vengeance and, at the same time, to give the opportunity to those responsible for human rights violations to admit that abuses were committed.

The reconciliation of the country is an ethical issue of the highest importance. Yet reconciliation is only possible if the truth is proclaimed and justice is sought: truth is the social debt owed to the victims and the accomplishment of justice is a basic need of social dignity. Reconciliation implies that never again – *nunca más* – should certain things be permitted in Chile. No politics, no government, no ideology, no amount of force should ever justify abuses against human rights and inflict death, pain, and loss of dignity on any citizen.

The return to democracy has meant that we can be sure again of living without fear in our own country and can feel that we have regained our status as citizens with corresponding rights and responsibilities. But the real challenge consists in creating a culture of respect towards human rights. An this means education, this means conviction, this means commitment. It simply cannot be taken for granted.

6 Conclusion: And the president wept

On 9 May 1990, barely two months after taking office, Patricio Aylwin, the newly elected president of Chile, created a National Commission on Truth and Reconciliation, to contribute to the establishment of the truth regarding cases of human rights violations which resulted in the death of the victim. Nine months later, the report of the Commission, covering 2,279 cases and filling six volumes, was officially given to the president. On 4 March 1991, President Aylwin presented the *Informe Rettig* (named after the person who headed the Commission) to the nation.

Everyone listened. Till this very day, no one has dared question the authenticity of the report's contents. The lethal truth of the existence of political victims during the period of the military government is beyond dispute; it has become a common truth among all sectors. However, interpretations differ. The military still maintain that the killings occurred in a time of war and therefore were inevitable for political reasons based on national security.

The social truth has been established; but what about social justice? In this concrete political situation, axiological conviction, based on ethical principles, and political prudence, preoccupied with the consolidation of the democratic system, enter into conflict. The trouble is that so far the social realities of "power," "force," and "legitimacy" are not invested in a single political agent or institution, since the military forces still retain considerable social power and the possibility of a military intervention cannot be disregarded. This shows that the political situation in Chile is not strictly one of democracy, but rather one on the way to democracy.

As regards the process of reconciliation of the country, so far the following steps have been completed:

1. The social truth regarding the past events has been established. This is of extreme importance in so far as no nation is able to survive if a common truth about its past is lacking.
2. The *Informe Rettig* has done justice to the victims, since their good name has been restored. The dead are not criminals but political victims. Also, the Commission has suggested to Parliament concrete measures for material reparation to the families of the victims.

3. The report in itself has been accepted and received by the vast majority as the national conscience of the country. The Commission's lack of judicial power enhanced its ethical testimony as a moral condemnation of the violations against human rights which occurred during the military government.

The question of penal justice, however, is still unresolved. Will the perpetrators of human rights violations be brought to the law courts? This implies another question: will the military authorities permit the political authorities to pass judgment on their men in uniform? In other words, can the newly gained democracy stand up against the military forces without endangering its very existence?

The global truth has been established and some measures of justice have been implemented. These are concrete signs in the process of reconciliation. Important steps have been taken, but as yet not all is accomplished.

On the night of 4 March 1991, when President Aylwin was pronouncing his much-expected and long-awaited speech, the television cameras remained fixed on him as tears rolled down his cheeks, while he solemnly, as President of the Republic, begged forgiveness of the victims' families for the atrocities committed against their dear ones. This plea for forgiveness was long overdue, and many identified with this new representative of the people in such a memorable moment in the history of Chile. The authenticity of Aylwin's tears on behalf of the nation may be a sign of a popular promise that *nunca más* will the pages of Chilean history be filled with massive violations against human rights.

Note

1. I have given a systematic presentation of the doctrine of national Security in *Moral de discernimiento*, vol. 4 (Santiago: Paulinas, 1988), pp. 447–57. One may also consult: J. Comblin, "La doctrina de la seguridad nacional," *Mensaje* 247 (1976), 96–104; M. Ruz, "Doctrina de seguridad nacional en América Latina," *Mensaje* 261 (1977), 418–26; Vicaría de la Solidaridad, *Estudio bibliográfico sobre seguridad nacional* (Santiago, 1977), and *Seguridad nacional y régimen militar* (Santiago, 1977); J. Comblin and A. Methol Ferre, *Dos ensayos sobre seguridad nacional* (Santiago: Vicaría de la Solidaridad, 1977); J. Comblin, *El poder militar en América Latina* (Salamanca: Sígueme, 1978); H. Montealegre, *La seguridad del estado y los derechos humanos* (Santiago: Academia de Humanismo Cristiano, 1979); J. Tapia Valdés, *El terrorismo de estado* (Mexico: Editorial Nueva Imagen, 1980); SELADOC (Servicio Latinoamericano de Documentación), *Iglesia y seguridad nacional* (Salamanca: Sígueme, 1980); J. Chateau, *Seguridad nacional y guerra subversiva* (Santiago: FLACSO, 1983); H. Pozo, *La seguridad nacional: raices internacionales* (Santiago: FLACSO, 1983).

Contributors

Xavier Albó, b. 1934, La Garriga, Catalunya; Ph.D. in Philosophy, San Gregorio School of Philosophy, Quito, and in Anthropology–Linguistics, Cornell University. Co-founder (1972), Centro de Investigación y Promoción del Campesinado (CIPCA), where he is currently a member of the research department. Has published extensively, including 15 books on Bolivian rural and Indian issues, and is currently national coordinator for Bolivia of an international project on violence in the Andean region, sponsored by the Peruvian Peace Research Association (APEP), Lima.

Luis Pedro España N., b. 1962. Colegio de San Ignacio de Loyola, Caracas; Licentiate in Sociology from the Catholic University Andrés Bello, Caracas; Master in Political Science, Simon Bolívar University, Caracas. Presently professor and researcher at the Institute for Economic and Social Research of the Catholic University Andrés Bello, where he is coordinator of the Socio-Political Department. National coordinator for Venezuela, since 1991, of an international project on violence in the Andean region, sponsored by the Peruvian Peace Research Association, Lima.

Bruce Kapferer trained at Sydney University and later at Manchester University, when the anthropology department was headed by Prof. Max Gluckman. Concentrated specifically on the role of symbolism in political and ritual systems. Developed a comparative approach in anthropology which is highly informed by currents within European structuralism and phenomenology through his wide field experience in Zambia, Sri Lanka, and Australia. He is concerned in establishing a critical anthropology to address major human issues and has focused his work on myths and legends of state nationalism and their role in ethnic prejudice and violence. Has had teaching posts in Australia, Sweden, and Sri Lanka, and is currently at the University College Anthropology Department, University of London.

Edward Khiddu-Makubuya, LL B (Hons), Makerere University (Uganda); LL M and Doctorate in the Science of Law (JSD), Yale University; Diploma in Legal Practice (Dip. LP), Law Development Centre, Uganda. Advocate, High Court of Uganda; Associate Professor of Law, Makerere University. Member, Uganda Human Rights Commission and Uganda Constitutional Commission.

Felipe E. MacGregor, s.j., President, Peruvian Peace Research Association; Director, Universidad del Pacífico; Council member, United Nations University; member,

Commission on Cultural and Social Origins of Violence, UNESCO; Professor of Ethics and Rector Emeritus, Catholic University of Peru. Formerly President, Union of Latin American Universities; Vice-President, International Federation of Catholic Universities; member, Executive Council of the International Association of Universities; Rector, Catholic University of Peru (1966–1977); President, Peruvian National Commission of Peace Education. Has edited the following publications: *Violencia y paz en el Perú, Siete ensayos sobre la violencia en el Perú, Violencia estructural en el Perú* (7 vols), *Cocaína: Problemas y soluciones andinos*, and *Impacto macroeconómico de los gastos militares en el Perú*.

Tony Mifsud, s.j., b. 1949, Malta. Has lived in Chile since 1974. Graduated in English literature, University of Malta, philosophy, Gallarate, Italy, and theology, Catholic University, Santiago de Chile; then specialized in Christian Ethics at the Universidad Pontificia de Comillas, Madrid, Spain. Author of a 4-volume work, *Moral de Discernimiento*, dealing with the principal ethical issues in Latin American society. President of a National Civic Education Programme, 1987–1989; participated in 1990 in the Consultative Commission on Human Rights for the newly-elected government. Presently director of ILADES, a Jesuit academic centre of post-graduate studies and research on social problems in South America.

Irene Rizzini is Professor at the Santa Úrsula University and Coordinator of CESPI/USU (Coordination for Studies and Research on Childhood, Santa Úrsula University).

Francisco J. de Roux, s.j., was educated at the Javeriana University, the London School of Economics, and the University of Paris. A Colombian Jesuit and currently director of the Centro de Investigación y Educación Popular (CINEP, Centre for Social Research and Education), Bogotá, he has published extensively on peace, violence, economics, ethics, and politics.

Marcial Rubio Correa, b. 1949, LL M, Pontificia Universidad Católica del Perú (Catholic University of Peru); Professor of Law, Department of Law, Catholic University of Peru; President, Centro de Estudios y Promoción del Desarrollo (DESCO); General Secretary, Asociación Peruana de Estudios e Investigación para la Paz (Peruvian Peace Research Association, APEP), Lima, Peru.

Kumar Rupesinghe, b. 1943, Ph.D. in Sociology, City University, London; London School of Economics; Secretary General, International Alert, London; Senior Researcher, International Peace Research Institute, Oslo (PRIO); Chair, International Peace Research Association's Commission on International Conflicts and their Resolution (ICON); Coordinator, United Nations University Programme on Governance and Conflict Resolution. Has published and edited many articles and books, including *Conflict and Resolution in Uganda* (London: James Currey, 1989); *Ethnic Conflicts and Human Rights, a Comparative Perspective* (United Nations University, 1989); and a three-volume ICON book series published by Macmillan, London, in 1992.

Robert Brent Toplin, BA, Pennsylvania State University; MA and Ph.D., Rutgers University. Author of a number of books dealing with violence as it relates to slavery and race relations in the United States and Latin America, including *The Abolition of Slavery* (1972), and *Unchallenged Violence: An American Ordeal* (1975); editor of *Slavery and Race Relations in Latin America* (1974). Has had several televised dramatic documentaries and films which examine the problem of violence, including "Denmark Vesey's Rebellion" (1982), "Solomon Northup's Odyssey," and "Charlotte Forten's Mission."

MILES D. WOLPIN, BA (Economics), Wharton School, University of Pennsylvania; MA, Ph.D., and Doctor of Law, Columbia University. Professor, Department of Political Science; State University College of Arts and Science, New York. Previously a researcher with the International Peace Research Institute, Oslo (PRIO), and has taught at the National University of Mexico. His most recent publication is *America Insecure: Arms Transfers, Global Interventionism and the Erosion of National Security.*